LESSONS AND LEGACIES XIV

LESSONS AND LEGACIES XIV

The Holocaust in the Twenty-First Century: Relevance and Challenges in the Digital Age

Edited and with an introduction
by Tim Cole and Simone Gigliotti

NORTHWESTERN UNIVERSITY PRESS EVANSTON, ILLINOIS

Northwestern University Press
www.nupress.northwestern.edu

Holocaust Educational Foundation
of Northwestern University
Founded by Theodore Zev and Alice R. Weiss

Printed in the United States of America

10 9 8 7 6 5 4 3 2 1

ISBN 978-0-8101-4273-2 (cloth)
ISBN 978-0-8101-4272-5 (paper)
ISBN 978-0-8101-4274-9 (ebook)

Cataloging-in-Publication data are available from the Library of Congress.

♾ The paper used in this publication meets the minimum requirements of the American National Standard for Information Sciences—Permanence of Paper for Printed Library Materials, ANSI Z39.48–1992.

Contents

Theodore Zev Weiss

Foreword

ONCE AGAIN IT IS MY PLEASURE TO THANK THOSE WHO HAVE MADE THE publication of another volume in the Lessons and Legacies series possible. This is the fourteenth volume of the series of scholarly papers to be published as an outgrowth of three decades of Lessons and Legacies conferences sponsored by the Holocaust Educational Foundation in partnership with universities. The Lessons and Legacies conference is the most important conference for scholars in the field of Holocaust studies, and the Lessons and Legacies volumes highlight some of the best scholarship presented at each conference.

Emanating from the 2016 conference held on the campus of Claremont-McKenna College, the chapters contained herein broadly reflect the conference's theme, "The Holocaust in the Twenty-First Century: Relevance and Challenges in the Digital Age." This volume includes not only recent research by renowned scholars in the field but also the innovative work of young academics. Our primary objective is to assist, support, and encourage scholars and future scholars in teaching about the Holocaust in order to ensure that Holocaust education is included in as many colleges and universities as possible throughout the United States and around the world.

I am grateful to Professors Tim Cole and Simone Gigliotti for their commitment of time and energy in bringing this volume to publication. I also want to express my deepest appreciation to the conference co-chairs, Professors Hilary Earl and Wolf Gruner, as well as conference co-conveners Professors Wendy Lower and Jonathan Petropoulos.

Also, many thanks to my wife, Alice, and my children, Deborah and Gabriel and Danny and Jodi, and my grandchildren, Tamar, David, Matthew, Benjamin, Jacob, and Zoey. As my oldest grandchild, Tamar Aizenberg, begins her pursuit of a Ph.D. in Jewish studies focusing on modern Jewish history and the Holocaust, may she bring new light to future generations.

LESSONS AND LEGACIES XIV

Tim Cole and Simone Gigliotti

Introduction: The Holocaust in the Twenty-First Century

IN NOVEMBER 2016, THE FOURTEENTH BIENNIAL LESSONS AND LEGAcies conference, "The Holocaust in the Twenty-First Century: Relevance and Challenges in the Digital Age," drew scholars and attendees from the around the world to the beautiful campus of Claremont McKenna College on the outskirts of Los Angeles. Over several days, scholars presented their research that offered new locations and disciplinary perspectives from which to examine the nature and impact of the Holocaust. Some of these perspectives have been commissioned for publication in this volume, which focuses on critiques of core themes which have sustained the field's intellectual contours, investigations that map the Holocaust as a migratory persecution, and responses to the conference theme of the "relevance and challenges" presented by the "digital age." The eleven chapters in this latest volume of the associated Lessons and Legacies series represent but a fraction of the tremendously diverse and transnational range of papers submitted at the conference. These chapters affirm new directions in Holocaust studies and marked gender shifts in its authorship. They also speculate about the virtues and cautions of the impact of digital technology, whether in the form of online digital archives, social media, or quantitative software applications.

In compiling this volume, the editors were guided by the theme of traditional humanities scholarship's coexistence with the scholarship that is currently engaged in interdisciplinary research collaborations and investigations of the "digital age." We do not need reminders of the digital age's much-discussed and already visibly disruptive impacts on scholarship and models of student learning. That age's effect on institutional approaches to the digitization of testimonies and archives, and global museums' engagement with influential social media in curating visions of the Holocaust, is also marked. If digital technology has required institutions to invest millions of dollars in staff and infrastructure into making various Holocaust archives more accessible and available for study, research, and re-witnessing, does this development mean that the historical and geographical record of the Holocaust is more advanced, secure, and comprehensive than without it? There is no straightforward answer to this question, as demonstrated by some authors in this volume, and indeed a reluctance by others to engage with digital methods in favor of thick description and biographical narratives.

Although the chapters differ markedly in their embracing or eschewing of digital methods, a number of shared themes are explored: first, the tracing of experiences of persecution, escape, and resistance at different scales (individual, group, and systemic); second, methodological innovation through the adoption and tracking of "microhistories" of movement and displacement; third, experiments with Saul Friedländer's call for an integrated history and an integrated methodology to underwrite it; fourth, the mainstreaming of oral history; and fifth, local to transnational emphases in the geographies of the Holocaust. Alongside these five overarching themes that connect the chapters, lies the unforeseen and very welcome prevalence of women as contributors, and their increased role in shaping the future contours of Holocaust studies scholarship.

In relation to the first theme of scales of investigation, there tends to be, as noted by Anne Knowles and her coauthors, a "gap in Holocaust studies between the microhistory of the individual, the mezzohistory of social groups, and the macrohistory of the systemic, political-economic project of the Nazi regime." The chapters collected in this volume focus in the main on the first of these two scales of analysis—the microhistory of the individual and the mezzohistory of social groups—as well as exploring the potential of digital methods to bridge the gaps between the micro and mezzo. The relative absence of macrohistories of the Nazi regime—and indeed the relative absence of the perpetrators (aside from those standing trial in Israel and Germany)—in this volume is striking. That trend was certainly not evident in the first volumes emerging from the Lessons and Legacies biannual conferences.

The early historiography of the Holocaust tended to draw on the paperwork and documentary record of the perpetrators to explain how and why genocide was enacted by the Nazi state and its collaborators during the Second World War. This volume's focus on the individual victim (whether as an individual or as part of a network or social group) as the target of those policies is a clear and consistent feature. The research sources that have enabled this paradigmatic and subjective shift provide significant impetus to the subfield of Jewish and social histories of the Holocaust, as can be found in the chapters' notes. Their depth and diversity confirm the benefits of accessing previously inaccessible archives, making use of the very large collections of oral history interviews with survivors, and the prevalence of nuanced and interdisciplinary scholarly influences.

To underscore the significant effect of this transformation, one need look no further than the documentary record that Raul Hilberg utilized in his groundbreaking 1961 work, *The Destruction of the European Jews*.[1] Hilberg's research, which provided the most enduring vision of the Holocaust's tropes of perpetrator, victim, and bystander, was predominantly based on confiscated German documents that were presented at the postwar Nuremberg trials. That documentary record is largely absent from the authors' research in this volume. Instead, scholars' use of perpetrator documentation has been displaced by increasing use of the massive global projects to interview Holocaust survivors in the 1980s and 1990s.

Drawing as they do on the words of the victims, these chapters push new questions into the mainstream of Holocaust studies. The authors of these chapters are not primarily concerned with how or why the Nazi state implemented a policy of mass murder, but rather with the nature of the experiences of those targeted for murder, and how they sought to evade the genocide. Indeed, in this case, the authors engage in what might be termed a "distant dialogue" with Hilberg, providing the missing "text" of the embodied voice in order to reenergize his influential work. They also showcase alternative intellectual conversations to develop Friedländer's model of "integrated history" in ways that he most likely would not have anticipated.[2]

The first part of this volume, "Tropes Reconsidered," contains four chapters that take readers into the worlds of complicity, suffering, social taboos, and judicial accountability. The role of women as inhabitants of the "gray zone" has been largely absent from Holocaust historiography. This hypermasculine zone receives an overdue re-gendering in Andrea Rudorff's chapter, "Reimagining the 'Gray Zone': Female Prisoner Functionaries in the Gross-Rosen Subcamps, 1944–45." Rudorff draws on hundreds of oral history interviews with women who were prisoners in the Gross-Rosen subcamps, and nuances Primo Levi's notion of the "gray zone."[3] In particular, Rudorff suggests that this way of thinking about prisoner functionaries in the camp system has tended to draw solely upon the experience of the male prisoners in men's camps. By focusing on the women's camps, Rudorff suggests a need to reimagine the "gray zone" as a gendered concept. The situation that she uncovers in the Gross-Rosen subcamps at the end of the war simply does not fit with this rather monolithic concept. As she argues, when it comes to "discussing camp societies and prisoner behavior, it is important that we do not follow the widespread assumption that the well-documented experiences of male inmates, which reflect their specific experience in the main camps, are universal." Moreover, the notion of "choiceless choices" developed by Laurence Langer, again within the context of thinking primarily about the responses by male members of the ghetto Jewish Councils, do not translate to a time and place where "although in a situation of compulsion, they could decide whether they wanted to collaborate or not."

Rudorff's insights are suggestive. If the "gray zone" has been located principally as a concentrationary camp norm, how does its character migrate, mutate, or become irrelevant across the subcamp's social network and its hierarchies of administration, interactions with the local population, and constantly changing labor force? Given that subcamps remain relatively understudied in historiography, and that scholars continue to privilege well-known concentration and extermination camps as Holocaust epicenters of persecution and thus of witness history, Rudorff's attention to the experience of female prisoners in Gross-Rosen subcamps is an important, multifaceted contribution. She cites Ruth Klüger's call to investigate the "nuances of reality and gritty surfaces" of camp experiences as an inspiration.

The last year of the war and of the "Final Solution" saw the mass transfer and evacuation of guards across existing concentration camps, and also a shortage of experienced female prisoners to supervise an expanding subcamp system. This deficit led the SS to appoint functionaries from the first prisoner transport arriving at subcamps. Rudorff charts the arrival, recruitment, and tasks of these inexperienced female prisoner functionaries. She also outlines their "rewards," which included better food and clothes, less intrusive accommodation, and exemption from strenuous work. The prisoner functionaries sustained a short-term support network based on first arrivals, their transport group, and national belonging, and did not exhibit the violent kapo regime that was often found in concentration camp administrations. Rudorff's attention to female prisoner functionaries insightfully reveals the redundancy of using enduring popular philosophical markers of behavior and judgment such as the "gray zone" to describe the panorama of coerced behavior in the highly complicated network of the subcamps. As with the other chapters that adopt a microhistorical approach, Rudorff warns against an approach to the Holocaust that is overly monolithic and insensitive to the particularities of time and place, and—as many chapters in this volume suggest—most strikingly, gender.

Primo Levi's influence in Holocaust memory and scholarship is again rethought in Sharon B. Oster's analysis of that multidimensional signifier of the Holocaust, the *Muselmann*. In "The *Muselmann* Liberated: Impossible Holocaust Metaphors in Survivor Memoirs and Photography," Oster asks readers to rethink the damaging abstraction of the term *Muselmann* and sets out to extract the experience from the symbol of the "living dead" prisoner that it has become. As she insists, "we must reexamine our repeated, uncritical recirculation of the term to see it as a category invented in the 'logic' of the Nazi hierarchy. What if, indeed, there are multiple categories of *Muselmänner*: the dying or dead, the suicidal, and the liberated?"

Oster argues that *Muselmann* was a term adopted by survivors as they sought to narrate their wartime experiences and thus could be—and was—seen as a "temporary" "condition." However, this "fluidity of meaning and metaphoricity" was lost with the widespread adoption of Primo Levi's dominant use of the term. But it is not only Levi whom Oster seeks to challenge. She also critiques the choice and captioning of photographs of survivors taken by the western Allies when they liberated the camps in Germany. The dominant and most widely circulated images offered a co-joined *Muselmann*—the living and the dead—but other photographs offered very different renderings of survivors. These tended not to be recirculated, precisely because they did not show what Oster identifies as the dominant "de-individuating uniformity" of images of "the silent, uniform, skeletal, zombie-like figure of the living dead."

To reclaim the experience from the trope, Oster charts the evolution of physiological definitions of a *Muselmann*; and the philosophical, literary, and visual uses and abuses of the figure of the *Muselmann* in its singular and crowd formations (*Muselmänner*), places of residence (the barbed wire fence, the hospital barracks), ambiguous humanity (the liberated and the living dead), and his social death through inmates' determined efforts at physical segregation. She then turns her attention to photographic documentation of the liberated survivors, which complements the earlier focus on the semantic decline of the individual.

Liberation photos, Oster asserts, had visualized the *Muselmann* long before Levi's phrase, "the demolition of a man," took hold in popular literary discourse. As she suggests, "It is as if the closer an image, or expression, can go to showing life on the very brink of death—life in death, or as death, human as nearly matter—the more powerfully one can convey a sense of the extremity of the atrocity that was the Nazi genocide." In short, "the iconic images illustrate the story told by the *Musselmänner*," but as Oster shows, both survivors themselves as well as a large number of relatively unseen photographs offered rather different visions of this figure.

The obsession with bodily waste, and the inability to suppress its visual return once seen, is the topic of Holli Levitsky's "Absent Presence, Pathological Afterimages, and the Aesthetics of Excrement." Levitsky focuses on that nondiscriminatory measure of degradation—excrement—and she charts scholars' refusals to see its olfactory power to strip bare the uncivilizing and filthy truths of the Holocaust. Though the topic of excrement has featured in numerous scholarly works about the Holocaust, Levitsky mounts a philosophical investigation of excremental aesthetics using a range of philosophical, literary, testimonial, and visual sources.[4] Levitsky follows the flow of excrement from Holocaust bodies to Holocaust representations. She asserts that the stench of excrement has yet to be grasped or understood as a site of "olfactory information" about the Holocaust. She uses perspectives from psychoanalysis and post-structural criticism to work through the figurative and literal meanings of excrement and abjection, and ultimately, the elimination of the Holocaust body. Similar to Oster, Levitsky uses visual evidence of photographs and newsreels taken by the western Allies when they liberated the camps. She traces the emergence of what she dubs an "excremental aesthetics" in postwar representations of the Holocaust. Focusing in particular on literary sources, she points to the centrality of human excrement as material object and metaphor in narratives of the Holocaust. However, as she suggests, "excrement may be the only metaphor that makes metaphor itself impossible."

The elimination of the Holocaust body took many forms and involved an inestimable number of perpetrators, accomplices, and institutions across Europe. Bringing one of those accused and well-known individuals to belated justice is the focus of Yehudit Dori Deston's chapter, "When One Door Closes, Another Opens: The Demjanjuk Trials in Israel (1986–1993) and in Germany (2009–2011)." In this chapter, Dori Deston focuses on what might be considered the perpetrator trope of low-level, "unthinking" participation. She compares the legal proceedings in Israel and Germany that were brought against the Ukrainian John Demjanjuk for his wartime work as a camp guard in extermination camps. Demjanjuk had been living a comfortably submerged life in the United States until it was discovered by the U.S. Office of Special Investigations in 1976 that he had failed to declare his participation in Nazi crimes on his citizenship application. Thus began proceedings to bring him to justice. Dori Deston charts the protracted proceedings in Israel whereby Demjanjuk was charged with being the gas chamber operator at Treblinka. Acquitted at trial in Israel in 1987 due to reasonable doubt, he returned to the United States whereupon he was extradited, after four years of waiting, to Germany in 2009 to stand trial for his role as a guard in Sobibor. As Dori Deston notes, Demjanjuk has the dubious honor of being the "first person in history whose American citizenship was revoked twice." Demjanjuk appealed the guilty verdict that was delivered at his trial in Germany in 2012, and as Dori Deston notes, he died, in the eyes of German law, an innocent man. The chapter contributes to the literature on late twentieth-century Holocaust justice, and the transnational legal cultures that surrounded so-called Holocaust trials through the prosecution of low-level perpetrators—as well as the pedagogic, documentary, and "extralegal" objectives of Israel and Germany that contributed to the trials' different outcomes. Dori Deston's microhistorical and biographical approach characterizes the chapters that make up the second part of this collection.

The second part of this volume, "Survival Strategies and Obstructions," contains three chapters that focus on trajectories of survival, adaptation, and obstruction using different scales of experience and methodological approaches to advance new contributions to Holocaust studies and geographies through the lens of microhistory. Susanna Schrafstetter's chapter, "The Geographies of Living Underground: Escape Routes and Hiding Spaces of Fugitive Jews in Germany, 1939–1945," examines experiences of mobility and improvised living constructed while under threat. Her analysis of the constant mobility of Jews—especially Jewish women—in hiding in Berlin suggests mobility as an example of hiding, linking that concept to studies of isolating movement as a key norm of the Holocaust experience.[5] But as well as pointing to the broader continent-wide significance of motion, Schrafstetter signals the importance of paying attention to specific geographies. Strategies of hiding in Bavaria differed from those in Berlin in important ways, leading Schrafstetter to ask whether the rural population in Bavaria was "less prone to denounce suspicious individuals than Germans in other regions."

The focus on subterranean experiences merits further comment. Although testimonies, literature, and film have long construed the "underground" through resistance associations, other experiences of the "underground" reveal it as an especially vast and complicated topography of resistance, insurgency, and improvised living.[6] This subterranean mobility, which is undoubtedly a spatial strategy of survival, entailed finding livable urban and rural locations in order to evade capture. Oftentimes, these locations were not suitable for human habitation, such as sewers and caves. These broadly defined subterranean spaces were pursued and secured with desperation, improvisation, and immense dependence on others. Schrafstetter's example of this subterranean mobility occurs on the escape routes and in the hiding spaces of fugitive Jews in Germany during World War II. She invokes a term of marine exploration, "submarines," which has been used by survivors to describe themselves in this novel but actually transnational phenomenon.[7] Schrafstetter points out that these Nazi-era Jewish "submarines" in Germany were not isolated across Europe, given the prevalence of social networks of support that aided Jews' survival in a multitude of hiding contexts, escape routes, and concealed identity schemes across France, Belgium, the Netherlands, and Denmark. The term "submergence" is, therefore, an updated word for an old practice that Jews undertook to avoid persecution in Europe and to aid their assimilation into Gentile society.

Her analysis of the spatial patterns of hiding in rural and urban environments through these submarines' support networks, through identity concealment in public, through the provision of physical hiding places, or through frequency of movement and obstruction, is ripe for geo-visual development in the future.

The under-explored participation of women in Jewish resistance is the subject of Dalia Ofer's chapter, "Bella Hazan Ya'ari: A Member of the Jewish Resistance in Pursuit of Self and a Future." She takes one Polish Jewish woman—Bella Hazan Ya'ari—and follows her journey through ghettos and camps, a journey marked by her growing understanding of the threat that Jews faced, as well as the options for resistance. Adopting the concept of "tipping points" that Ofer developed in earlier work with Lenore Weitzman, the chapter explores the moments in Hazan Ya'ari's transformation of thinking, acting, and identity.[8] Hazan's story is of particular interest to Ofer in affording a singular biography of a much wider story of the transformation of Jewish women's identities during the course of the war as they moved into entirely new and previously unimaginable spheres of influence that included armed resistance.

Indeed, Hazan Ya'ari's courageous life is waiting for a biopic: as a courier for the Dror Zionist underground movement in World War II, she undertook dangerous missions across Poland and Vilna before her incarceration in Auschwitz, eventual liberation, and emigration to Palestine. It was there in Palestine—and later Israel—that Hazan Ya'ari became a major commentator about the Jewish resistance. Ofer reads Hazan's life as that of a forensic biographer, scoping her decisions in their heroic and bitter impacts. The tipping points in Hazan Ya'ari's life were not only spatially anchored, for example through adaptation to ghettoization, but they were also most profoundly affected by news of death from ghettos and other locations. These tipping points evolve in emotional intensity and epic risk-taking as Ofer traces the cartography of Hazan's childhood and teenage years from Poland, to ghettoization in Vilna, living as a "submerged" Jewish woman on Polish papers, and her first recruitment into underground activities. Hazan Ya'ari embodies the Polish-Jewish variant of Schrafstetter's German Jews living on the run—except with couriers and the Jewish resistance, until her capture and torture by the Gestapo in Warsaw. Ofer's use of the term "tipping points" is an organizational compass which concludes with an analysis of Hazan Ya'ari's postwar construction of her wartime self in resistance movements, and her responsibilities to her family and friends.

In "Migration Narratives of Holocaust Survivors in Chile, Colombia, and Mexico," Lorena Avila, Nancy Nicholls, and Yael Siman take readers to the impact of Jewish emigration to Latin America, namely Chile, Colombia, and Mexico. The authors consider the different motivations of émigrés, including their routes, stopovers, and eventual trajectories, and try to situate this persecution-induced migration within the field of transnational histories of the Holocaust. The authors—drawing on digital methods—develop innovative "circular migration plots" to visualize refugees' trajectories of migration, attempting to give them a spatial agency, which they assert is currently lacking in studies of Jewish refugees of Nazism. These plots effectively track the changing itineraries of refuge and re-migration, as well as providing an emotional topography of political obstruction and frustrated ambition. The authors effectively suspend the migration narrative as a transit capsule in itself; though the journeys are "completed" through arrival at the migration destination, the refugee-survivors carry with them a displacement and memory archive that becomes the norm of their new lives, motivating multiple re-emigration attempts to anchor themselves in that ever-elusive place of belonging, whether in Latin America or the United States. Through their use of mobility plots and a finely nuanced analysis of the language of exiles, Avila, Nicholls, and Siman further sensitize readers to the semantic dimensions of migration and show how these dimensions play out along global routes of cosmopolitanism, professional development, and cultural adaptation.

The digital methods adopted by Avila and her coauthors are joined by other digital methods in the final part of the volume, "Digital Methods, Digital Memory," which contains four chapters that most directly engage with the conference theme of the "relevance and challenges" of the Holocaust in the "digital age." In "A Different Approach to Microhistory: The Arrests of the Jews of the Vaucluse as Seen through Quantitative Prosopography," Adrien Dallaire adopts a quantitative approach to take on what he sees as a numerical anomaly about the "French–foreign" dichotomy that characterizes much historiography about the Holocaust in France; namely, the belief that more foreign-born Jews residing or interned in France than French-born Jews were victims of the "Final Solution" through arrest and eventual deportation. His use of "prosopography—the investigation of the common background characteristics of a group of actors in history by means of a collective study of their lives," provides the direction that Schrafstetter's focus on submerged mobilities could follow. With this method, Dallaire has constructed a database on the lives of 2,826 Jews of the Vaucluse region, which contains information on their country of origin, age, personal and professional backgrounds, movements, education, and careers. He pays particular attention to the birth countries of arrested Jews and the variable of "nationality" as a means to unpack and destabilize the prevalent assumption among historians that "foreignness" was a fixed category that determined one's fate as a Jew in wartime France.

In "Mind the Gap: Reading across the Holocaust Testimonial Archive," Anne Kelly Knowles, Paul B. Jaskot, Tim Cole, and Alberto Giordano, alongside a wider technical team, work with digital methods to expand on Friedländer's model of "integrated history." The chapter showcases how digital humanities methods can bridge the gap between the individual and the systemic. In order to bridge this gap—or at least the gap between micro and mezzo scales of analysis—they offer up an experiment in using corpus linguistics methods to scale up and across from the individual victim's narrative to the fate of social collectives. Their use of digital methods mirrors Dallaire's use of prosopography to make visible the "traits and characteristics of the population as a whole" and the use of circular migration plots in Avila et al.'s chapter to chart the migration patterns of central European Jewish emigrants to and in Latin America. In particular, their chapter is suggestive of the value of "distant reading" in identifying, for example, the gendering of survivor narratives.[9]

The chapters by Avila et al., Dallaire, and Knowles et al. advocate the adoption of digital humanities approaches to make a metastatement on the field. They showcase how microhistory is profiting from the direct integration of software, technical competencies, and applications that are required to capitalize on the digital moment, and orient new directions in future scholarship. The goal of biographical curation at the individual and group level (or the micro and mezzo scales) in Avila et al.'s study delivers comparative analysis over time and space at the scale of the continent, revealing distinct spatial patterns in emigration; in Dalliare's chapter, it delivers new patterns of scaling chance, fate, and nationality to challenge the conventional historiographic wisdom concerning the different fate of French-born and foreign-born Jews; and in the case of Knowles et al., it delivers new insights into gendered narratives and experiences.

Although they work with digital methods, these chapters do not eschew close reading altogether. As Dallaire is careful to spell out, "prosopography is . . . a hybrid of sorts: a qualitative approach is used to extract information contained in the sources, while a quantitative one is at the heart of the statistical analyses performed on the collected data." Although all three chapters can be seen as offering methodological challenges or invitations to scholars in Holocaust studies, they suggest that the adoption of digital methods will be more a case of adding new tools, rather than discarding existing ones. There are sections of all three chapters that point to the careful and close reading of survivor testimony that brings the individual and his or her story to the fore, as well as the contextualizing and placing of that individual within the broader "mezzohistories" that digital humanities methods are well positioned to uncover.

However, Hannah Pollin-Galay's chapter, "When the Index Is Wrong: Exploring Black Holes in Victim Memory," sounds a note of critical caution and offers a "reversal" to the rush to adopt digital humanities methods in Holocaust research, pedagogy, and memory. In particular, she juxtaposes the neat, topographical view of the world rendered by the Google map that accompanies survivors' testimony in the USC Shoah Foundation's Visual History Archive interface with the far more chaotic geography that characterizes the ways that survivors retell their pasts through landscapes of what Pollin-Galay dubs "black holes." While the digital map orienting the twenty-first-century viewer can pinpoint the subcamp where Hana Golani worked, its flattening of this place to another point on the earth's surface contrasts markedly with Golani's description of this subcamp as "darkness" and "a field in no-place," which Pollin-Galay reads as a loss "to self-orient, to know where she was" that the digital map effaces. Pollin-Galay suggests that "to lose personal navigation capacities was a real part of what it meant to be a victim of Nazi violence for many people." Hana Golani's experience of one of the camps where she was incarcerated as a "no-place" is particularly significant given the geography of retelling in 1990s Israel. As Pollin-Galay argues, retelling the Holocaust through "black holes" not only challenges the digital map of the Shoah Foundation interface, but also the dominant Israeli narrative of *amidah*, or "resistance" at the time of retelling. As she suggests, "contextualizing these memories of disorientation within these witnesses' testimonies as a whole, geography becomes significant once again. The witness's current location of testimony puts specific conceptual pressures on the conversation, giving each memory of geographic rift a different meaning." Pollin-Galay's insistence that space and place matter characterizes the approach of all the scholars in this volume.

As readers know, Holocaust studies encompasses more disciplines than just history, and the Lessons and Legacies conferences and volumes have been no exception to this principle of multidisciplinary gathering. As well as thinking through the impact of digital humanities methods on historical research on the Holocaust, the Lessons and Legacies XIV conference paid attention to the nature of Holocaust memory practices in the digital age. Meghan Lundrigan's contribution to this volume, "People, Places, Things: Considering the Role of Visitor Photography at the United States Holocaust Memorial Museum," identifies the somewhat belated beginning of the digital age in the preeminent memory institution in the United States—the United States Holocaust Memorial Museum—as the year 2015, when the museum lifted its prohibition on visitors taking photographs within the exhibition space. This decision was not about changing attitudes toward the ethics of tourist behavior vis-à-vis photography and Holocaust museums and memorials. Rather, it was a response to, if not a reluctant embrace of, the rise of social media as a key tool to amplify the museum's global impact and storytelling mandate, instantaneously. The resulting proliferation of social media images offers, Lundrigan convincingly argues, a dynamic new source to explore the visceral self-construction of Holocaust tourists as active agents in shaping Holocaust memory in—and through—the digital age. Her chapter is an important and perhaps uncomfortable reminder that it is not simply historians who wield the tools of the digital humanities to influence and innovate prescient and temporal genres of Holocaust digital archiving. It is also the museumgoer with her cell phone in hand who stands "at the front line of visitor engagement with Holocaust memory" and plays a role in co-curating versions of the Holocaust that scholars cannot ignore.

As is evident in this narrative overview of the chapters, a shared set of concerns synergizes the volume, some of which bear reemphasizing. As already mentioned, the ubiquitous presence of survivors' voices marks an important historiographical shift. From the complete absence of oral history narratives in the footnotes of the foundational historiography, they have become increasingly central to historiography, memory, and criminal proceedings.[10] This volume reflects the mainstreaming of oral history within Holocaust studies. It is clear, however, that oral history is used in a range of different ways within Holocaust studies, reflecting wider differences in approach, listening competency, "testimonial literacy," and scholarly influences.[11] In part, oral history interviews offer access to the kind of knowledge that was never written down, or even if it was, ended up being destroyed in the context of the Nazi retreat. As Andrea Rudorff shows, to get inside the subcamps of Gross-Rosen in the final chaotic year of the war when the subcamp system grew exponentially, oral histories are essential data. There are doubtless numerous other places and experiences that can only be accessed and recounted through careful analysis of the oral history record.

The quantitative and multilingual scale of the oral history archives which have been created over the last two or three decades is, admittedly, daunting. As Knowles et al. signal, distant reading and the use of corpus linguistics methods is one answer to this dilemma. Another, as in Rudorff's study, is sampling. She used approximately 150 of the close to 2,000 interviews that the Shoah Foundation undertook with former female inmates of the Gross-Rosen subcamps. But oral histories afford richer challenges, and opportunities, than simply those of scale. They also demand the kind of close reading that characterizes many of the chapters in this volume. The importance of oral history lies not simply in what is said, but also—and most crucially—in the meaning given to events. For example, Pollin-Galay shows the ways that narratives can work against dominant frameworks, and Oster points to the complex ways that survivors use the concept of the *Muselmann* as a temporary condition to highlight their own sense of vulnerability and guilt.

The richness of oral history as sources, as well as the potential of digital approaches, characterize the innovation of the chapters in this volume. The chapters here may not be the kind of integrated history that Friedländer imagined. But they do offer a repurposing of what methodological "integration" requires and how new concepts that expand on integrated histories are needed to accommodate the Holocaust as a complex and multilayered history beyond perpetrators, victims, and bystanders. This volume clearly connects the micro, mezzo, and macro, while unashamedly choosing to begin analysis at the micro. Mapping and interpreting the experiences of individuals and groups should not be read as a retreat to minutiae for minutiae's sake. As Matti Peltonen has suggested, "micro historians are actually trying to discover very big things with their microscope and magnifying lenses."[12] This is certainly the case for the chapters here which invite readers to reconsider broader understandings of the Holocaust.

But as well as the striking use of oral histories as sources, microhistory as methods, and the embracing of digital tools, this volume is distinctive not simply by dint of the contents of the chapters, but also the nature of the authors. As we have already noted, the majority of the authors are women. Also significant, two of the chapters are coauthored by large collaborative research teams. Indeed, the shift toward collaborative modes of working is one explicitly signaled by Knowles et al., who call for an integrating of "scholarly practice" in order to develop "integrated histories" of the Holocaust. Looking back through earlier volumes of the Lessons and Legacies series, the sole-authored scholarship model of the traditional humanities dominates, as indeed it does in this volume, and Adrien Dallaire's chapter shows that not all digital humanities scholarship requires multi-person and multidisciplinary teams. However, the collaborative chapters authored by Avila et al. and Knowles et al. indicate one important way that digital humanities methods are transforming scholarly practice and findings. The scientific model of teams of researchers is becoming more the norm within the digital humanities, and these multi-authored chapters represent the arrival of that approach within Holocaust studies. As demonstrated in this volume, the evolving contours of the Holocaust in the digital age offer profound opportunities—as well as ongoing and new challenges—for scholarly and memory work alike.

NOTES

1. Raul Hilberg, *The Destruction of the European Jews* (Chicago: Quadrangle Books, 1961).

2. Saul Friedländer, *Nazi Germany and the Jews*, vol. 1, *The Years of Persecution 1933–39* (New York: HarperCollins, 1997) and vol. 2, *The Years of Extermination 1939–45* (New York: HarperCollins, 2007).

3. The "gray zone" was an area of extreme moral ambiguity occupied by those prisoners in the camps who collaborated with their Nazi persecutors to

various degrees in exchange for minor privileges. In this zone, many prisoners were forced to make—or chose to make—disturbing moral compromises with their tormentors in order to lengthen their short life expectancy.

4. See, for example, Terrence des Pres, *The Survivor: An Anatomy of Life in the Death Camps* (New York: Oxford University Press, 1976); and Simone Gigliotti, *The Train Journey: Transit, Captivity, and Witnessing in the Holocaust* (Oxford: Berghahn Books, 2009).

5. Gigliotti, *The Train Journey*; Tim Cole, *Holocaust Landscapes* (London: Bloomsbury, 2016).

6. See especially Gunnar S. Paulsson, *Secret City: The Hidden Jews of Warsaw, 1940–1945* (New Haven, Conn.: Yale University Press, 2002).

7. See, for example, Bob Moore, *Survivors: Jewish Self-Help and Rescue in Nazi-Occupied Western Europe* (Oxford: Oxford University Press, 2010).

8. Dalia Ofer and Lenore Weitzman, "The Sequential Development of Jewish Women's Coping Strategies in the Ghettos during the Holocaust: A New Theoretical Framework," in *Women and the Holocaust: New Perspectives and Challenges*, ed. Andrea Peto, Louise Hecht, and Karolina Krasuska (Warsaw: Wydawnictwo Instytut Badán Literackich PAN, 2015), 27–63.

9. Franco Moretti, *Distant Reading* (London: Verso, 2013).

10. See in particular the use of oral history interviews by one of the leading historians of Holocaust perpetrators, in Christopher Browning, *Remembering Survival: Inside a Nazi Slave-Labor Camp* (New York: W.W. Norton, 2010).

11. Noah Shenker, *Reframing Holocaust Testimony* (Bloomington: Indiana University Press, 2015).

12. Matti Pentonen, "Clues, Margins and Monads: The Micro-Macro Link in Historical Research," *History and Theory* 40 (2001): 350.

I. T·R·O·P·E·S R·E·C·O·N·S·I·D·E·R·E·D

Andrea Rudorff

Reimagining the "Gray Zone": Female Prisoner Functionaries in the Gross-Rosen Subcamps, 1944–45

SOON AFTER LIBERATION, SURVIVORS OF THE NAZI CONCENTRATION camps began providing detailed descriptions of the social dimensions of incarceration, the moral dilemmas and ambiguities faced by camp inmates, and the hybrid roles of prisoner functionaries.[1] It is from these early testimonies that we learned about the SS's perfidious organization of power and its exploitation of a "kapo system" that entailed the delegation of responsibility for discipline to selected inmates. This method of privilege and terror not only allowed mass numbers of prisoners to be controlled by just a few SS commanders and guards, it also stifled solidarity between prisoners. Authors like Benedikt Kautsky described the brutality of long-term prisoners, mostly Germans, who were categorized as "common criminals" and "repeat offenders." Regarded as incurable, they were subjected to preventive detention in a concentration camp. In the role of camp functionaries, they executed SS orders and tortured fellow inmates. Their powerful position within the camp hierarchy arose not only from the authority they were granted by the SS, but also through their use of force and their position as Germans and so-called Aryans, who often held antisemitic views.[2] It took some time before historians and sociologists acquired a deeper understanding of the camps' internal social organization.[3] Although most scholars tried to present a differentiated view and warned against making generalizations, their analyses were often based on the available survivor reports, which predominantly reflected the experience of male prisoners in the main camps (*Stammlager*). Furthermore, Wolfgang Sofsky's monolithic and static model of "absolute power," which left little room for an analysis of changing social patterns or variations and flexibility of structures within concentration camp society, influenced the scholarly discourse.[4]

My research on the Gross-Rosen women's subcamps suggests the need to revise this impression of the kapo system. In their testimonies, former female prisoners and former female guards presented a very different view of prisoner collaboration in these camps. The study of the role of prisoner functionaries in women's subcamps had not yet entered the discussion, not only because female persecution experiences did not receive scholarly attention until the 1980s,[5] but also because there was a general lack of knowledge about the subcamps, despite the fact that the majority of concentration camp prisoners were imprisoned in this type of camp in 1944 and 1945.[6]

In discussing camp societies and prisoner behavior, it is important that we do not follow the widespread assumption that the well-documented experiences of male inmates, which reflect their specific experience in the main camps, are universal. Ruth Klüger, who was imprisoned in a Gross-Rosen subcamp, has criticized the unwillingness of the public to take a differentiated view of camp experiences. She accuses people of being "caught up in a kind of chamber of horrors cum melodrama, where the nuances of reality and its gritty surfaces disappear in a fog, and you can't make out any details, so why try?"[7] It is precisely this empty space that my work on the Gross-Rosen subcamp system takes as its starting point.[8] Working with a wide range of sources, I adopt a multi-perspectival approach that not only locates the Gross-Rosen women's subcamps within the system of concentration camps, but also explores—in detail—the varied historical actors in this place (prisoners, guards, companies' employees, and the local population) and the framework for their actions and interactions.

The basis for this analysis of the Gross-Rosen women's subcamps is the examination of the remaining written documentation of the camps (which is not complete, since the SS destroyed numerous documents in 1945); material from more than 140 investigation proceedings against female guards, which took place after the war in Poland and Czechoslovakia, as well as in East and West Germany; and survivor testimonies. Several thousand former female prisoners in Gross-Rosen subcamps have testified about their imprisonment in many different contexts and at different times. Some had already begun to write down their experiences during or shortly after the war.[9] Others reported immediately after their liberation in surveys by Jewish organizations in Poland and Hungary. In Poland, the Central Jewish Historical Commission (Centralna Żydowska Komisja Historyczna) devoted itself to this work, and set up regional offices in several cities. In Hungary, the Deportáltakat Gondozó Országos Bizottság (DEGOB) recorded some 5,000 memoirs of survivors who returned to Hungary in 1945 and 1946. Institutions such as the Wiener Library, Yad Vashem, and the U.S. Holocaust Memorial Museum also collected survivor reports. Due to the increasing interest of the public, several former female prisoners of Gross-Rosen have published their memoirs, especially since the 1980s. I also used about 150 of the approximately 2,000 interviews of the USC Shoah Foundation with former female inmates of Gross-Rosen subcamps, which were conducted in the 1990s.

This multitude of testimonies makes it possible to capture many different perspectives and to create samples for different groups of prisoners within a camp. The heterogeneity of postwar reports and testimonies makes them particularly valuable for research given that, depending on personality, context, and time of creation, they focus on different aspects of the camp experience. While the early postwar reports tended to be very fact-oriented and strove for precise documentation of the camp conditions, the later reports and interviews tend to tell us more about everyday life and emotional states. In the video interviews of the 1990s, it is particularly striking how general Holocaust narratives, which had evolved over the preceding decades, influenced the story. Many of the survivors who gave interviews for the Visual History Archive of the USC Shoah Foundation did not spend the longest period of their captivity in the better-known camps such as Auschwitz, but in one or more subcamps. During the interviews with the former Gross-Rosen prisoners, it was noticeable that misunderstandings and indifference toward the subcamp experience were quite prevalent. The interviewers often urged the survivors to speak more about the better-known camps and were less interested in the women's experiences in lesser-known subcamps.[10]

Despite this, many female survivors of the Gross-Rosen subcamps present narratives about the role of prisoner functionaries that do not correspond to general expectations, which were formed through the aforementioned early camp literature that tended to privilege male camps and the experiences in the main camps. To prevent Holocaust research and education from being reduced to a simple black-

and-white model of prisoner relations, their experiences in subcamps need to be taken more seriously and further historical research must be conducted to close the gaps. This chapter seeks to do some of that gap-closing through an analysis of the experiences of female prisoners in the Gross-Rosen subcamps in 1944 and 1945. In doing so, it aims to challenge and nuance dominant understandings of prisoner societies and gender roles.

FEMALE PRISONERS IN THE SUBCAMPS OF GROSS-ROSEN: SOCIETY AND AUTHORITY

From spring 1944, companies in Lower Silesia, the Sudeten territory, Lusatia, and East Brandenburg established 100 subcamps—among them 45 camps for female prisoners—as part of the comprehensive exploitation of concentration camp prisoners by the German armaments industry.[11] These were subordinated to the administration of the Gross-Rosen concentration camp. Approximately 26,000 Jewish women, most of them from Poland and Hungary, but also from western Europe, Czechoslovakia, Germany, and Austria, were imprisoned in these camps and forced to work in the armaments industry. From October 1944 onward, they were also deployed in the construction of fortifications designed to hinder the advance of the Red Army. Most of the young women were selected for work while on the ramps of Auschwitz-Birkenau. They had been deported some days, weeks, or months earlier from Hungary, from Theresienstadt, from the Litzmannstadt ghetto, from Plaszow concentration camp, from Majdanek subcamps, and—in the case of a smaller group of women—from camps in western Europe such as Westerbork, Vught, and Drancy.

There were, however, 6,200 Polish Jewish female prisoners in the Gross-Rosen camp system who did not share the Auschwitz experience. Since 1942–43, they had been inmates of the camps of Organization Schmelt—an institution established to exploit the labor of the Jewish population of the Zagłębie region.[12] Between March and September 1944, thirteen women's camps of Organization Schmelt were converted into Gross-Rosen concentration subcamps. Most of the women stayed where they were in these camps. They were simply assigned a concentration camp number and became Gross-Rosen prisoners. The Schmelt camps already had preexisting structures of prisoner collaboration, such as a camp eldest (*Lagerälteste*) and block eldest (*Blockälteste*), in place. In many cases these structures remained after conversion to a Gross-Rosen subcamp—systematic changes in personnel did not occur.

In 1944, when women's subcamps were being established throughout the Reich, SS-camp administrators were faced with a new challenge. They lacked experienced female prisoners who could serve as functionaries. Among the male prisoners, there were enough long-term prisoners who had already proven their willingness to follow SS instructions. They were sent as functionaries to the men's subcamps, where they demonstrated the same behavior as in the main camps. But most of the main camps did not have a female prisoner population, and the women's camps in Ravensbrück, Auschwitz, Majdanek, and Stutthof did not have enough female functionaries to meet the new needs. Forced to improvise, the SS appointed functionaries from the first prisoner transport arriving at any given subcamp. This practice led to the appointment of women as functionaries who did not belong to a special prisoner group, but instead shared a common background with the other prisoners.[13]

In most cases, SS officers recruited women who could speak German and who appeared tough and able to assert themselves. Language skills and appearance were the most important criteria, but in many cases the criteria for selection were vague and arbitrary. Two Hungarian survivors of the Schlesiersee subcamps described their arrival in the camp together with 1,000 other women: "We had to stand for roll call until late in the evening and the SS man picked out women for different positions. If the prisoner made a friendly face she got a better position."[14] Edith K., a survivor from the Breslau-Hundsfeld subcamp, stated in a testimony after the war: "My sister Eva was beautiful. She spoke German fluently. The *Oberaufseherin* [female guard in charge] chose her during arrival and said, 'You are my secretary, the camp eldest.'"[15] The more or less random selection of functionaries led to a high fluctuation in the following weeks. Either women realized that they were unable to fulfill the tasks, or the camp leader decided they were not suited for the job. Several women quit their assigned jobs after a few days or weeks. They stayed in the camp and led the life of a "normal" prisoner—without privileges, but relieved of the moral pressure of being a functionary. Several prisoners who had only held this function briefly spoke after the war about conflicts of loyalty and the difficulty of balancing the expectations of the SS with their own moral sensibility. Isabella Katz, a 24-year-old from Kisvárda, recognized the ambivalence of the function, for which she had initially volunteered.

> The German genius had, of course, variations of evil, one of which was to appoint torturers from among the inmates themselves. Brother against brother. Sister against sister. And if you survived long enough, you realized that the minutest advantage might help you make it through. In many cases the Germans realized their intentions. They suceeded in brutalizing some of us. But only some.[16]

Isabella felt a moral obligation to keep herself and her three sisters alive and took the position so that she could assign her sisters to less strenuous work. However, the SS ousted her after a few days when they discovered that she did not exert enough pressure or hit her fellow prisoners.

Lore Herzberger, a 21-year-old Jewish woman from Mönchengladbach, arrived with her mother via Theresienstadt and Auschwitz at the Sackisch camp in Silesia. In her interview for the Visual History Archive in 1995, she recalled:

> When we got there, we were the only two German Jews, my mother and I. The others were all Polish Jews. And the Germans thought we would make good *Lagerälteste*, my mother and I, because they could talk to us. And we did it for one whole day. But we just couldn't do it.—Why?—Because of the things they asked us to do to the other prisoners, we couldn't do it. . . . And we did that for one day and then they took somebody else. . . . We gave it up. I mean, it would have been good for us, because we would have had more to eat, we would have been in a better position, but we couldn't do it.[17]

It is notable that Lore Bruch did not specify exactly what "things they asked us to do to the other prisoners." What were the tasks given to these hastily elected functionaries?

DUTIES AND PRIVILEGES

The group of prisoner functionaries was hierarchically structured and had to operate in two areas: inside the camp (as *Lagerälteste*/camp eldest, as *Blockälteste*/block eldest, or as *Stubenälteste*/room eldest) and outside the camp (as *Kolonnenälteste*/column eldest, also called "*Schieberin*"). The camp eldest wore a badge on her left arm with the inscription "*Judenälteste*" and was the liaison between the camp leader, the guards, and the prisoners. She had to pass on the orders from the camp leader and make sure they were carried out. Her job also involved organizing the line-up for roll call and planning the work columns. She selected each of the block eldest and was responsible for overseeing their work. The block eldest was in charge of a single barrack, and was responsible for upholding law and order and guaranteeing that the barrack was kept tidy and clean. She had to wake up the prisoners in the morning and organize the distribution of food in the mornings and evenings. The column eldest was in charge of one work unit outside the camp. They made sure the prisoners kept moving forward on their way from the camp to the factory, which was in some cases several kilometers away from the camp.

We have no evidence that further types of functionaries which are documented in other camps existed in the women's subcamps. There were, for example, no female forewomen or kapos *inside* the factories. German civil foremen and forewomen maintained control over the workers at the work sites (as was also the case in other female camp complexes, like Ravensbrück), rather than there being a well-developed kapo system as was the case in the factories linked to the men`s camps.[18] In the Gross-Rosen subcamps, female SS guards, who had often worked in the same factories before being designated camp guards,[19] kept an eye on the door so that nobody escaped from the factory. They regulated who could go to the toilet—only one visit per shift. In short, the system of functionaries in the Gross-Rosen subcamps was not very complex, certainly when compared against the male camps. But it was also less complex than, for example, the system in Ravensbrück, where a camp police had been established in 1942 to guard new transports and arrange work details. No equivalent structure was established in the Gross-Rosen women's subcamps.

Besides the various "eldest" roles, women prisoners in the Gross-Rosen subcamps worked in offices, infirmaries, and kitchens or food stores—the so-called *Lagerinnendienst*. They were privileged prisoners, but had no authority to give instructions or orders to other prisoners. The number of the *Lagerinnendienst* fluctuated: a camp report from the Hochweiler camp shows that regularly anywhere between 52 and 96 of 1,000 women were assigned to it.[20] Most of the prisoners in the offices, infirmaries, and in the kitchen had fixed positions. In the offices and infirmaries this was because certain skills were required.[21] In the case of kitchen staff, they needed to be free of infectious diseases and therefore had to be checked regularly. Blood, urine, and bowel samples were sent to the SS Institute of Hygiene in Auschwitz for this purpose.[22] In addition to the permanent kitchen staff, there were temporary kitchen workers who volunteered for kitchen services after the factory work in order to gain access to additional food in this way.[23]

The functionaries enjoyed many privileges and received preferential treatment, such as better food and clothes. They were exempt from performing the strenuous work in the factories and were often provided better accommodations, such as a double or triple room with other privileged prisoners. By contrast, the other prisoners had to sleep with up to a hundred people in rooms furnished with three-story bunk beds. Sala Neustätter, who served as camp eldest in Parschnitz, shared a special room with two other female prisoners, one of whom worked as a typist and the other as a nurse in the prisoner infirmary. She testified after the war: "We had iron beds, a wardrobe, a table and a desk in the room. The room was equipped with a gramophone and a collection of German and Czech records."[24] The ordinary prisoners could only dream of this kind of luxury. In many camps, the difference in housing conditions between ordinary and privileged prisoners was extreme. In the Schlesiersee camp, the prisoners lived in unheated barns or tents while the functionaries lived with the camp guards in farmhouses. The Hungarian Jewish prisoner Aniko K. from the Schlesiersee camp remembered the block eldest sitting in the warm house: "They were laughing, they had warm clothes on and were comfortable and we were outside in the freezing cold."[25]

ATTITUDES OF FUNCTIONARIES TOWARD THE ORDINARY PRISONERS

To analyze the behavior of functionaries toward their fellow prisoners, it is necessary to understand the individual's affiliation with a specific subgroup within prisoner society. Three factors influenced membership in these subgroups: nationality; previous experience of Nazi persecution; and perhaps the most important factor in determining a prisoner's position in the camp hierarchy, the time of her arrival in the subcamp. People on the first transport always had an advantage in securing the important functions in the camp. A particularly dramatic situation occurred in the former camps of Organization Schmelt where Polish Jewish women had been imprisoned for one or two years. When hundreds of "new" women, mostly from Hungary, arrived in these camps in May 1944, they had a very poor chance of obtaining a privileged position. A list of kitchen personnel in the Ober Altstadt camp in January 1945 shows that fifteen former Schmelt prisoners and only two Hungarian women (Deutsch Kati and Gutmann Jolan) worked in this privileged position, despite the fact that there were 200 Hungarian women who had already been in the camp for several months.[26] In this case, the Hungarian Jews who were deported much later were at a disadvantage.

However, in the camps that were created in the summer and autumn of 1944, the situation could be very different. In the Breslau-Hundsfeld camp, for example, Hungarians and Slovaks made up the first transport to arrive at the camp in August 1944. In postwar testimonies, several former Polish inmates who arrived on a second transport in October 1944 complained about them. Upon their arrival, according to the Polish Jew Sonja C. from Lodz, the Hungarian women had "all favorable work arrangements" in their hands, and as a result, the Polish women were disadvantaged in the distribution of food.[27] After a few weeks the SS replaced the camp eldest, a Slovakian woman named Eva L., with a German Jew. As a consequence of this change, the conditions for the Hungarian and Slovak Jews worsened. In postwar interrogations these women testified that Eva L. was removed because of the solidarity she showed with the prisoners.[28] By contrast, the Polish prisoners did not recall acts of solidarity on the part of Eva L.

My analysis of postwar testimonies reveals that the prisoners on the first transport were judged quite negatively by the later prisoners who did not belong to this group. Due to the scarcity of resources, every incoming transport worsened the living conditions in the camp, and new arrivals were exposed to the mistrust of the already resident prisoners for this reason alone. But because the women from the first transport had better opportunities to save influential positions for their own group, they also secured a better supply of material resources for themselves. The functionaries in the subcamps had many opportunities to look out for and provide for their relatives and acquaintances, in particular the distribution of food and clothes, but also in the assignment to privileged work details. The so-called camp family, a close circle of four to five people, enjoyed the greatest advantage, but some of its actions also benefited the larger group. Although group membership was primarily based on national origin, persecution experiences and deportation routes also played a major role, which did not always coincide with the national origin of the prisoners. This becomes particularly evident in the example of Polish Jewish women. The difference in experience between those who had been imprisoned in forced-labor camps of the Organization Schmelt for several years and those who had experienced life in the ghettos or in the concentration camps Plaszow, Majdanek, and Auschwitz could hardly be greater. The Polish Jewish woman Anna Freilich, who survived the ghetto in Szydlowiec and the camps Starachowice and Auschwitz, met Organization Schmelt prisoners—also Polish Jews—in the former Schmelt camp in Zillerthal-Erdmannsdorf, where she was deported in July 1944. In contrast to her own experiences of the ghettos and camps, she recalled that they lived "a normal life": they had their own clothes, relatively orderly conditions, and above all almost no idea of the mass murder of Polish Jews. The newcomers from Auschwitz could hardly believe what they saw in Zillerthal-Erdmannsdorf.[29] Paula Gruber-Herszkopf, who, like many of the Schmelt prisoners, came from Sosnowiec but was deported to a subcamp via Auschwitz, also felt more connected with the "women from Auschwitz," as they were called in the Langenbielau II camp (where they were also housed in a separate barrack), than with the Jewish women who had been imprisoned in Langenbielau since 1942–43. Although they came from her hometown, their very different experience of persecution had separated her from them.[30]

To develop dominance, a certain group size was necessary. German and Austrian Jews were a minority in these camps and always arrived as part of another subgroup, mostly via Theresienstadt. Although they were preferred by the supervisors because of their origin and language skills, they were unable to assume a dominant position as a group in the camp hierarchy. Instead, they were mixed with the national group with whom they arrived at the camp. As the German Jewish prisoner Ursula Pawel—who was deported via Theresienstadt to Auschwitz and then to the Sackisch subcamp—reported: "There were certain tensions between the Czech and the Polish prisoners. I was part of the Czech contingent."[31]

Despite the "certain tensions," most survivors in my sample testify that the functionaries in the women's subcamps played a predominantly positive role, especially in comparison with the situation they experienced in Auschwitz, where the female functionaries tended to be very violent. The functionaries in the Gross-Rosen subcamps were "nicer and much more relaxed."[32] The Polish prisoner Maria H. testified after the war that the block eldest did not act against the prisoners—"they were one of us."[33]

Survivors mentioned situations in which functionaries used their position to alleviate difficult situations, for example, when they tried to mediate in conflicts with the SS or when they looked after prisoners who needed support coping with imprisonment and forced labor. Sara Plager-Zyskind, a former inhabitant of the Litzmannstadt ghetto, who was later deported to the subcamp in Mittelsteine, recalled in her memoirs that Hella, the camp eldest, took care of the youngest prisoners and supplied them with additional bread.[34] If the SS forced them to punish other prisoners, they developed ways to pretend that they were inflicting punishment. Many succeeded in defusing situations to the benefit of the prisoners or improving conditions in the camps. The German Jewish prisoner Hilde Isaak wrote about the camp in Reichenbach: "The uniformed pushed a stick into the hand of the camp eldest. She refused to hit anybody. Banished the stick. And even more: she cared that we had a bearable life."[35] This was possible only because in the last year of the war, businesses and the SS leaders had an interest in satisfactory labor output. Functionaries, for example, were able to complain to the camp administration of Peterswaldau camp about beatings from a female SS guard.[36] The mere fact that prisoners were able to issue a complaint is an indication of the new conditions.

However, in the case of a few camps, prisoner functionaries almost entirely replaced the SS leadership. One of these camps was Parschnitz in the Sudetes, where more than 1,000 prisoners were housed in an unused factory building and forced to work in several textile and armament enterprises. The camp eldest, Sala Neustätter, a Polish Jew in her late thirties from Szczakowa, had a far-reaching influence. How much power the camp eldest was able to acquire depended on her personal ambition, her self-assertion, and the personality of the camp leader. In Parschnitz prisoners feared Neustätter more than the female camp leader, Else Hawlik, whom they did not see daily. Sala Neustätter abused her power, beat prisoners with lashes, truncheons, and belts, denounced them to the camp leader, stole food rations, and made suggestions as to which of the sick prisoners should be sent to Auschwitz. The prisoners remembered the cynical and insulting comments that Neustätter made while beating a woman. They hardly differed from typical SS slogans. The camp leader is said to have told Neustätter: "Too bad that you are a Jew, you could have been such a good SS camp guard."[37]

In 1954, former prisoners brought Sala Neustätter, who at the time went by the name Chana Lender, to court. She was accused of beating prisoners, stealing food rations, and participating in selections, and she ended up serving a custodial sentence in Poland from 1955 to 1958. Although the court recognized the basic dilemma facing functionaries, it argued that Neustätter was not a spineless victim who had blindly followed the orders of the camp leader. And difficult circumstances, it continued, do not absolve a person of responsibility for her own behavior, especially when there was no order to behave cruelly. Neustätter was not charged with the third point of the indictment—participation in the selections and sending weak or sick prisoners to Auschwitz—because the court was not convinced that she had any role in the decision-making process. Neustätter was initially sentenced to prison for five years. After her appeal to the Supreme Court, the term was raised to eight years. Her poor health and good behavior in prison led to her early release on parole in 1958 after she had served less than three years of her sentence.[38]

I was able to find only one other proceeding against female functionaries from the Gross-Rosen women's subcamps. Both had taken place in postwar Poland, where a controversial discussion of the role of functionaries had taken place.[39] The second accused *Lagerälteste,* Dora Luks (she became Dora Brawer after marriage) from Ober Altstadt camp, admitted in her court testimony on September 19, 1947, that she had acted against the prisoners, for example by waking them up at night to clean rooms and toilets. After six former prisoners made strong allegations against her, the defense found another twenty-four former prisoners to testify on her behalf and praise her behavior in the camp. The trial ended in an acquittal.[40]

CONCLUSIONS

In conclusion, functionaries in the Gross-Rosen women's subcamps were a vital component in the management of the camps, helping to stabilize the system of forced labor and exploitation. Most strove to carry out the administrative tasks assigned to them, which contributed to the functioning of everyday life in the camp. Unlike in the main camps where a pronounced system of terror existed, and prisoners became accomplices to camp leaders and helped persecute their fellow prisoners to their own advantage, this conduct remained the exception here. There are several reasons for this. First, when the number of women's camps grew in 1944, the SS did not have experienced long-term female prisoners to serve as functionaries. In each subcamp, the SS had to establish new structures of power that required time to develop. Because functionaries were recruited from the general prisoner population, most tried to act to the benefit of their fellow prisoners. They risked losing their jobs, however, if their bias became too apparent. Second, since most of the women's subcamps were relatively short-lived and did not exist for even a year, even when a sympathetic camp eldest was only in place for a few weeks or months, this short period of solidarity could make an important difference in the lives of the women in the camp. Third, the low fluctuation rate of prisoners helped establish stable group structures in the Gross-Rosen subcamps. Together, these factors meant that the role of the functionary, however complex and ambivalent, could help to uphold a certain humanity in the camp. In general, it can be stated that while the women in the subcamps suffered from malnutrition, hard work, and the maltreatment of the SS, in most cases they did not suffer from a violent kapo regime.

This contrasts with the wider historiographic discussion over prisoner collaboration, mostly inspired by Primo Levi's conception of the "gray zone."[41] This dominant literature focused on camp conditions that are not comparable with the situation in the women's subcamps. The female prisoners in these subcamps in the late stages of the war were not forced to help in mass killing like the members of the *Sonderkommando* in Auschwitz. They were not exposed to these kinds of "choiceless choices,"[42] as Lawrence Langer phrases it. Instead, they faced choices over whether to collaborate or not. Although they were in a situation of compulsion, they could decide whether they wanted to collaborate or instead stay in the background. The decision to collaborate was motivated by the will to survive, to exercise power, or at least to improve their own living conditions, but sometimes also from a sense of responsibility for their own particular group: because during the performance of their functions, they had the opportunity to act more or less in favor of the prisoners. The specific experience of the women functionaries in the Gross-Rosen subcamps points to the need for a more nuanced understanding of the moral ambiguities in the camp system.

NOTES

1. Eugen Kogon, *Der SS-Staat: Das System der deutschen Konzentrationslager* (Munich: Verlag Karl Alber, 1946); Primo Levi, *Se questo è un uomo* (Turin: De Silva, 1947); Paul Martin Neurath, *Social Life in the German Concentration Camps Dachau and Buchenwald* (New York: Columbia University Press, 1951); Bruno Bettelheim, *The Informed Heart; Autonomy in a Mass Age* (Glencoe, Ill.: Free Press, 1960); Hans G. Adler, *Theresienstadt 1941–1945: Das Antlitz einer Zwangsgemeinschaft* (Tübingen: J.C.B. Mohr, 1955); Herrmann Langbein, *Menschen in Auschwitz* (Vienna: Europa Verlag, 1972).

2. Benedikt Kautsky, *Teufel und Verdammte: Erfahrungen und Erkenntnisse aus sieben Jahren in deutschen Konzentrationslagern* (Zürich: Büchergilde Gutenberg, 1946), 8–9, 141–45, 160–61.

3. Falk Pingel, *Häftlinge unter SS-Herrschaft: Widerstand, Selbstbehauptung und Vernichtung im Konzentrationslager* (Hamburg: Hoffmann und Campe, 1978); Falk Pingel, ed., *Abgeleitete Macht, Funktionshäftlinge zwischen Widerstand und Kollaboration: Themenheft der Beiträge zur Geschichte der nationalsozialistischen Verfolgung in Norddeutschland 4* (Bremen: Edition Temmen, 1998); Maja Suderland, *Ein Extremfall des Sozialen: Die Häftlingsgesellschaft in den nationalsozialistischen Konzentrationslagern* (Frankfurt am Main: Campus, 2009).

4. Wolfgang Sofsky, *Die Ordnung des Terrors: Das Konzentrationslager* (Frankfurt am Main: S. Fischer Verlag, 1993).

5. Esther Katz and Joan Ringelheim, eds., *Proceedings of the Conference, Women Surviving: The Holocaust* (New York: Institute for Research in History, 1983); Renate Bridenthal, Atina Grossmann, and Marion Kaplan, eds., *When Biology Became Destiny: Women in Weimar and Nazi Germany* (New York: Monthly Review, 1984); Carol Rittner and John K. Roth, eds., *Different Voices: Women and the Holocaust* (St. Paul, Minn.: Paragon House, 1993); Dalia Ofer and Lenore J. Weitzman, eds., *Women in the Holocaust* (London: Yale University Press, 1998); Judith Tydor Baumel, *Double Jeopardy: Gender and the Holocaust* (London: Valentine Mitchell, 1998); Gisela Bock, ed., *Genozid und Geschlecht: Jüdische Frauen im nationalsozialistischen Lagersystem* (Frankfurt am Main: Campus, 2005).

6. Almost all existing studies about female functionaries refer to the main women's camp, Ravensbrück. See Irmtraud Heike and Bernhard Strebel, "Häftlingsselbstverwaltung und Funktionshäftlinge im Konzentra-

tionslager Ravensbrück," in *Frauen in Konzentrationslagern: Bergen-Belsen—Ravensbrück*, ed. Claus Füllberg-Stolberg, Martina Jung, Renate Riebe, and Martina Scheitenberger (Bremen: Edition Temmen, 1994), 89–98; Renate Riebe, "Funktionshäftlinge in Frauenkonzentrationslagern 1933–1939," in Pingel, *Abgeleitete Macht*, 51–56; Bernhard Strebel, "Unterschiede in der Grauzone? Über die Lagerältesten im Frauen- und Männerlager des KZ Ravensbrück," in Pingel, *Abgeleitete Macht*, 57–68; Annette Neumann, "Funktionshäftlinge im Frauenkonzentrationslager Ravensbrück," in *Tod oder Überleben? Neue Forschungen zur Geschichte des Konzentrationslagers Ravensbrück, Bulletin für Faschismus- und Weltkriegsforschung,* Supplement 1, ed. Werner Röhr and Brigitte Berlekamp (2001): 25–87.

7. Ruth Klüger, *Still Alive: A Holocaust Girlhood Remembered* (New York: Feminist Press at the City University of New York, 2001), 73.

8. Andrea Rudorff, *Frauen in den Außenlagern des Konzentrationslagers Groß-Rosen* (Berlin: Metropol, 2014).

9. Diaries of Fela Szeps, Aliza Besser, and Hella Kantor, in Yad Vashem Archives (hereafter YVA), 033/747; 0.33/3394; 0.33/1269; Ana Novac, *Les Beaux Jours de ma jeunesse* (Paris: Édition Balland, 1996).

10. On the institutional context of the Shoah Foundation interviews, see Noah Shenker, *Reframing Holocaust Testimony* (Bloomington: Indiana University Press, 2015).

11. Anne Kelly Knowles, Paul B. Jaskot, Benjamin Perry Blackshear, Michael De Groot, and Alexander Yule, "Mapping the SS Concentration Camps," in *Geographies of the Holocaust*, ed. Anne Kelly Knowles, Tim Cole, and Alberto Giordano (Bloomington: Indiana University Press, 2014).

12. Andrea Rudorff, "Arbeit und Vernichtung Reconsidered: Die Lager der Organisation Schmelt für polnische Jüdinnen und Juden aus dem annektierten Teil Oberschlesiens," *Sozial.Geschichte Online* 7 (2012): 10–39, http://duepublico.uni-duisburg-essen.de/servlets/DocumentServlet?id=28067.

13. Rudorff, *Frauen*, 250–54.

14. DEGOB-protocol 2820, Rozsi and Helen F. (July 16, 1945).

15. BArch B 162/20491, Edith K. (June 19, 1967).

16. Isabella Leitner, *Fragments of Isabella: A Memoir of Auschwitz* (New York: Crowell, 1978), 45. See also USC Shoah Foundation VHA 1918, Interview with Isabella Leitner (April 3, 1995).

17. USC Shoah Foundation VHA 2999, Interview with Lore Bruch, née Herzberger (June 6, 1996).

18. Bernhard Strebel, *Das KZ Ravensbrück: Geschichte eines Lagerkomplexes* (Paderborn: Schöningh, 2003), 454.

19. About the recruitment of female guards in the Gross-Rosen subcamps, see Andrea Rudorff, "'Der Unsinn und die Leere einer solchen

Tätigkeit': Rekrutierung und Arbeitsmotivation von Aufseherinnen in Groß-Rosener Außenlagern," in *Zentrum und Peripherie: Die Wahrnehmung der nationalsozialistischen Konzentrationslager*, ed. Roman Fröhlich et al. (Berlin: Metropol, 2013), 77–94.

20. BArch NS 4/GR 7, Lagerrapport Hochweiler (November 1, 1944).

21. About one functionary's work as a *Schreiberin* (writer) in Grünberg, see USC Shoah Foundation VHA 1059, Interview with Nelly Blumner (January 31, 1995). About the infirmaries, see Rudorff, *Frauen*, 203–22.

22. Accompanying sheets in APMAB, Bestand des SS-Hygieneinstituts.

23. See, for instance, USC Shoah Foundation VHA 29327, Interview with Ray Langer (May 20, 1997).

24. AIPN, GK 304/194, Testimony of Chana Lender (February 28, 1955).

25. DEGOB-protocol # 3544, Aniko K. (November 15, 1945).

26. ITS, Doc.-ID 563170, File 1.1.2.1/0337/0088.

27. BArch B 162/20940, Testimony of Sonja C. (May 22, 1967).

28. BArch B 162/20490, Testimony of Zipora R. (May 22, 1967), Lillie R., Edith K. (June 19, 1967), Helen S. (August 8, 1967).

29. USC Shoah Foundation VHA 20030, Interview with Anna Freilich (September 25, 1996).

30. Paula Gruber-Herszkopf, *Pozostał ból: Wspomnienia o moim życiu w Polsce* (Warsaw: Zydowski Instytut Historyczny, 2007), 183.

31. Ursula Pawel, *My Child Is Back!* (London: Valentine Mitchell, 2000), 86.

32. Gruber-Herszkopf, *Pozostał ból*, 183.

33. BArch B 162/20491, Testimony of Maria H. (August 1, 1967).

34. Sara Plager-Zyskind, *Stolen Years* (Minneapolis, Minn.: Lerner, 1981), 209, 227–28.

35. Hilde Isaak, *An Philips*: *Wir leben! Die Philipsgruppe und ihre Irrfahrten 1943–1945* (Stuttgart: Rimon-Verlag, 2004), 95; YVA, 033/2449, 22, Inge Weinberg, Nicht erlebte Erlebnisse.

36. AIPN Wr 488/233, Testimony of Adela U., Gustawa G., Emilia F., Anna F., Golda F.; BArch B 162/5850, Testimony of Karl Ulbrich (February 25, 1968).

37. AIPN, GK 304/194, 62, Testimony of Chana P. (August 19, 1954).

38. AIPN, GK 304/194, Trial against Chana Lender.

39. Zofia Wójcicka, *Arrested Mourning: Memory of the Nazi Camps in Poland, 1944–1950* (Frankfurt am Main: Peter Lang, 2013), 128–62; Gabriel N. Finder and Alexander V. Prusin, "Jewish Collaborators on Trial in Poland 1944–1956," *Polin* 20 (2008): 122–48.

40. AIPN Wr 488/1267, Trial against Dora Brawer.

41. Primo Levi, *The Drowned and the Saved* (New York: Schocken Books, 1989) 53; Jonathan Petropoulos and John Roth, eds., *Gray Zones: Ambiguity and Compromise in the Holocaust and Its Aftermath* (New York: Berghahn Books, 2005).

42. Lawrence Langer, *Versions of Survival: The Holocaust and the Human Spirit* (Albany: State University of New York Press, 1982).

Sharon B. Oster

The *Muselmann* Liberated: Impossible Holocaust Metaphors in Survivor Memoirs and Photography

IN *SURVIVAL IN AUSCHWITZ* (*SE QUESTO È UN UOMO*, 1958), PRIMO LEVI describes a problem of post-Holocaust language: "Just as our hunger is not that feeling of missing a meal, so our way of being cold has need of a new word. We say 'hunger,' we say 'tiredness,' 'fear,' 'pain,' we say 'winter' and they are different things. They are free words, created and used by free men who lived in comfort and suffering in their homes. If the lagers had lasted longer a new, harsh language would have been born." This language actually *was* born in the Nazi concentration camps, an elaborate form of doublespeak that masked the quotidian violence of the camps. Victor Klemperer called it LTI, *Lingua Tertii Imperii*, the "language of the Third Reich."[1] One unique euphemism born of that system is the peculiar camp moniker for the emaciated and dying, the "Muslims" (*Muselmänner*), arguably the *Ur*-figure of reduced humanity in concentration camp testimony.[2] In Auschwitz survivors' accounts, the term typically refers to the masses of starved, emaciated, near-dead concentration camp victims, the lowest of the low in the camp hierarchy. Yet for many survivor-writers the term *Muselmänner* slips into a more symbolic register, so that these "living dead" function as "impossible metaphors" to capture the routine nearness and ubiquity of death in "killing centers" like Auschwitz.[3] For Primo Levi, the term *Muselmann* becomes a designation and a metaphor: from the retrospective point of view of the "saved," the *Muselmänner* are "the drowned," all those whom "nothing [could] save . . . from selections or from death by exhaustion," the "complete witnesses" who are nonetheless "mute."[4]

Levi's account has been profoundly influential. To Giorgio Agamben, for example, the *Muselmänner* constitute the "lacuna" in every testimony, the ethical aporia of Auschwitz that has come to symbolize the existential condition of the camps: a basic human inability to adapt to brutality; inevitable death; and a consequent inability to testify to the experience of atrocity.[5] Such analyses treat the category of the *Muselmann* as objective. However, a close examination of attempts to define it (by survivors, historians, sociologists, philosophers, and others) reveals a surprising complexity regarding what is essentially a *condition*, one that was, in some cases, temporary. In what follows I will present examples of survivors who claimed, "I was a *Muselmann*," and I contend that when used to describe others, the term helped to deflect and contain the abject, profane interpenetration of life and death that was a daily fact of one's own camp experience. If so many survivors came to see themselves as one-time *Muselmänner*, or to have a kind of "*Muselmann*" double (a group that may include those who did not recognize it as such, or called it something else), then it makes sense to view the designation *Muselmann* as a rhetorical construction, one that in survivor testimony is often rendered, according to Levi, as a silent, embodied figure of death-in-life, the ultimate product of radical evil.[6] In other words, we must reexamine our repeated, uncritical recirculation of the term to see it as a category invented in the "logic" of the Nazi hierarchy. What if, indeed, there are multiple categories of *Muselmänner*: the dying or dead, the suicidal, and the liberated?

If the *Muselmann* provides a literary trope for narrating Holocaust abjection, in liberation photography we find its visual analogue. Although originally an Auschwitz trope of the "living dead," the *Muselmann* also helps us explain the relationship between text and image in liberation photographs of camps in Germany, those liberated by Allied forces at the war's end, well before the *Muselmann* was immortalized by survivor-memoirists.[7] The most widely circulated visual images from Holocaust liberation photography, like the literary *Muselmann*, capture the paradox of the "living dead," and consequently have become symbolic, iconographic images of collective memory. Yet this, too, is problematic. Viewed in the context of a wider range of liberation photos, such images risk simplifying the incredibly disturbing scene of intermingled life and death that confronted the liberators, and the military photographers and journalists who arrived at camps in Germany and Austria in April and May of 1945. They developed their own "double vision" to distance themselves from what Robert

Abzug describes as "some of the most frightening scenes in modern history," involving "the unimaginable suffering of others."[8]

The term *Muselmann* captures a paradox that is also taboo: the everyday commingling of death and life, human body and corpse, and the breakdown of human solidarity between those deemed *Muselmänner* and other Auschwitz prisoners. In her study *Values and Violence in Auschwitz* (1979), survivor and sociologist Anna Pawelczynska describes Auschwitz as "a landscape of death": for the living, death "constituted a permanent element of camp life," with the descent of *Muselmänner* to the bottom of the camp structure and into speedy death an inevitability.[9] This hierarchy functioned largely because other prisoners avoided those deemed *Muselmänner*, however difficult this might be, since in Auschwitz one could not help but see them wherever one looked:

> Some of the *Muselmänner* died in the hospital barracks and at least had a place to lie down, but generally they died everywhere: standing at roll call, being herded to work, in barracks and outside barracks, on the camp roads and in the camp toilets; they died unassisted or they were beaten to death. Of all the various kinds of death, the *Muselmann*'s was one of the worst.[10]

From an ethical standpoint, Pawelczynska suggests that the designation *Muselmann* announced a renunciation of those one saw everywhere yet who were deemed beyond humanity. The category might logically have included *all* sick and emaciated prisoners—medically speaking, all prisoners at some point—but according to Auschwitz accounts, the term was used to designate a distinct group whom no one wanted to become. The term thus refers at once to a figure, a medical designation, an anthropological type, an ethical category, or all of these.

In post-Holocaust critical discourse, the fluidity of meaning and metaphoricity of the term *Muselmann* has been lost. We have largely adopted Levi's formulation from *The Drowned and the Saved*:

> I must repeat: we, the survivors, are not the true witnesses . . . we are those who by their prevarications or abilities or good luck did not touch bottom. Those who did so, those who saw the Gorgon, have not returned to tell about it or have returned mute, but they are the "Muslims," the submerged, the complete witnesses, the ones whose deposition would have a general significance. They are the

> rule, we are the exception. . . . We who were favored by fate tried, with more or less wisdom, to recount not only our fate but also that of others, indeed of the drowned . . . Even if they had paper and pen, the drowned would not have testified because their death had begun before that of their body. Weeks and months before being snuffed out, they had already lost the ability to observe, to remember, to compare and express themselves.[11]

For Levi, the *Muselmann* is the "complete witness" but one who has no story; we must speak "in their proxy." Agamben calls this "Levi's paradox."[12] As we have adopted this specific interpretation of the *Muselmann*, we have overlooked not only contradictions within Levi's own work, but also those narratives in which survivors *refer to themselves* as one-time *Muselmänner*, who witness and tell their stories.

Moreover, we overlook the continuity between the phenomenon of *Muselmänner* in Auschwitz during the war, and that of survivors who were photographed by U.S. Army Signal Corps members in German and Austrian camps immediately upon liberation. In captions given to these photographs, the same paradoxical language of lifelike matter ascribed to *Muselmänner*, of "living death," reappears. In both cases we see the same radical commingling of life and death, and the near elimination of the divide between human and matter. Yet where we might expect the liberated to be valorized, image and language combine once again to alienate those deemed fated to die, those nearest to death, and those "beyond help or hope." The publication (and recirculation) of specific images reflects the dehumanizing view liberators eventually took of the liberated, part of the "psychic closing-off" needed to distance themselves from the dead and liberated alike. As Abzug explains: "if the liberator defined the helpless victims of Nazis as not quite human, then he could defend himself against thinking that this might have been his own fate . . . that anyone could be brutalized into such a state, that one's normal existence and even life was so fragile."[13] The *Muselmann* as visual metaphor transforms corpselike bodies into miraculous material evidence of Nazi atrocity, and a symbol of human fragility. As "survivors," the "mummy-men" in these images may have held a new status, but they were no less objectified or metaphorized: they were photographed and filmed as specimens, exhibits, and as embodied, authenticating proof that what the Signal Corps photographers Arnold Samuelson and J. Malan Heslop witnessed was real, especially for a viewing public back home that was reluctant to believe it. These liberation photos comprise a visual lexicon of death in life, materialized not in words alone, like the discursive *Muselmann*, but also, we will see, in the meaning generated between caption texts and images of their miraculously reduced bodies.

"I WAS A MUSELMANN"

Although the term *Muselmann* was used to describe others, the near-death or life-in-death condition of the *Muselmann* was one that perhaps all concentration camp prisoners endured to some extent, and that, given testimonies of former *Muselmänner*, some apparently survived. For example, survivor Herbert Treitel (R) describes himself as a former *Muselmann*:

> I: How did you keep your strength up to work every day?
>
> R: That friend was working by the SS. He brought me the SS pieces of bread, the crust of the bread they throw in the garbage can and cheese with worms they throw in the garbage can. He brought me that cheese. I washed the cheese and washed the crust from the bread. A big help to me. A big help the first year.
>
> I: Did you lose a lot of weight?
>
> R: Oh, I was thin already. I had later an accident on my toes. Somebody dropped a piece of crystal (?) on my foot and I lost a lot. I was a muselman.
> (Wife added, "It's a term well known.")
> Yah, very well known. Muselman is the end. They are ready to go to the oven.
>
> I: People that were in such a debilitated condition.
>
> R: Deteriorated. This I had already from what I still lost a lot of weight. It was too hard . . .[14]

When Treitel was chosen by an "SS man" for work as an electrician, he claims, it "saved my life. Then I was already a person. A prisoner, but a person."[15] As a "Muselman," Treitel was socially dead, as if sentenced to die. But when he became useful again and was recognized as such, his status changed; he felt himself a "person" once more. That so many people were thus deemed and dismissed as fated to die is central to what we call "the atrocity," since this condition turns out to have been, in some cases, temporary. If the term *Muselmann* is a misnomer, a simplification of what was actually a heterogeneous phenomenon that many survivors experienced, but for practical and ethical reasons they avoided using the term *Muselmann*, then we might see the term as effectively creating the category of prisoner it sought to describe, more metaphor than actual type.

The term *Muselmann* has been understood to identify concentration camp prisoners who were on the brink of death from severe malnutrition. But some definitions include an ethically loaded qualifier that those designated as *Muselmänner* were also fated, or were fatally resigned, to die: "doomed to selection."[16] It is this sense of being "fated" that for many scholars has provided the basis for the connection to the word "Muslim" or to Muslims themselves. Yad Vashem's lexicon entry for "*Muselmann*," for example, connects the hunched, reduced prisoner to the image of a praying, "fatalist" Muslim "prostrating himself on the ground in prayer":

> German term widely used among concentration camp inmates to refer to prisoners who were near death due to exhaustion, starvation, or hopelessness. The word *Muselmann* literally means "Muslim." Some scholars believe that the term originated from the similarity between the near-death prone state of a concentration camp *Muselmann* and the image of a Muslim prostrating himself on the ground in prayer.
>
> Many victims, totally lacking the wherewithal to adapt, reached this stage soon after arrival in a camp. Other prisoners succumbed to sickness, physical abuse, hunger, and overwork. One could identify *Muselmanner* [*sic*] by their physical and psychological decline; they were lethargic, indifferent to their surroundings, and could not stand up for more than a short period of time. Most other prisoners avoided contact with *Muselmanner*, in fear of contracting the condition themselves.
>
> The Nazis running the camps considered the *Muselmanner* undesirable, because they could not work or endure camp rule. Thus, during selections, these victims were the first to be sentenced to death. A person at the *Muselmann* stage had no chance for survival; he or she would not live for more than a few days or weeks.[17]

Presenting the connection to actual praying Muslims as a way of explaining the term's etymology seems not only tendentious (based on the vague belief of "some scholars") but also morally problematic. The religious studies scholar Gil Anidjar takes this view in a book-length study of Arab-Jewish relations, in which the "Muslim," long a "figure of absolute subjection," finds new iteration in the stereotypical fatalistic Muslim projected onto concentration camp victims.[18] Yet this symbolic association with fatalism is common: writers like Jean Améry see the *Muselmänner* as the camp's quintessential victims, fated to die by definition. Wolfgang Sofsky describes "'living skeletons'" as the mark of the Nazi regime's "absolute power," the "genuine inventions of the concentration camp."[19] In these examples, we see a move from description into prescription, and finally into metaphor, raising ethical implications for a slippage between the physical and metonymical. If near-dead prisoners were called *Muselmänner* because they allegedly contributed to their own fate, or worse yet, because they had actually renounced their will to live, they become synecdochic stand-ins for passive Jews, another iteration of those who, as Abba Kovner famously implied in his 1941 call for revolt in Lithuania, went "like sheep to the slaughter."[20]

Yet this prescription was not solely about renunciation and surrender to fate. The Yad Vashem entry raises another, contradictory claim in the second paragraph, namely that *Muselmänner* were rather victims of *others'* renunciation, as if they carried a terminal, contagious condition: "Most other prisoners avoided contact with *Muselmänner*, in fear of contracting the condition themselves." Pawelczynska corroborates this, noting that the *Muselmann* was despised, reviled, and abandoned by other inmates:

> Only in exceptional cases could a sympathetic person help. By imagining their own fate prisoners lost the remains of their psychic strength, which they needed for self-defense. Prisoners who relegated the dying to the world of the dead could look the other way and pass them by or take their shoes and ration of bread. [21]

Naming other people *Muselmänner* thus seems to have been a survival strategy. Since, as the Yad Vashem definition explains, "during selections, these victims were the first to be sentenced to death," projecting the condition of the *Muselmann* onto others was a way of trying to fend off death and promise oneself more life.[22]

Zdziław Ryn and Stanisław Kłodziński, who published the first study of the "*Muselmann* phenomenon" in 1987, describe the *Muselmänner* as victims of physical malnutrition and psychological overload, which led many to lose all hope or desire to live.[23] They enumerate physical stages from "weight loss" and "muscular asthenia" to pronounced forehead and eye sockets, slowed breathing, edemas on the body, and to psychological changes, an attitude of indifference and self-exclusion from social relations. Yet even as they note the many signs of becoming a *Muselmann*, they cannot pin down precisely when one is actually there. Furthermore, they argue that the *Muselmann's* social death was a symptom of "approaching death," that dying came first, ostracism after.[24] But dying was also apparently a symptom, a consequence, of having been deemed a *Muselmann*—social death first, actual death to follow, since only a few rare individuals helped and sometimes saved their lives.

Ryn and Kłodziński's study includes a section titled "*Ich war ein Muselmann*" ("I was a *Muselmann*"), later excerpted by Agamben, containing testimonies of at least ten survivors who called themselves former "*muselmänner*."[25] The survivors describe their temporary transformation, and their subjection to an entirely different treatment from others. Feliksa Pierarska explains: "I personally was a *Muselmann* for a short while. I remember that after the move to the barrack, I completely collapsed as far as my psychological life was concerned . . . I was overcome by a general apathy; nothing interested me." Bronislaw Goscinki describes his physical afflictions, obsession with food, and how others avoided him, but eventually his ability to "win the trust of the other inmates" gained him extra rations of food, which saved him from what he calls "*Muselmannhood*." Jerzy Mostowsky, apparently a *Muselmann* from 1942 to early 1943, says: "I wasn't conscious of being one. I think that many *Muselmänner* didn't realize they belonged to that category. . . . In many cases, whether or not an inmate was considered a *Muselmann* depended on his appearance."[26] From the U.S. Holocaust Memorial Museum's Oral History Project, Shemshihu Spivack, Lou Dunst, Shaul Sadan, Jan Van Den Berg, and several others also testified, "I was a Muselmann"; and survivor David Matzner titled his memoir *The Muselmann: The Diary of a Jewish Slave Laborer*.[27] These accounts challenge Levi's figure of "sublime silence" as the "complete witness," and as a synecdoche for the most heinous aspects of Nazi atrocity—the reduction of human beings to matter. How many other prisoners were also, unknowingly, perceived as and deemed to be *Muselmänner*? Describing the experience of "selection," the process that gave the term *Muselmann* its meaning, Levi's words echo—"You will be chosen. I will be excluded"—and we see the designation for what it is: no mere neutral description of reality, but a performative utterance—in effect, a death sentence.[28]

At times Levi seems aware of the term's metaphorical nature, suggesting that we may have taken him too literally, absorbing parts of his account of the *Muselmann* uncritically into our cultural lexicon as an actual reified "type," the other who did not survive:

> All the musselmans who finished in the gas chambers have the same story, or more exactly, have no story; they followed the slope down to the bottom, like streams that run down to the sea. On their entry into the camp, through basic incapacity, or by misfortune, or through some banal incident, they are overcome before they can adapt themselves; they are beaten by time, they do not begin to learn German, to disentangle the infernal knot of laws and prohibitions until their body is already in decay, and nothing can save them from selections or from death by exhaustion. Their life is short, but their number is endless; they, the *Muselmänner*, the drowned, form the backbone of the camp, an anonymous mass, continually renewed and always identical, of non-men who march and labor in silence, the divine spark dead within them, already too empty to really suffer. One hesitates to call them living: one hesitates to call their death death, in the face of which they have no fear, as they are too tired to understand.[29]

Levi's attempt to describe *Muselmänner* results in a proliferation of metaphors: most profoundly, "the drowned," the fated, but also "an anonymous mass . . . of non-men," "the divine spark dead within them . . . One hesitates to call them living: one hesitates to call their death death."[30] Lacking the "divine spark," they seem mere moving bodies, automata. Not calling their death "death" makes this more palatable. That even Levi cannot pin down the precise condition suggests its fluid, changing nature. His range of metaphors suggests the metaphoricity of the concept itself, attempting to name not a "them"—but a state they inhabit, for a time.

Levi then contradicts his own view.[31] His essay "Shame," which gets far less attention on the matter, suggests that we might see the *Muselmann* metaphorically, here as Levi's own deceased double: how he "might be alive in the place of another, at the expense of another."

> Almost everybody feels guilty of having omitted to offer help. The presence at your side of a weaker—or less cunning, or older, or too young—companion, hounding you with his demands for help or with his simple presence, in itself an entreaty, is a constant in the life of the Lager. The demand for solidarity, for a human word,

advice, even just a listening ear, was permanent and universal but rarely satisfied.[32]

The *Muselmann* is Levi's reminder that he "failed in terms of human solidarity."[33] He suggests that to witness *Muselmänner* go to their deaths created for prisoners an ethical crisis, and feelings of complicity and guilt. Writing the literary *Muselmann* retrospectively invokes this metaphor for life in death, death in life, as a way to register, atone, for this ethical crisis.

THE "LIVING DEAD": THE *MUSELMANN* IN LIBERATION PHOTOGRAPHY

The silent figure of the *Muselmann* allows survivor-memoirists to convey death in life, to explain their own survival, and possibly assuage their feelings of complicity or shame. The impossible metaphor of the *Muselmann* therefore says as much about death as it does about life, both during and after the Holocaust. Even as the passage into death of so-called *Muselmänner* kept others alive, the mundane production of corpses that defined camp life passed death onto (indeed, into) the living—a commingling of the profane and whatever remained of the sacred. In the discourse of liberation photography—that is, in image captions, photographers' eyewitness accounts, news articles, and museum displays—we see the same impossible metaphors of the "living dead."

Barbie Zelizer, a leading interpreter of atrocity photographs, argues that the proliferation and circulation of postwar liberation photographs represented a breakthrough in visual culture, providing the images at the heart of the "collective memory" of the Holocaust formed immediately after the war, although often decontextualized.[34] For Zelizer, the most widely circulated among these images took on a symbolic, and eventually iconic, function apart from their specific referential meaning: as a synecdoche for the entire atrocity.[35] This is because they function, as the literary *Muselmänner* do, as visual tropes for the paradox of living death. Atrocity photographs, Zelizer shows, encouraged viewers to bear witness, or to witness others bearing witness: survivors, soldiers, German civilians subjected to "denazification," or foreign leaders and diplomats, often shown looking at bodies.[36] The photographs aimed to dispel skepticism in viewers tainted by the exaggerated reportage of World War I, by antisemitism, or by simple disbelief. But they also created problems for collective memory: unlike the meticulously detailed written news accounts of the liberation, which prioritized the accuracy of what journalists saw and where, many photographs were published referring to the wrong camps, or lacking descriptive information like names, accurate captions, attribution, or other frames for understanding the depicted activity. Photographed prisoners and victims were instead generalized in captions, rendered "voiceless and anonymous," like a 73-year-old Frenchman at Buchenwald who, like the *Muselmann*, was described by a reporter as showing "a sign of vitality among the living dead."[37]

Photo captions exacerbated the problem of misinformation, resulting in ever more metaphorical language. At a loss for words for what they saw, as in a statement for the American Society of Newspaper Editors titled "Words Cannot Describe Horrors," journalists used photographs to tell their story where words failed. Images of starved bodies served as graphic documentary proof, but also, as Zelizer notes, as anonymous embodiments of a universalized story.[38] Margaret Bourke-White's biographer Vicki Goldberg describes how when Bourke-White photographed survivors, "not one of them reacted . . . Buchenwald had stripped away self-consciousness and ordinary response. Liberated, the skeletal figures stared from her photograph with the eyes of men who have seen too much, their faces framed by wire, their lives by an unbearable past and an unimaginable future . . . *it is as if they have died and yet are keeping watch*."[39] Goldberg's description could be that of a *Muselmann*. But where depictions of the *Muselmann* rely solely upon words, here the image of the emaciated survivor visually authenticates the trope of the miraculous living dead with concrete bodily materiality.

As the story of the liberation moved from the 1940s to the 1950s, Zelizer shows, the gap between documentary realism and iconography widened. Not only were images still printed with misinformation, but the variety of visual representations "was laundered" so that only a "few familiar shots made repeated rounds across different domains of representation."[40] What surfaced less frequently were images of confrontations between perpetrators and survivors, Nazi perpetrators, and those complicating depictions of witnessing. Instead, two categories appeared most often: the accoutrements of atrocity, and survivors, typically small groups of liberated survivors, looking full face into the camera from behind the barbed wire of unidentified camps.[41] In spite of the carnage, disease, rot, stench, and death that liberating troops and journalists confronted, a handful of posed images of uniformly arranged, emaciated survivors made the news rounds in a simplification that cemented certain dimensions of the story in the popular imagination, and continued to circulate well into the 1990s.[42] So why did *these* particular images make the rounds, and what dimension of the story did they tell?

As the German and Austrian camps were liberated, atrocity photography proliferated. The U.S. Army Signal Corps photographers made the majority of photographs at camps like Buchenwald, Nordhausen, Wobbelin, Dachau, and Mauthausen, their material laboratory in the United States making over one million prints.[43] Soldiers with cameras often accompanied tours of dignitaries, news members, politicians, and military officials around the camps and were "encouraged to 'sightsee'" as they went, yet they found it difficult to show at home photos that were dismissed as fabrications or too shocking. Some images, however, were shown and circulated widely, such as the now-famous photo of rows of prisoners in the barracks at Buchenwald that has become iconic (figure 2.1).

This image taken by Margaret Bourke-White is perhaps best known for presumably depicting a young Elie Wiesel, pictured in the second row of bunks, seventh from the left, next to the vertical beam.[44] Bourke-White titled the photo "Inside Dormitories, Buchenwald," but when it first appeared in the *New York Times* and *Los Angeles Times* in 1945, it depicted unnamed prisoners in an unidentified camp, moving from signifying Buchenwald to symbolizing liberation in general. In Carol Zemel's view, the image as icon represents the "Holocaust sublime," edging us "into barely imagined terrors."[45] The assemblage of figures binds them into a unified "assertive human force," creating a "dramatic tableau," or still life. The centerpiece, the man at the right, "frontal, naked for no reason," is less a person than a "stand-in for the others." For Zemel, the image is sublime because it reveals the "forbidden and unknown," bringing us to the "brink of human existence," that is, to the "space between life and death," a space limning the human-material divide that we often identify with the *Muselmann*.[46]

Zelizer, meanwhile, chronicles the image's biography. A 1979 *Maclean's* story used the image to illustrate a reunion of former Buchenwald prisoners, although none at the reunion were in that photo. The image gained new life in 1981, when Los Angeles businessman Mel

Fig. 2.1. Former prisoners of the "little camp" in Buchenwald stare out from the wooden bunks in which they slept three to a "bed." Photograph 74607. United States Holocaust Memorial Museum, courtesy of National Archives and Records Administration, College Park.

Mermelstein identified himself in it. *Newsweek* featured an image of Mermelstein pointing to himself in the Buchenwald photo with the caption "Footnote to the Holocaust." In 1982, a journal repeated earlier errors by using the photo to illustrate a critical piece on the British Holocaust revisionist David Irving with the incorrect caption "death-camp survivors" (Buchenwald was not a death camp). In a 1993 art installation, Judy Chicago embroidered pastel-colored figures above the faces of the men to highlight women's experience at the hands of men, and their lack of representation in the popular imagination. Chicago's piece makes explicit how the image was becoming synecdochic for the entire atrocity of the Holocaust, one that is gendered male. By 1995, the image detached from Buchenwald altogether when *Newsweek* featured a cover story on the 50th anniversary of the liberation of Auschwitz, accompanied by this image.[47]

The ongoing fame of this image is deeply ironic, given Abzug's account of the "Little Camp" at Buchenwald: "a section of crude barracks" made specifically for Jews, Roma, Sinti, and the ill that by liberation, with the entire camp population grown to almost 50,000 with evacuees from the eastern death and labor camps, was plain "dismal."[48] With mostly barns (not buildings), a ditch for a latrine, and an awful stench from stacks of the dying and dead, the Little Camp, which was separated from the rest of the camp by barbed wire, was disdained by the entire camp hierarchy. American liberators, perhaps despite themselves, eventually avoided the Little Camp and ignored the prisoners there in favor of healthier ones. Two American psychological warfare observers, Egon Fleck and Edward A. Tenenbaum, wrote of the worst cases: "'They are brutalized, unpleasant to look on . . . It is easy to adopt the Nazi theory that they are subhuman, for many have in fact been deprived of their humanity. It would be easy to continue favoring the big camp in the distribution of food, as had been done in the past, and, more important for the wretches of the small camp, in the distribution of medicine.'"[49] Abzug explains how, anonymous, emaciated, and craven, "Little Camp prisoners could easily be both pitied and avoided. These worst cases became symbols of horror, the stuff of nightmares, but otherwise remained in dangerous anonymity."[50]

If these prisoners continued to be regarded as untouchable even as survivors, it begs the question: what made their images such amenable visual tropes? The caption accompanying the Buchenwald photo (figure 2.1), as found in the U.S. Holocaust Memorial Museum's digital photography collection, offers some insight. It describes its subjects in precisely the same terms as the *Muselmann*, suggesting that mere days before liberation when it was taken, these same men might have been deemed *Muselmänner*:

> Slave laborers peered from their *tomb-like*, wooden bunks at the concentration camp at Buchenwald, near Weimar, Germany, when U.S. troops liberated the area. Approximately 21,000 inmates—Russian, Polish, French, Italian, and Czechoslovakian—were freed. They were described as "*the living dead*."[51]

This reference to the "tomb-like" bunks and the "living dead" inhabiting them in the original photo's caption is echoed in another photo, taken on June 30, 1945.

Fig. 2.2. Visitors view a photomural of survivors in their barracks in Buchenwald at the "Lest We Forget" exhibition at the Library of Congress. June 30, 1945. Photograph 10621. United States Holocaust Memorial Museum, courtesy of the Martin Luther King Memorial Library and *Washington Star*.

Since journalists covering the liberation feared the public would not believe what they had seen, Joseph Pulitzer, editor of the *St. Louis Post-Dispatch*, set out to change this in April 1945, after joining an American congressional delegation on visits to Buchenwald and Dachau.[52] There he overcame his own skepticism and found the reality to be worse than the rumors. This led to the June 30, 1945, opening of "Lest We Forget," a two-week exhibition at the Library of Congress of "life-size" photomurals depicting the horrors of the Nazi concentration camps (figure 2.2).[53]

Cosponsored by the *St. Louis Post-Dispatch* and the *Washington Evening Star* (Washington, D.C.), the exhibition came to the Library of Congress from St. Louis. The *Washington Evening Star* later reported that the exhibition broke all records—88,891 people had seen it within three weeks, and 5,229 on the opening day alone.[54] The photomurals consisted of enlarged photographs made by the U.S. Army Signal Corps, the Associated Press, and the British Information Service, depicting liberation scenes from the concentration camps of Buchenwald, Nordhausen, Ohrdruf, Leipzig-Thekla, and Bergen-Belsen.[55] In the photograph of spectators confronting the Buchenwald image (figure 2.2), we see how the atrocity of mass death was symbolized by a photo literally in one's face, as Janina Struk puts it, enlarged to more than double life-size.[56] Unsurprisingly, Buchenwald is not mentioned in the photo's caption; rather, the title on the wall reads "The Living Dead," suggesting that the image of the survivor was meant to capture the paradox of the precarious line between life and death, which was comparable to the *Muselmann* for so many writers. This comparison, however, works both ways, extending our notion of the *Muselmann* into the category of the "survivor," and blurring the line between them. In both cases, humans become objects—human evidence, living relics, material embodiments of a universal trope of atrocity—but each with a very different status in the public imagination. Even more than in the literary *Muselmann*, here silent authenticity lies in the photographed material body.

While visitors perhaps came to "Lest We Forget" out of "morbid curiosity," responses from some of them suggest that the images served as opportunities for public witnessing to mass atrocity, with little attention given to the specificity of those whose bodies served as evidence.[57] One visitor did register their humanity in this comment: "It's unbelievable, but true. It's not just the piles of dead prisoners. Look at the expressions on the faces of those living people!" But many also viewed the images as representing "the atrocities" in general, so that others should see them to believe, to "learn," or in order to "love democracy more."[58] Liberation newsreels of the camps also met with mixed responses, with theater owners in Britain and the United States finding them too shocking to show moviegoers.[59] Such images may have provoked empathy, but more often they had the reverse effect. In a Mass-Observation report in the United Kingdom, for example, several who saw similar photographs in the papers and were interviewed, admitted that they began to be disgusted with images of liberated prisoners, with "their cracked faces, and their skinniness and sloppiness and horribleness."[60] Struk explains how such views may have been

> encouraged by the dehumanizing way in which those liberated were often described in the press: "pitiful specimens," "the living

> dead," "ape-like living skeletons," "skeletons held together with rags," "wrecks of humanity." Photographer David E. Scherman described how he and Lee Miller "held flashbulbs for each other while photographing stripe-clad skeletons who had just been freed." He added: "A few of them simply died of exhaustion, or perhaps excitement, before we could get their pictures."[61]

Here, as in literary descriptions of *Muselmänner*, we see a proliferation of metaphors—"the living dead," "ape-like living skeletons," "skeletons held together with rags," "stripe-clad skeletons"—all conveying a paradox of the intermingling of humanity and materiality.

I will now show how this dominant pattern among now-iconic photos is complicated by some of the more obscure photographs taken by two U.S. Army Signal Corps photographers, Lt. Arnold Samuelson and J. Malan Heslop, at the liberation of the Ebensee concentration camp in Austria. Lt. Samuelson's unit of photographers documented the advance of American troops through France, Belgium, Germany, and Austria, including the liberation of concentration and POW camps, and on May 8 they entered Ebensee and photographed its survivors.[62] Ebensee, a subcamp camp of Mauthausen, was created in 1943 to provide labor to construct underground factory tunnels, but by 1945 it had become a dumping ground for dying prisoners transported from other locations.[63] Abzug describes how "bodies, ashes, the living dead riddled the compound, and even those who could stand sometimes just collapsed and died."[64] Samuelson's men could hardly believe the state to which the inmates had been reduced. For the image of a large group of emaciated former prisoners of Ebensee, taken by Samuelson one day after liberation, the men came out of the infirmary barracks to be photographed, among them the 21-year-old Jewish survivor Joachim Friedner from Krakow (center-left holding his metal name tag, in figure 2.3).[65]

In this image, we see a wide range of expressions on the men's faces: some appear confused, some wondering, and many perhaps on the edge of death. According to Zelizer, this photograph gained wide circulation, conforming as it did to the visual pattern she describes: a group shot of anonymous emaciated survivors with the central figure staring directly at the viewer. Although Zelizer does not specify where it was published, the photo exemplifies those photos published without specific mention of location, perpetuating the problem of

Fig. 2.3. One day after their liberation, a group of former prisoners at the Ebensee concentration camp pose outside for U.S. Army Signal Corps photographer Arnold Samuelson. May 7, 1945. Photograph 66297. United States Holocaust Memorial Museum, courtesy of National Archives and Records Administration, College Park.

misinformation that informed collective memory, as noted by Zelizer and Struk. By contrast with how the photo was apparently published, the original caption from the donated photograph, according to the U.S. Holocaust Memorial Museum photo archive, is quite specific:

> Starved prisoners, nearly dead from hunger, pose in the Nazi concentration camp in Ebensee, Austria. In the Austrian Alps the Nazis had one of their largest camps. Large numbers of inmates were starving to death and dying at the rate of 2000 per week. The camp was reputedly used for "Scientific" experiments. It was liberated by the 80th Division, 3rd U.S. Army.[66]

The afterlife of the image, moreover, followed that of the Buchenwald photo: it was recycled in late 1945 in a military newspaper and was said to depict the effects of planned starvation, a theme that persisted into the 1960s when *Time* magazine captioned it "Starving Jewish Prisoners" in an article about the Eichmann trial, signifying simply "liberation." By the 1990s, the photo had been published in three separate *Newsweek* articles with the following captions, illustrating its symbolic significance and function: "Concentration Camp Survivors," "Prisoners on Liberation Day," and wrongly, "Death-Camp Survivors" (in 1983, 1975, and 1980, respectively).[67] The photo even appeared as the cover image for the catalog of a 1995 U.S. Holocaust Memorial Museum exhibit commemorating the 70th anniversary of the liberation of the camps titled "Liberation 1945."[68]

Unlike Samuelson's ultimately iconic photo, those taken by J. Malan Heslop, one of the five other U.S. Army Signal Corps photographers in the 123rd Combat Unit, did not gain as wide a circulation, if published at all.[69] Many of them are group portraits of emaciated survivors, some behind barbed wire, standing in rows, so that they nearly match the composition and content of the ones widely circulated. Yet significantly, they disrupt the narrative created by more iconic images of the miraculous, silent "living dead," the *Muselmann*-like "non-men," through subtle deviations in composition, and in the gazes and expressions of the men portrayed. For example, one portrait of four survivors does show their emaciation and deprivation and was originally captioned "These living skeletons are young boys" (figure 2.4).

Yet unlike in other group photos, these men are seated, they are both facing and looking away from the camera, and toward something off in front of them. They are engaged, and are perhaps even talking, rather than confronting the viewer directly with a silent gaze of admonishment, as in the Buchenwald "Lest We Forget" photo. To Heslop, these men may have appeared as "living skeletons," but for public circulation, perhaps they seemed too human to be chosen to embody that metaphor.

Other group photos further disrupt the uniform, collective gaze of survivors that would directly confront spectators and demand that we witness. One portrait of two men even disrupts the subjects' silence, refuting Levi's commonly accepted notion of the mute *Muselmann* (figure 2.5). Instead, in this image we see men as they might have been, naked—perhaps too naked for public viewing—hungry, wasted, still behind barbed wire, but also with expressions of relief rather than of suffering, one even smiling in the sun, the other like he is about to say something.

Fig. 2.4. Group portrait of emaciated survivors of the Ebensee concentration camp. 1945. Photograph 78920. United States Holocaust Memorial Museum, courtesy of Ron Leidelmeyer.

In a large group portrait taken in the infirmary barrack, clearly posed for the viewer's inspection, most of the men look at the photographer, and hence at the viewer, but a tall man, standing third from the left, stares off to his right, smirking at something or someone (figure 2.6). This detail creates what Roland Barthes called the "*punctum*" of the image, the "accident which pricks" the viewer, the "detail" that has "a power of expansion."[70] Here, this detail expands our view of the spontaneity and individuality concealed by the orderly rows of naked bodies uniformly arranged for the shot, not unlike their formerly ordered arrangement in the *appelplatz*, or roll call arena. Behind the tall man, seated on the bunk, the second and fourth men from the left also wave to the camera. These minor disruptions in gaze, facial and bodily expression, and composition reveal these men's humanity, individuality, and agency.

Likewise, an image of a small group seated on the floor of the

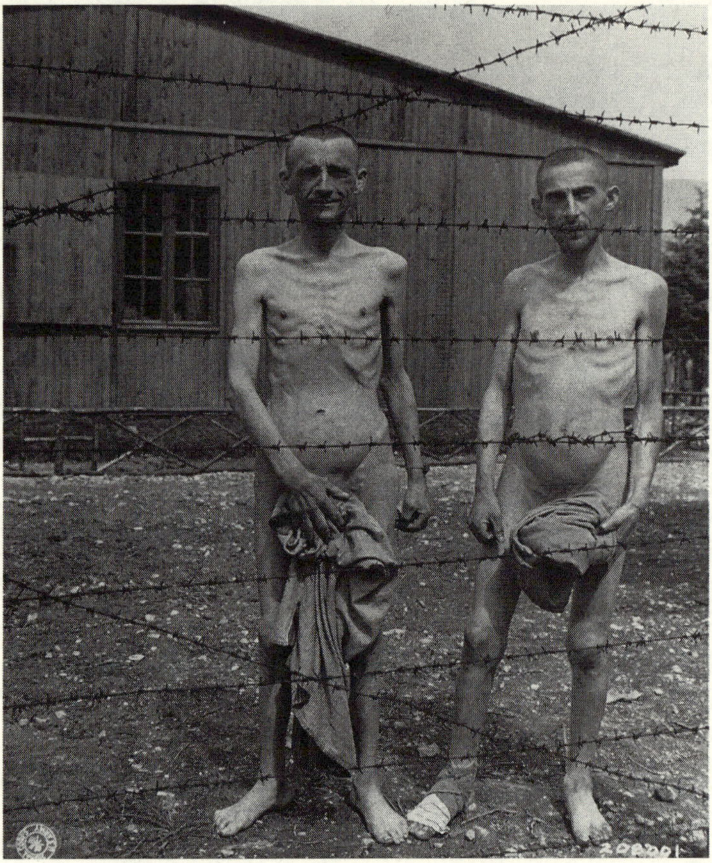

Fig. 2.5. Two emaciated survivors stand behind a barbed wire fence in the hospital compound at the Ebensee concentration camp. May 8, 1945. Photograph 78361. United States Holocaust Memorial Museum, courtesy of National Archives and Records Administration, College Park.

infirmary shows former prisoners in an array of positions and expressions, a candid shot perhaps, with one man off to the right smiling, and another in the center holding his hands in a gesture of prayer, or gratitude (figure 2.7). Like the previous examples, this photo lacks the de-individuating uniformity of those shots which lend themselves to symbolic rather than referential meaning. Its lack of wider circulation, moreover, suggests that such images would not serve collective memory as well as the silent, uniform, skeletal (and naked), zombie-

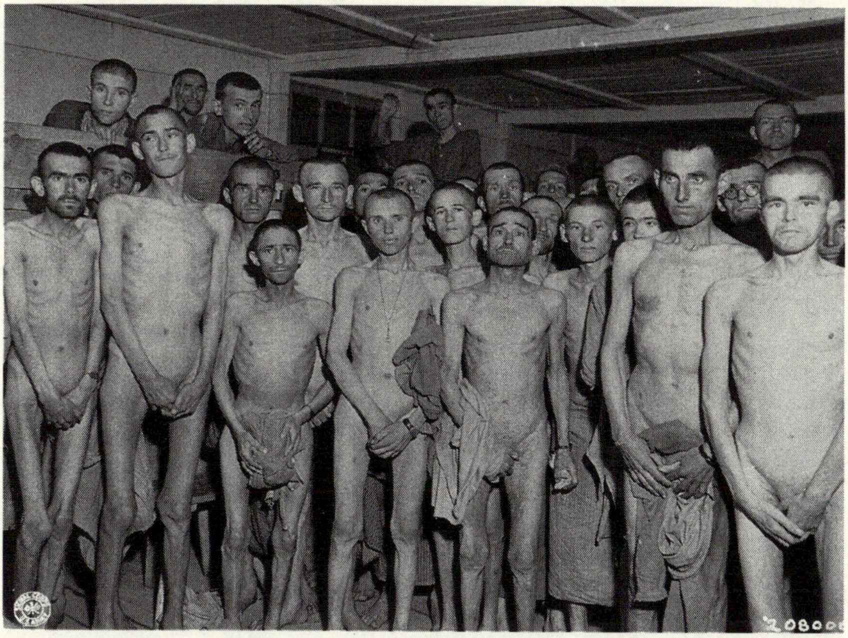

Fig. 2.6. Group portrait of emaciated survivors in the infirmary barrack for non-Jewish prisoners in the Ebensee concentration camp. May 8, 1945. Photograph 74964. United States Holocaust Memorial Museum, courtesy of National Archives and Records Administration, College Park.

like figures of the living dead for capturing the "worst." It is as if the closer an image, or an expression, can get to showing life on the very brink of death—life in death, or *as* death, human as nearly matter—the more powerfully it conveys a sense of the extremity of the atrocity that was the Nazi genocide.

Finally, one last image captures a moment of survivors in the infirmary barracks at Ebensee smiling, waving, and cheering at their American liberators (figure 2.8). This image perhaps proves the point most effectively: unlike this image, the photographs that matured into symbolic icons of Nazi atrocity, and received the widest circulation, were not those depicting cheering prisoners, those with individual voices, unique smirks on their faces, or hands expressively in prayer, but those who best visualize, as Levi put it, "the demolition of a man."[71] In other words, the iconic images illustrate the story told by the *Musselmänner*, according to Levi: that of "the drowned . . . an

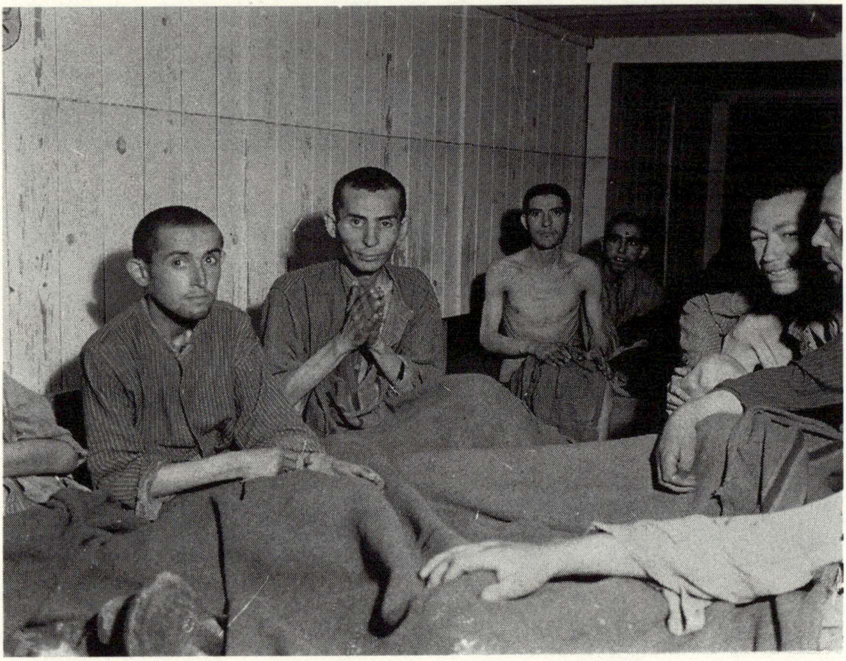

Fig. 2.7. Survivors sit on the floor in the infirmary barracks for Jewish prisoners in the Ebensee concentration camp. May 8, 1945. Photograph 74962. United States Holocaust Memorial Museum, courtesy of National Archives and Records Administration, College Park.

anonymous mass, continually renewed and always identical, of non-men who marched and labor in silence," silently embodying atrocity for those who come after, to convey to us that place, or moment, where the border between life and death was brought to the brink of collapse.[72] Perhaps this is why thousands of spectators came to see just such images of miraculous embodiment in "Lest We Forget." To look at "the Living Dead" was effectively to look at the miraculous *Muselmann* by another name: "survivor."

To conclude and reiterate, although Levi's account of the *Muselmann* has been most influential, even he contradicted himself, reserving the "right to inconsistency."[73] Well before he introduces the "musselmanns, the men in decay," in *Survival in Auschwitz*, he describes himself like a *Muselmann*, though in different terms, entering the Ka-Be as "naked and last again in a queue of human skeletons."

Fig. 2.8. Survivors wave to American liberators from their bunks in the infirmary barracks for Jewish prisoners in the Ebensee concentration camp. May 8, 1945. Photograph 78359. United States Holocaust Memorial Museum, courtesy of National Archives and Records Administration, College Park.

He recounts a horrid moment with a "non-Jewish Pole" and a nurse "who resembled him like a twin," who points to Levi's ribs "as if I was a corpse in an anatomy class," pinches his flesh "as if it was wax," and finishes his anatomy "demonstration" by declaring, "'*Du Jude, kaput. Du schnell Krematorium fertig*.' (You Jew, finished. You soon ready for crematorium)." Even before the death sentence is pronounced, social death is complete: says Levi, "I feel as if I had never in all my life undergone an affront worse than this."[74] For all intents and purposes, in this moment—discursively, socially, ethically—Levi is made a *Muselmann*, and possibly he knows it himself. In this light, his description of the *Muselmänner* as those with whom "it is not even worth speaking," as those who are "only here on a visit," seems not his own view, but more likely his ironic, deeply cynical ventriloquizing of the Nazi attitude, the "logic" of those who were engaged in the "demolition of a man," rather than that of the humans who bore their relentless affronts and physical blows.

As we have seen, the *Muselmann* inhabited, in some cases (perhaps many, maybe even that of Levi himself), a reversible condition on the continuum of prisoner starvation and deprivation. However, the repetition of the image over time—as the purportedly silent, fated embodiment of the Nazi genocidal effort—reveals its universalizing, iconic potential, but also its ultimate opacity: an image no longer able to refer or to represent anyone, only to reiterate and to signify nothing but itself. Given the history of liberation photography, this assertion places the iconic image of the *Muselmann* at the heart of Holocaust collective memory. To avoid reproducing the logic of Nazi euphemism ourselves, and the dangerous reading practice upon which it depends, we must not confuse metaphor with denotation. Of course, so many concentration camp prisoners were literally on the edge of death by the end of the war. However, in its figurative sense, the *Muselmann* also points to the lived experience of death's proximity that all prisoners shared, a condition that one could not change. Critically reading the literary *Muselmann*, as we have done here, demands that we recognize this distinction in order to hear the survivor's story: the stark confrontation with the gradual extinction of life, with the fragile tension between life and death; and the accusing voice, for which *Muselmänner* stand, not as silent others resigned to death and beyond human reach, but as those who are also part of the survivors, and who could have been, under different circumstances, part of us. The *Muselmann* figures at once the other, *and* the survivor's own shadowy "Auschwitz double," an impossible metaphor for living death, and thus for the very impossibility of truly "surviving" a place from where, as Charlotte Delbo puts it, "none of us was meant to return."[75]

NOTES

Deepest thanks to Valerie Hébert of Lakehead University for organizing the June 2017 USHMM summer research workshop, "Regarding Atrocity: Photography, Memory and Representation," where I researched Holocaust liberation photographs, and to the participants in that workshop for their generous feedback, in particular, Dan Magilow. Thanks also to the receptive audience at the 2016 Lessons and Legacies conference panel, and to Simone Gigliotti and Tim Cole for incisive suggestions for revision.

1. Victor Klemperer, *LTI: Notizbuch Eines Philologen* (Leipzig: Reclam Verlag, 1975).

2. Because the word *Muselmann* is a cognate in multiple languages, we see various spellings in oral transcripts and written accounts: "muselman," "musselman," "Muselman," "musulmann," "Muselmann," sometimes capitalized, sometimes not. I have kept the original spellings found in each source, and have somewhat arbitrarily chosen Primo Levi's spelling, "*Muselmann*," plural "*Muselmänner*."

3. See Sharon B. Oster, "Impossible Holocaust Metaphors: The *Muselmann*," *Prooftexts* 34, no. 3 (Fall 2014): 302–48. "Killing centers" is Doris Bergen's phrase. See Doris L. Bergen, *War and Genocide: A Concise History of the Holocaust* (Lanham, Md.: Rowman and Littlefield, 2016).

4. Levi, *Survival in Auschwitz*, 90. Primo Levi, *The Drowned and the Saved* (New York: Vintage, 1989), 83–84.

5. Giorgio Agamben, *Remnants of Auschwitz: The Witness and the Archive* (New York: Zone Books, 1999), 81–82.

6. See David Simpson, *9/11: The Culture of Commemoration* (Chicago: University of Chicago Press, 2006), 162.

7. According to Wolfgang Sofsky, the term *Muselmann* was most commonly used in Auschwitz, "from where it spread to other camps as well . . . In Majdanek, the word was unknown. The living dead there were termed 'donkeys'; in Dachau they were 'cretins,' in Stutthof 'cripples,' in Mauthausen 'swimmers,' in Neuengamme 'camels,' in Buchenwald 'tired sheikhs,' and in the women's camp known as Ravensbrück, *Muselweiber* (female Muslims) or 'trinkets.'" See Wolfgang Sofsky, *The Order of Terror: The Concentration Camp*, trans. William Templer (Princeton, N.J.: Princeton University Press, 1999), 329, n. 5.

8. Robert Abzug, *Inside the Vicious Heart* (New York: Oxford University Press, 1985), 3, xi.

9. Anna Pawelczynska, *Values and Violence in Auschwitz: A Sociological Analysis*, trans. Catherine S. Leach (Berkeley: University of California Press, 1979), 74.

10. Pawelczynska, *Values and Violence*, 42.

11. Levi, *The Drowned and the Saved*, 83–84.

12. Agamben, *Remnants of Auschwitz*, 82.

13. Abzug, *Inside the Vicious Heart*, 40–41.

14. Transcript, interview with Herbert Treitel, survivor, interviewed in 1986 by the National Council of Jewish Women (Holocaust Oral History Project, United States Holocaust Memorial Museum, 2007), https://collections.ushmm.org/oh_findingaids/RG-50.154.0028_trs_en.pdf.

15. Transcript, interview with Herbert Treitel.

16. Levi, *Survival in Auschwitz*, 88, in footnote. Glossing the term

Muselmänner, Levi admits that he "does not know why" it was used in the camps in this way.

17. Yad Vashem is the Center for Holocaust Research, Documentation, Education and Commemoration in Jerusalem, Israel. Shoah Resource Center, International School for Holocaust Studies, "Muselmann," n.d., http://www.yadvashem.org/odot_pdf/Microsoft%20Word%20-%206474.pdf.

18. Gil Anidjar, *The Jew, the Arab: A History of the Enemy* (Stanford, Calif.: Stanford University Press, 2003), 119.

19. Jean Améry, *At the Mind's Limits*, trans. Sidney Rosenfeld and Stella P. Rosenfeld (Bloomington: Indiana University Press, 1980), 9; Sofsky, *The Order of Terror*, 25.

20. Abba Kovner used this phrase in his famous pamphlet of December 13, 1941/January 1, 1942, calling for underground revolt against the Nazis, as a metaphor for what Vilna youth should not do. See Kovner, "A First Attempt to Tell," in *The Holocaust as Historical Experience: Essays and a Discussion*, ed. Yehuda Bauer and Nathan Rotenstreich (New York: Holmes and Meier, 1981), 81–82. As Berel Lang has rightly pointed out to me, Kovner directed his criticism at those he thought could have resisted but did not, but he couldn't at that time have known of the condition of the *Muselmänner*. My intention with this analogy is to point out the harmful logic of the fatalist assumption

21. Pawelczynska, *Values and Violence in Auschwitz*, 77. On "social death," see Orlando Patterson, *Slavery and Social Death: A Comparative Study* (Cambridge, Mass.: Harvard University Press, 1985).

22. It allowed the "Jew near death" as David Simpson puts it, to turn the "Jew nearer death" into a non-Jew, a Muslim, the Jew's religious and political "other." See Simpson, *9/11*, 163.

23. Based on a questionnaire survey of eighty-nine Auschwitz survivors, the German title translates as "At the Border between Life and Death: A Study of the Phenomenon of the *Muselmann* in the Concentration Camp." I am relying upon quoted versions of this study in other accounts. Zdzislaw Ryn and Stanslaw Kłodziński, *An der Grenze zwischen Leben und Tod: Eine Studie uber die Erscheinung des "Muselmanns" im Konzentrazionslager, Auschwitz-Hefte*, vol. 1 (Weinheim: Beltz, 1987), quoted in Gottfried Kössler, Matthias Naumann, Werner Renz, and Jörg Thums, "Muselmanner," glossary entry, website of the Wollheim Memorial, I.G. Farben Building, Frankfurt, Germany, http://www.wollheim-memorial.de/en/muselmaenner.

24. Ryn and Kłodziński, *An der Grenze zwischen Leben und Tod*, 147; qtd. here: http://www.wollheim-memorial.de/en/muselmaenner.

25. Agamben, *Remnants of Auschwitz*, 186.

26. Agamben, *Remnants of Auschwitz*.

27. David Matzner, *The Muselmann: The Diary of a Jewish Slave Laborer* (Hoboken, N.J.: Ktav, 1994). The others named above gave interviews for the Holocaust Oral History Project, the transcripts of which are in the U.S. Holocaust Memorial Museum's Center for Advance Holocaust Studies archive.

28. Levi, *Survival in Auschwitz*, 126.

29. Levi, *Survival in Auschwitz*, 90.

30. Levi, *Survival in Auschwitz*, 90.

31. Levi is aware of this. In a 1986 conversation with Philip Roth, he says, "Please grant me the right to inconsistency . . . The coherence I think one notes in my books is an artifact, a rationalization a posteriori." "A Conversation with Primo Levi by Philip Roth," in *Survival in Auschwitz*, 180–81.

32. Levi, *The Drowned and the Saved*, 82, 78.

33. Levi, *The Drowned and the Saved*, 78.

34. Barbie Zelizer, *Remembering to Forget: Holocaust Memory through the Camera's Eye* (Chicago: University of Chicago Press, 1998), 140.

35. On the cultural force of liberation photos as icons, see Carol Zemel, "Emblems of Atrocity: Holocaust Liberation Photographs," in *Image and Remembrance: Representation and the Holocaust*, ed. Shelley Hornstein and Florence Jacobowitz (Bloomington: Indiana University Press, 2003), 201–19.

36. On the forced confrontations of German civilians with dead bodies at atrocity sites in German villages and towns, and the Signal Corps photographs of them, see Christopher E. Mauriello, *Forced Confrontation: The Politics of Dead Bodies in Germany at the End of World War II* (Lanham, Md.: Lexington Books, 2017).

37. Barbie Zelizer, "The Liberation of Buchenwald: Images and the Shape of Memory," in *Cultural Memory and the Construction of Identity*, ed. Dan Ben-Amos and Lilian Weissberg (Detroit, Mich.: Wayne State University Press, 1999), 145.

38. Zelizer, "Liberation of Buchenwald," 146.

39. Cited in Zelizer, "Liberation of Buchenwald," 149.

40. Zelizer, *Remembering to Forget*, 160.

41. Zelizer, *Remembering to Forget*, 160. This kind of photo is typified in the famous image taken by *Life* photographer Margaret Bourke-White, titled "Survivors behind Barbed Wire, Buchenwald, 1945." The image was subsequently redrawn by Art Spiegelman in his first version of *Maus*, an image taken up by Marianne Hirsch as the cornerstone of her theory of "postmemory." See Hirsch, "Surviving Images: Holocaust Photographs and the Work of Postmemory," *Yale Journal of Criticism* 14, no. 1 (Spring 2001): 9–13.

42. Zelizer, *Remembering to Forget*, 162–63, 168.

43. Janina Struk, *Photographing the Holocaust: Interpretations of the Evidence* (London: I. B. Tauris, 2004), 128.

44. Zelizer, *Remembering to Forget*, 186.

45. Zemel, "Emblems of Atrocity," 211.

46. Zemel, "Emblems of Atrocity," 211. This is problematic for Zemel, and I would agree, precisely because it seals a "murdered Jewish population . . . timelessly, essentially, and reverentially into another's sacralized space" (217).

47. This summary is taken from Zelizer, *Remembering to Forget*, 183–88.

48. Abzug, *Inside the Vicious Heart*, 46–47.

49. Quoted in Abzug, *Inside the Vicious Heart*, 58.

50. Abzug describes similar reactions by American liberators to the extreme mingling of life and death at Nordhausen, Bergen-Belsen, and other camps. See Abzug, *Inside the Vicious Heart*, 40–41, 84–86. For example, American Curtis Mitchell, who screened Signal Corps photos for public release, said of liberated prisoners at Bergen-Belsen: "'You got over the feeling that these were people any more. They were so thin and so dried out that they might have been monkeys or plaster of Paris and you had to keep saying to yourself, these are human beings, and even when you said it, your mind was not believing it because nothing like this had ever happened before and it just couldn't happen.'" Interview with Curtis Mitchell, witness to the Holocaust, and narrative of Mitchell in "The Valley of Death, the Armies of Life," *Moment* (May 1981): 14, 17–19; quoted in Abzug, *Inside the Vicious Heart*, 86.

51. U.S. Holocaust Memorial Museum (henceforth USHMM) Collections, Photograph 74607, emphasis mine, https://collections.ushmm.org/search/catalog/pa6164.

52. Struk, *Photographing the Holocaust*, 131.

53. USHMM Collections, Photograph 10621, https://collections.ushmm.org/search/catalog/pa1045552.

54. Struk, *Photographing the Holocaust*, 132; Abzug, *Inside the Vicious Heart*, 132–34.

55. See Mark Philip Bradley, *The World Reimagined: Americans and Human Rights in the Twentieth Century* (New York: Cambridge University Press, 2016), 78–80.

56. Struk, *Photographing the Holocaust*, 132.

57. Quoted in Bradley, *The World Reimagined*, 80.

58. Bradley, *The World Reimagined*, 80. Struk notes how the exhibition flyer for "Lest We Forget" and later, the book compiled by the *Daily Mail, Lest We Forget*, were also full of misinformation: the book attributing death camp techniques to all the camps, and citing mistaken statistics; the

American flyer not mentioning Auschwitz at all; and little mention that the majority of victims were Jews (Struk, *Photographing the Holocaust*, 133–34).

59. Struk, *Photographing the Holocaust*, 126.

60. Struk, *Photographing the Holocaust*, 133.

61. Struk, *Photographing the Holocaust*, 133.

62. USHMM Collections, Photograph 62762. https://collections.ushmm.org/search/catalog/pa1151523.

63. Abzug, *Inside the Vicious Heart*, 108.

64. Abzug, *Inside the Vicious Heart*, 121.

65. Also pictured are William Hauben (second row from the front between the survivor holding his name tag and the one wearing a blanket) and Bernard Smilovic, located second from the left, first row wearing a blanket. USHMM Collections, Photograph 66297, https://collections.ushmm.org/search/catalog/pa9117.

66. USHMM Collections, Photograph 66297. The catalog also notes that the original caption from a donated photograph reads: "Starved prisoners, nearly dead from hunger, pose for the photographer in their rags." https://collections.ushmm.org/search/catalog/pa9117.

67. Zelizer, *Remembering to Forget*, 181.

68. *Liberation 1945* (Washington, D.C.: United States Holocaust Memorial Council, 1994).

69. Born in Taylor, Utah, and raised as a Mormon on a farm in West Weber, Utah, Heslop showed interest in photography as a young boy and learned the art on his own before studying photography at Los Angeles City College. From there he was recruited into the U.S. Army Signal Corps in Los Angeles in 1942. UHHMM Collections catalog, Photograph 62475, https://collections.ushmm.org/search/catalog/pa1151506.

70. Roland Barthes, *Camera Lucida: Reflections on Photography*, trans. Richard Howard (New York: Hill and Wang, 2010), 27, 42, 45.

71. Levi, *Survival in Auschwitz*, 26.

72. Levi, *Survival in Auschwitz*, 90.

73. See Levi's conversation with Philip Roth in Levi, *Survival in Auschwitz*, 180.

74. Levi, *Survival in Auschwitz*, 48–49.

75. Charlotte Delbo, *Auschwitz and After*, trans. Rosette C. Lamont (New Haven, Conn.: Yale University Press, 1995), 114.

Holli Levitsky

Absent Presence, Pathological Afterimages, and the Aesthetics of Excrement

As part of your equipment have something to dig with, and when you relieve yourself, dig a hole and cover up your excrement. For the Lord your God moves about in your camp to protect you and to deliver your enemies to you. Your camp must be holy, so that he will not see among you anything indecent and turn away from you.

—*Deuteronomy 23:13–15*

Seventy days during which we haven't taken our dresses off . . . They must stink but we don't notice because our nostrils are full of the smell of the crematoria . . .

—*Charlotte Delbo,* Who Will Carry the Word?

The relation between what we see and what we know is never settled.

—*John Berger,* Ways of Seeing

"NOTHING IS MORE QUOTIDIAN THAN EXCREMENT AND ANALITY,"[1] writes Gene A. Plunka. In Holocaust imagery, excrement materializes in achingly human stories, mired in quotidian detail, yet potent enough to scorch. For example, Lina Wertmüller's film *Seven Beauties* seems to come alive in a whirling vortex with its abhorrent image of an anarchist jumping into a pool of feces. This is not a vision of reality, but the representation of a world so criminally brutal that it cannot be accurately represented except through shit. Steven Spielberg's *Schindler's List*, groundbreaking in so many ways, with its black-and-white cinematography was able to bring an unnerving sharpness and clarity to the portrayal of such abject scenes as the small boy hiding in the latrines, standing in excrement up to his chest. Laszlo Nemes's film *Son of Saul* opens in a feverish pitch of routine life in a *Sonderkommando* unit: a brutal cycle of gathering, gassing, and incineration. The gas chambers, cleaned of the excrement and vomit, begin to erase the remnants of Jewish life that ended there.[2]

In reality, human waste overflowed in the camps. Terrence Des Pres saw it as nothing less than an "excremental assault," leaking from the open toilet pits into the prisoners' barracks, where one bucket held the product of the entire block.[3] At night, prisoners necessarily repurposed their soup bowls as toilets. Outside, the human material spewing forth from the crematoria night and day—a combination of gases, ashes, and mineral fragments—constituted human waste of a different kind. Falling over the camp grounds, dusting the head, bodies, and entering the orifices of the prisoners, it was an assault of the kind that poet Paul Celan imagined every morning as the "black milk of daybreak . . . [which] we drink and we drink."[4]

In *The Train Journey: Transit, Captivity, and Witnessing in the Holocaust*, Simone Gigliotti links her analysis of the experience of the deportation trains to the visual and embodied dimensions of survivor experiences, what she terms "sensory witnessing." The smell of and closeness to excrement was a "condition of literal defilement."[5] As she suggests, in the experience of deportation trains, Des Pres's excremental assault resulted in the unmaking of bodies, exposing a profound crisis of witnessing. Gigliotti's notion of "sensory witnessing" reminds us that no aspect of the Holocaust should be ignored; that even such socially taboo topics as excrement, urine, human waste, and their accompanying stench should be accounted for. Witnesses expressed terrifying contact with excrement and its stench in deportation trains, and in the camps, and their testimonies were corroborated by historical accounts.

Indeed, many of the images of excrement and human waste in Holocaust films and in literary accounts, as seen in the examples above, have become as iconic as they are ubiquitous. In consideration of the camps, we see (or can imagine) such waste products in the muddy, excrement-covered grounds, the references to diarrhea and its gruesome and painful effects, and in the smeared remains—even relics—of the prisoners in their final moments. They remind us, as does Daniel Goldhagen,[6] of the physicality of the Holocaust, gradually reducing the body to excrement, or eliminating it completely. Robert Jay Lifton, too, reminds us that the term for Auschwitz—*anus mundi*—"accurately reflects the Nazi vision of the necessity to sweep clean the world"[7] of undesirables, which for the Nazis were biomedical waste material.

In this chapter I am seeking to identify—and thus help the reader imagine—what I am calling pathological afterimages of human waste, from the excremental to the remnants of bodily erosion. Beyond the visible image of a child hiding in an Auschwitz latrine, or of the gas chambers smeared with human waste, lay the remnants that are not seen. By using the word "afterimage," I am recalling the fairly normal optical condition caused by the continued activation of the visual system after exposure to the original image has ceased. A pathological afterimage is an abnormal phenomenon, where the image does not eventually disappear. This clinical condition, palinopsia, results in images that recur to such a significant degree that they become difficult or impossible to ignore. The pathology which leads to palinopsia can be observed in a variety of forms, as it is thought to be a brain-related disorder that results from traumatic experiences.

This discussion of seen and unseen excrement and human waste furthers an understanding of the limits of representation, underlining the need to return again and again to the imagery of the not-seen alongside the seen. The absent presence—a phantasm of history—emerges from the massive archive of survivor testimonies. Here, I want to cite Giorgio Agamben, who writes that the "testimony contained at its core an essential lacuna . . . commenting on survivors' testimony necessarily meant interrogating this lacuna."[8] In consideration of this lacuna, I want to interrogate the ongoing moments of contact between people and shit. In the imagery, the forced contact reveals a variation of copraphagia, the ingestion of excrement. That excrement could enter our mouths is an idea routed through the brain, that records itself in and on our bodies as revulsion, abjection, impurity, and taboo. Under this investigation, even the lacunae are seen as abject.

Pursuing the relationship between shit as metaphor and the "reality" of human waste underscores the "impossibility of metaphor" as an axiom of Holocaust representation. Indeed, literature and film present powerful examples of the real olfactory consequences of an ongoing excremental assault in the camps, ghettos, and in hiding. The images suggest the "unbearable stench" evoked by the poet Edmond Jabés, inasmuch as they suggest a metonymic connection between the seen and the unseen, the smelled and the unsmelled. Olfactory information is powerful, unfacilitated knowledge that reaches deep into our sciences and our mythologies, just as the words "witness" and "testify" originate in the fragments of the biological humanity that we excrete. The reality of excrement as an "absent presence" in the visual imagery has become, to an extent, a metaphor. The exposure of its presence in the frame highlights the "uncontained" nature of shit as fragmentary, remnental, piecemeal, but also as fluid and without borders. Exposing the reality of the pathological "after-stench" even more forcefully sears the scene (and not seen) into the imagination of the non-witness, as this chapter seeks to do. But even before the literary imagination accepted the challenge of creating an imagery of the Holocaust, newsreels were being created about the atrocities and shown in real time. Typically presented in a cinema, newsreels were a source of current affairs, information, and entertainment for millions of moviegoers. Interrogating the scenes in newsreels for excrement gives us first access to what we mean by pathological afterimages.

THE NEWSREELS

In 2014, a British documentary titled *Night Will Fall*[9] debuted, compiling newsreel footage from 1945 that had never previously been released as a film.[10] Beginning with springtime shots of the German countryside, the narrator describes how the Allies advanced into the heart of Germany. "Neat and tidy orchards, well-stocked farms lined the wayside," the narrator intones, "and the British soldier did not fail to admire the place and its inhabitants. At least, until he began to feel a smell."[11] This was not a case of synesthesia, when one sense is experienced through another. The smell came from the concentration camp of Bergen-Belsen, near all those thriving German farms. The camp held burned and rotting bodies, disease-ridden prisoners, and a swampy stench of waste, accompanying and then overriding the seen images.

American photographers in the U.S. Army Signal Corps also filmed the liberation of the concentration camps. The short, stark newsreels that they produced were shown before feature films in major theaters across the United States. During the war, and for a few decades afterward, Americans watched these newsreels with great interest. They revealed the extent of a reality they could not get elsewhere. In the frames of such films, bodies were stacked in piles on the grounds of the camp, in mass graves, on carts. The chaos of limbs, heads, and torsos—death on a scale that could not be contained—sprawled into the edges of the films' frames in unholy disorder.

Contra Jewish tradition that dignity must precede all acts concerning the human body, the degraded bodies were stripped of all that was human, depositing their own biological matter over the camp landscape, people, and structures. The prisoners had become Agamben's "merely human—and, for this reason, non-human."[12] Lacking dignity even in death, the bodies were, as the Nazis indicated, *entwurdigen*, "deprived of dignity."[13] The mind, too, was worn away by the body's constant contact with waste. According to passages in the Babylonian Talmud, "if excrement is visible in the anus when a person sits or squats, he is not allowed to recite the Shema,"[14] nor can the Shema be recited "in the vicinity of human and animal excrement, urine, and other sources of foul odors" or "while one is defecating or in a toilet."[15] What kind of unholy ground had the Nazis created by abnegating the Jewish body?

Given Jewish law regarding the body, the raw nakedness of the exposed orifices presented a special problematic. The blessing to recite after one urinates or defecates, *Asher Yatzar*, specifies the holy relationship with the body's orifices: "Blessed is God who has formed the human body in wisdom and created many orifices and cavities. It is obvious and known before You that if one of them were to be opened or closed incorrectly, it would be impossible to survive and stand before You at all."[16] In consideration of such laws and traditions, the images from the camps appeared blasphemous, demonic. This brings to mind the figure of Belphegor in the Jewish Kabbalistic tradition, the demon associated with excretion, traditionally depicted as sitting on a toilet.[17]

In literature, photographs, films, paintings, and other representational forms of Holocaust testimony, the image of the piles of corpses has become iconic, as Barbie Zelizer's work emphasizes.[18] These images are potent symbols of the dehumanization, de-individualization, and extensive loss of bodies in the Holocaust. In the newsreels discussed earlier, the camera pans across the barracks of the *lager* to focus on one stack of cadavers, piled like thrown sticks. As the camera rests for a moment, one set of sunken eyes looks up, toward the camera, toward the viewer in the darkened theater. In that moment we are forced to look, to sink into those eyes and see in the unnamed faces and wasted bodies an excremental assault so complete they are as if one body: one Jewish body.

As they recorded the liberation of the camps, the filmmakers and cameramen seemed understandably focused on the massive number of corpses. The slow erosion degraded the formerly human men and women into mounds of sexless and de-animated body parts. Reduced to its most lifeless form, the body was, somehow, only matter. To those who hated Jews and saw their annihilation as the *end*-game, no distinctions carried any greater or lesser value. The bodies were already waste, or, in Agamben's understanding, merely human, and thus, non-human.

For Michael Steinlauf, the "vanished landscape"[19] of Jews and Jewish life in postwar Poland left behind a spectral and material presence of Jews. The newsreel images begged a similar question: as they were lifted, dragged, and carted away from these sites of violence, what did the bodies leave behind? In the background, like steam rising off fresh excrement, lay the material presence of Jewish waste products. Hovering over the unseen shit was olfactory revulsion as a spectral presence, trailing the corpses as a dark shadow.

In Jewish tradition, cleanliness is connected to a person's relationship with God.[20] Yet within spaces of containment—ghetto, train, camp—lay waste that forced the prisoners to break Jewish laws (and traditions such as "cleanliness is next to godliness"). The inescapable stench that resulted from such waste provided proof of its pervasiveness. If the camera had a device to record smell, like the "odorifics" machine that Holocaust survivor Maude shares with Harold in Hal Ashby's 1971 film,[21] no one would be able to watch these newsreels. Understandably, Maude records only scents that bring her joy.

The newsreels were recorded before a postwar vernacular and Holocaust cultural "industry" could emerge. But prisoners already had a camp lexicon, naming those who seemed to have lost the will to live "*Musselmänner*." The description of a whole class of prisoners as inherently helpless or hapless is not a topic I will discuss further in this chapter (but lies at the heart of Sharon Oster's chapter in this volume), but many questions about the classification persist. Were the *Musselmänner* less competent or courageous than others in the camps, or were they simply doomed from the start? Charlotte Delbo remembers the *Musselmänner* as a form of "life in death";[22] others have declared *Musselmänner* as the true witnesses to the final destruction of the Jews. My point is that these characteristics also describe the cadavers in the filmed images. They too are somehow neither dead nor alive, but rather matter itself that emerged from once live bodies and witnesses to their own destruction. History tells us what happened to most of the prisoners who died in the concentration camps. Left bloated or emaciated, life was strangled out of them like just another biological excretion. In the filmed images, the piles had become a blurred mass leaking across the screen, suggesting that the Jewish body that emerged from Auschwitz had *shit its own death*. The inhumane conditions of the camps led many prisoners to take their own lives rather than continue to suffer.

THE UNHOLY CAMP

Regulations governing bodily excretions, secretions, discharges, and even emanations were carefully outlined in the Hebrew Bible. Biologically bound acts and the resulting "waste" were understood to exist within the holy relationship between human and God. In the biblical injunction found in this chapter's epigraph, the highly specific processes for excrement are outlined: where and how to shit, and the procedures to follow after the fact to maintain holiness (digging a hole outside the camp with a trowel, then covering the used hole). The punishment for an "unholy" camp, where God might be exposed to excrement, would be the absence of providential protection and thus a lost battle against the Hebrews' enemies. The Nazis systematically forced Jews to violate these regulations.

The prisoners' shit befouled the camp grounds, which in turn became profaned space. Halakhic law not only delineates the process for waste elimination; it defines allowable sites and times of elimination. The Essenes were particularly concerned with impurity, and two of the Dead Sea Scrolls, the "War Scroll" and the "Temple Scroll," mandated that toilets be located outside of the military camp and outside of their "ideal future city" of Jerusalem. Interestingly, Jodi Magness cites that "the distances . . . placed the toilets . . . farther than Jews are allowed to walk on the Sabbath," and that, according to Josephus, "the Essenes did not defecate on the Sabbath."[23] They saw excrement as a source of ritual impurity, even though other scriptures identify instances of impurity without considering the act itself as ritually impure. Nonetheless, the groundswell of human waste that covered the concentration camp turned the entire site into a toilet in the inmates' midst. Naturally, in the camps it was impossible to practice Jewish laws regarding bodily excretions.

The latrines in the camps served multiple purposes. For prisoners, the latrine could function as a hiding space, the location of a clandestine meeting, or a site for suicide. Generally speaking, it was a befouled space. Still, art has the power to offer a kind of redemptive space (which history may not). In that way, the creative reimagining of a concentration camp latrine may be seen as a powerful testament to the force of imagination. For example, Hank Greenspan's 1992 play *Remnants*, based on years of collected testimony, offers redemptive moments even among the ruins. In the scene titled "The Vanity," a survivor narrates, with a kind of awe, what she saw in the Birkenau prisoners' latrine:

> In Birkenau there was the prisoners' latrine—you know, where we went to the toilet—which was really just a bench with a row of holes over a pit filled with quicklime. So this was where we went to the bathroom.
>
> . . . The SS took one lady, one of the prisoners, and they made her the Scheisskapo. This was a joke for the SS. It means "the shit commander." That was her title. It was on a sign that she wore around her neck. And her job was to watch the toilets and be like a kind of attendant. She had to keep it neat and clean.
>
> And one day I noticed that this lady, the Scheisskapo, had managed to find a few boxes. Somehow, she got a couple of old crates made of wood. And she put them together with the little one in front, so she could sit on it. And she also had a little mirror that she probably found in the clothes—from one of the prisoners who had been killed.
>
> So with the boxes and the mirror she made like a little bureau. She put the mirror over the big box and she sat on the little box and made like a little vanity in the corner of the latrine. A little vanity in the corner of the ladies' room.[24]

This scene provides a testimonial account of seeing within the deepest recesses of the camp—among the darkest places—thus allowing the imaginative writer to interrogate that darkness. In *Schindler's List* the small boy is saved by hiding in the latrine. So too in this play can the latrine be identified as "saving" the "Scheisskapo," reestablishing her humanity among and through the shit. Although laws of hygiene and holiness regarding excretion could not be followed, in the right context, maybe shit could itself be made beautiful. Perhaps the scene suggests that we are all shit, that the Holocaust opened up a space that can never again be covered up; thus, the excremental space is either left unholy or, as Emil Fackenheim insists, shit itself becomes holy. To again borrow lines from Jabes, in the case of Greenspan's play: "the words have disemboweled the words."[25]

EXCREMENTAL AESTHETICS

The word "aesthetics" derives from the Greek *aisthetikos*, meaning "of sense perception."[26] An excremental aesthetics would thus be concerned with creating a language for critical reflection on the mind and emotions in relation to olfactory imagery. The "literature of the body" suggested by this demand is not a new field of inquiry. There are roots traceable to Mary Douglas's work on purity and danger, Terrence Des Pres's work on the literature of survival, and Julia Kristeva's work on abjection.[27] Other theories about excrement and waste have emerged because the failure of conventional language to express the Holocaust experience demands an aesthetics that translates the experience into human, quotidian terms. "Fecopoetics," coined from "ecopoetics," explores the fecal in its material and symbolic aspect.[28] This theory is primarily interested in the scatological model of the medieval grotesque body, focusing on bodily fluids, excrescences, and decomposition more generally. Most pointedly delineated by Mikhail Bakhtin, the body is seen as existing in perpetual transformation and flux.[29] Susan Morrison adds the rhizome as a metaphor of the medieval body—an image that derives from Deleuze and Guattari's discussion of the rhizome as an organism growing in all directions, potentially endless, without head or center, exit or entry. Still, since the excremental exposes the clean, whole body as a "sham" and a "fiction,"[30] such an aesthetics brings us closer "to the 'real' of bodily human existence."[31] This theory also helps to understand how the concept of coprophagia emerges in a new form in Holocaust writing as forced contact with one's own or another's waste.

Excremental aesthetics is distinct from already formalized studies in psychoanalysis, in particular the concept of Freudian "anality," which is connected to a stage in psychosexual development. In this context, excremental aesthetics also differs from but is informed by the emerging field of "waste studies,"[32] which poses ethical questions about how we have disciplined ourselves in regard to dirt. For example, Douglas's work on the threat of excrement identifies a binary relationship between dirt and order. She reads excrement as impurity and disorder. The figuring of excrement as shit—low, horrifying, disgusting—is a manifestation of the mind-body split. For Douglas, reason is antithetical to excrement.[33]

Other terms have been used to describe literature of the body, though not necessarily with a focus on excrement. The "*aesthetics of agitation*,"[34] for example, a phrase used by Lawrence Langer (in his introduction to Charlotte Delbo's poetic trilogy *Auschwitz and After*), is itself a response to Adorno's dictum against writing poetry after the Holocaust. An aesthetics of agitation offers a poetics that reads against its own aesthetics, one which undercuts the clarity of narrative and struggles against the reader's potential over-identification with the author and the colonization of the victims' experience. Langer, along with poet of witness Carolyn Forche, also identifies a "*poetics of atrocity*," a category that includes the work of Holocaust poets.

To sum up, excremental aesthetics interrogates images of waste *seen and noted as such*, as well as seeking out the unseen but pathological afterimages that have leaked into the background. The "pathological afterimages," imprinted on the brain, are an effect of seeing deeply "into" a frame of reference for the waste material left behind.

EXCREMENTAL LITERATURE

While many testimonies and literary accounts include images of excrement, I have chosen to discuss several which highlight the role of copraphagia in their creation, since it is through the abject contact between people and shit that we find this particular pathology. Two texts in particular carry the burden of such pathological conditions: Charlotte Delbo's play *Who Will Carry the Word?* and Jerzy Kosinski's novel *The Painted Bird*. Overrun with images of bodily fluids emerging from sites of violence, putrefaction, and death, these texts assault us with copraphagic and transgressive imagery.

In 1943, Charlotte Delbo and 229 of her peers in the French Resistance against Nazi Germany were taken to Auschwitz. Based on her experiences, *Who Will Carry the Word?* follows twelve women as they struggle to find the will to survive when faced with the hellish world of the concentration camp. The play's title refers to the central crisis as their number falls due to attrition. Who will be the one to survive, defying all odds and carrying word of what happened to these women back to the unknowing world? The play is sparse. There are no sets, no makeup, and the faces and costumes do not matter. What does matter is the evocation of a "desolate landscape," described by the playwright as "nowhere . . . a place that no one can imagine."[35]

The unimaginable "nowhere" is established in the play's prologue by Francoise: "Because I have returned from where there was no return."[36] The haunting story begins with an attempt by Claire to keep Francoise from committing suicide. Francoise suggests that Claire seek out the bodies for a motive: "Ask their faces which are no longer faces; ask the sockets of their eyes which the rats have widened . . . Don't you believe that to become so scrawny, so ugly, so convulsed, so trapped in what remains of skin and flesh, you have to have suffered to the limit, a limit which no one reached before us?"[37] Facing the groundswell of ruined bodies wrenches all of the women closer to the one choice they have left, "becoming a cadaver . . . which will still be clean enough to look at."[38]

In its leaking, wasting state, the abject body violates the boundaries between the body and the camp. Mounette's fear is of "a lake of mire that extends as far as the other end of the horizon . . . I'm afraid to have it in my mouth."[39] The women's ongoing contact with the cadavers infects them with a kind of abject fear. These waste products test the notion of the self/other split upon which subjectivity depends.[40] The abjectness violates boundaries between the body and its excesses, obviating the desire for a "clean" and "proper" body.[41]

In the camps, and elsewhere in extremis, the absence of sanitary facilities was, as witness Pelagia Lewinska observed, a "deliberate way of erasing the humanity of [each person]; condemning them to die in and as excrement."[42] In his classic essay about excrement in the concentration camp, Terrence Des Pres identifies the extent to which prisoners were inundated with human waste. Dysentery and other diseases as well as rules about toilet usage left prisoners with little or no control over their natural functions. The demands of the bowels are absolute; without the ability to accommodate those demands prisoners soiled themselves and those around them, stepping in and sleeping on a fetid mixture of waste products. Of the ones too weak to move, Des Pres writes, they were "slowly enveloped in their own decomposition."[43] We do not feel the prisoners' dried diarrhea on the skin; we feel the debasement of one covered in shit. Yvonne states: "You can no longer look at yourself when you gradually dissolve, turning into dirty water, when diarrhea is dripping from you day and night . . . I am turning into dirty water . . . I am emptying. It is normal for life to expire through the lips. When it goes through the intestines—that's complete humiliation."[44] The regular and ongoing contact between people and excrement that we find in the text leaves us with the basest sense of horror, the sticky skin formed on spoiled milk that we take into our mouths without even noticing it there.

It is worthwhile considering why such images conjure the deepest level of "terrorized abjection,"[45] what Rudolf Otto describes as a "numinous unworth" and a "feeling of absolute profaneness."[46] At each stage of assault against the body, it was further degraded, its humanity diminished, always in a trajectory leading inevitably toward elimination. Soiled with their own filth as they sludged through the muddy grounds, the prisoners had to rise each day as if their life had meaning. One prisoner observes of the mud that it "retains odors. It smells of diarrhea."[47] What followed such threats to conventional bodily boundaries was abjection itself: self-disgust and loathing of one's own body. The breakdown in meaning, caused by the loss of the distinction between the body and its waste (the elimination of the body), was horrifying.

The fluid landscape of the bespattered camp, itself the result of an absence of sanitary facilities, broke down a number of conventional binary categories. In such an environment, what was "clean" or "dirty," "healthy" or "sick," "body" or "waste," or for that matter, "human" or "animal," normal or aberrant? A witness writes in *The Female Face of God in Auschwitz* that the effect of the excremental assault was a "deliberate means to fill us with contempt towards ourselves and our fellows . . . . The Germans . . . knew we were incapable of looking at each other without disgust."[48] Such a breakdown of meaning could be seen to be part and parcel of the Holocaust experience, where distinctions—particularly for Jews—were systematically broken down without repair.

Kosinski's novel *The Painted Bird* ostensibly fictionalizes the author's own experiences during the Holocaust. This account has been neither authenticated nor fully discounted, and readers are urged to research the story further. This chapter focuses on the novel as novel, which opens in the first weeks of World War II, in the fall of 1939, as a six-year old boy from a large eastern European city is sent away for safety by his parents. Though his identity is not revealed, his dark eyes and hair, olive skin, and city dialect make it clear to the peasants with whom he comes into contact that he is either a gypsy or a Jew.

The body of the boy sits in the space between *scheiss-stucke* ("pieces of shit"; used for corpses by German camp guards), and predatory or usurious. The ignorant and superstitious villagers see him as a physical and spiritual threat and defend themselves against his supposed sorcery. As the boy seeks shelter and care, he is repeatedly physically and emotionally assaulted in the most cruel and degrading ways. He is forced into contact with all kinds of fluids as he crawls, creeps, floats, and claws his way from village to village. After his first caretaker dies, he is found by other villagers and dragged about in a sack. He is hung by a hook and displayed like a sideshow freak. A folk doctor takes him in as her assistant, but then he is hurled onto a fish bladder floating down the river, and lands in another village. He winds up in the house of the miller, a deliriously jealous and violent husband, where he witnesses the gouging out of a plowboy's eyes. Meantime, the villagers engage in bestial and transgressive bodily acts with one another—fathers assault daughters, a young girl copulates with her brother and the family goat. Husbands brutalize and rape their wives. A man is thrown into a rat-filled pit and eaten alive. The villagers copulate, defecate, and urinate in the open without compunction. Overrun with images of bodily fluids emerging from sites of violence, putrefaction, and death, and so laden with excrement itself, the novel assaults the reader's sensibilities.

The "coprophagic narration" of *The Painted Bird* exposes the great threat that such assaults posed to the boy's identity. He has lost what he was, and carries only a vague sense of providence. Absent an identity of his own and a moral force with which to defend his ego, he internalizes the perversity of the villagers. He observes their deeply abject lives with wonder and awe; they are, in a word, shit. Images of shit thread through the novel as a bridge past conventional language, connecting the most base human act—the elimination of bodily waste—with the basest of acts—human defilement. As a result, the boy desires to be "shit," and begins to adopt his own pathology of violence.

Reading the symbolic against the literal, we can champion the imagination as a powerful tool of creation that furthers our understanding of the massive impact human waste had on the victims. Kristeva writes that, at a symbolic level, excrement is the confusing "abject" that is neither subject nor object, but, she writes, "not nothing either . . . A weight of meaninglessness, about which there is nothing insignificant, and which crushes me."[49]

The "crushing" meaninglessness of excrement is well illustrated in a scene from *The Painted Bird* where coprophagia might be understood as a visual ingestion of feces. The character called Stupid Ludmilla, a village outsider, is brutally attacked by a mob of local women. As the villagers hold her down, one of the women pushes a bottle filled with manure into her vagina. Ludmilla "began to moan and howl like a beast. The other women looked on calmly. Suddenly with all her strength one of them kicked the bottom of the bottle sticking out of Stupid Ludmilla's groin. There was the noise of glass shattering inside."[50]

Ludmilla had been the boy's protector; he witnesses the incident from a short distance away. The villagers seek to destroy the boy's body through these coprophagic acts, which are juxtaposed with such providential acts as the taking of the host during Mass. At one point, the boy believes the religion of the villagers might provide him with salvation. He embraces the opportunity to seek that providence when a sympathetic priest invites him to hold the sacred missal during the High Mass. When the weakened boy drops it, the horrified villagers descend on his body, staging a mock mass at an adjacent manure pit, then hurling him into it. In the Jewish tradition, the reason for covering excrement is not because excrement is like impurity and makes its surroundings impure; rather, it is forbidden to see it at the time of prayer. When the boy surfaces through the brown scum, he can no longer speak. Providence has failed him, and in replacement, he finds that he is, literally, shit.

Having lost his voice and his faith in providential protection, the boy decides to fully embrace the amorality of the villagers. In order to stop being shit, he must shit on others. Kosinski writes: "What mattered [to the boy] was that a man should consciously promote evil, find pleasure harming others, nurturing and using the diabolical powers granted him by the Evil Ones in a manner calculated to cause as much misery and suffering around him as possible."[51] "Now," the boy plans, "I would join those who were helped by the Evil Ones."[52] He translates the religious doctrine of the villagers into a diabolical plan. His forced, violent contact with the pool of excrement, which swallows his voice, conveys the significant defilement he has undergone.

Both Delbo's play and Kosinski's novel fixate on the transgression of bodily boundaries. Their anxiety with excrement and leakage brings to light the pathological displacement of these waste products as a form of traumatic representation. These stories help us tie together the literal use of human waste product, its symbolic potential as both humanizing and dehumanizing agent, and structural parallels between the grotesque and traumatic experiences. At the end of the novel, the boy is found by his parents, but he remains mute and psychologically fractured. After skiing into a deep gully he is knocked unconscious. After the chilling accident he regains his voice, but other traumatic symptoms remain.

Delbo's Francoise sees only one chance to escape the useless knowledge of the camp. She writes: "You must wait until my eyes do not see what they see."[53] But the physical assault on prisoners is brutal and dehumanizing. It weakens the body, and as the body erodes, the spirit becomes befouled. Excrement has left an absent presence, the images soiling the landscape and transgressing boundaries with their unholy excesses. The "pathological afterimages" of an excremental assault are retained in the mind's eye even after the abject and traumatic experience is visibly removed from the scene.

CONCLUSIONS

Unpacking these images of acts and products of elimination in Holocaust imagery summons us to see human waste as waste, that is, as a quotidian biological product. The shared stories testify to the great extent to which prisoners dwelled in their own and others' shit, and open a passage through which such pain can be approached. Yet each excretion also speaks to a transgressive body, a body in pain, as we know from the work of Elaine Scarry in *The Body in Pain* and Kali Tal. In her important essay "Speaking the Language of Pain," Tal writes that with all experiences of trauma, "reality so violates personal mythologies" that only the example of "the literal immersion of concentration camp victims in shit . . . of being forced to wear, eat or swim in excrement," can approximate the individual's totally abject sense of psychic and social "violation."[54] Achieving such an "approximation" of abjection has been the goal of this chapter. Projected into Agamben's lacuna, the excremental imagery refracts, emerging in the newsreels where we gain first access to the pathological afterimages. The corpses remind us that the Nazis forced the Jews to break the holy laws, reducing them to the "merely" human. The presentation of this argument, within an aesthetics of excrement, allows for a deeper understanding of the failure of conventional language to tell this harrowing story that in so many ways suggests the breakdown of civilization. But part of our civilizing process is to recognize the value of that which we deem uncivilized and to see ourselves in that threatening, filthy alterity. The language of excremental aesthetics engages that challenge by finding unity and humanity in the universal connection we share—in this case, excrement. What is more abject than human waste, and more horrifying than reading about the torture and murder of millions of people? Excrement may be the only metaphor that makes metaphor itself impossible.

NOTES

1. Gene A. Plunka, *Holocaust Drama: The Theater of Atrocity* (Cambridge: Cambridge University Press, 2009), 85.

2. *Seven Beauties, directed by Lina Wertmüller (1975, Medusa Film); Schindler's List,* directed by Steven Spielberg (1993, Universal Pictures); *Son of Saul,* directed by Laszlo Nemes (Hungarian National Film Fund, 2015)

3. Terrence Des Pres, *The Survivor: An Anatomy of Life in the Death Camps* (Oxford: Oxford University Press, 1976).

4. Paul Celan, "Todesfuge" (1948).

5. Simone Gigliotti, *The Train Journey: Transit, Captivity, and Witnessing in the Holocaust* (Oxford: Berghahn Books, 2009), 3.

6. Daniel Goldhagen, *Hitler's Willing Executioners: Ordinary Germans and the Holocaust* (New York: Knopf Doubleday, 2007)

7. Robert Jay Lifton, *The Nazi Doctors: Medical Killing and the Psychology of Genocide* (New York: Basic Books, 1986), 147.

8. Giorgia Agamben, *Remnants of Auschwitz: The Witness and the Archive*, trans. Daniel Heller-Roazen (Cambridge, Mass.: MIT Press, 2002), 13.

9. *Night Will Fall,* directed by Andre Singer (2014, Spring Films).

10. The story behind the film's long journey to publication will not be discussed here.

11. *Night Will Fall.*

12. Agamben, *Remnants of Auschwitz*, 68.

13. Agamben, *Remnants of Auschwitz.*

14. Jodi Magness, *Stone and Dung, Oil and Spit: Jewish Daily Life in the Time of Jesus* (Grand Rapids, Mich.: Eerdmans, 2011), 137.

15. Magness, *Stone and Dung, Oil and Spit*, 138.

16. Ronald H. Isaacs, *Every Person's Guide to Jewish Prayer* (Lanham, Md.: Jason Aronson, 1997), 109.

17. Ernest L. Abel, *Death Gods: An Encyclopedia of the Rulers, Evil Spirits, and Geographies of the Dead* (ABC-CLIO, 2009), 36.

18. See Barbie Zelizer, *Remembering to Forget: Holocaust Memory through the Camera's Eyes* (Chicago: University of Chicago Press, 1998), esp. 1, 90, 93, 106, 108, 133, 190, and 236.

19. Michael Steinlauf, *Bondage to the Dead: Poland and the Memory of the Holocaust* (Syracuse, N.Y.: Syracuse University Press, 1997).

20. See Leviticus 15:16 and 15:19 and Deuteronomy 23:10–15.

21. *Harold and Maude*, directed by Hal Ashby (1971, Paramount Pictures).

22. Charlotte Delbo, *Auschwitz and After* (New Haven, Conn.: Yale University Press, 1970), xi.

23. Jodi Magness, "What's the Poop on Ancient Toilets and Toilet Habits?" *Near Eastern Archaeology* 75, no. 2 (2012): 83.

24. Hank Greenspan, *Remnants*, directed by Hank Greenspan and Ann Klautsch (Ann Arbor: Michigan Radio Theater, 1992).

25. Edmond Jabès, *The Book of Questions* (Middletown, Conn.: Wesleyan University Press, 1991), 247.

26. Bharati Chand, *Advance Philosophy of Education* (Chennai: Notion, 2017).

27. Mary Douglas, *Purity and Danger: An Analysis of Concepts of Pollution and Taboo* (London: Routledge, 1966); Terrence Des Pres, *The Survivor: An Anatomy of Life in the Death Camps* (Oxford: Oxford University Press, 1976); Julia Kristeva, *Powers of Horror* (New York: Columbia University Press, 1982).

28. Susan Morrison, *Excrement in the Late Middle Ages: Sacred Filth and Chaucer's Fecopoetics* (New York: Palgrave Macmillan 2008).

29. Mikahil Bakhtin, *Rabelais and His World* (Bloomington: Indiana University Press, 1984).

30. Morrison, *Excrement in the Late Middle Ages*, 137.

31. Morrison, *Excrement in the Late Middle Ages*, 155.

32. See Susan Morrison, *The Literature of Waste: Material Ecopoetics and Ethical Matter* (New York: Palgrave Macmillan, 2015).

33. Douglas, *Purity and Danger*.

34. Delbo, *Auschwitz and After*, xvi.

35. Delbo, *Who Will Carry the Word?* 269.

36. Delbo, *Who Will Carry the Word?* 273.
37. Delbo, *Who Will Carry the Word?* 276.
38. Delbo, *Who Will Carry the Word?* 276.
39. Delbo, *Who Will Carry the Word?* 295.
40. Kristeva, *Powers of Horror*.
41. Kristeva, *Powers of Horror, 2.*
42. Melissa Raphael, *The Female Face of God in Auschwitz: A Jewish Feminist Theology of the Holocaust* (London: Routledge, 2003), 65.
43. Des Pres, *The Survivor*, 155.
44. Delbo, *Who Will Carry the Word?* 280.
45. Raphael, *The Female Face of God in Auschwitz*, 67.
46. Rudolf Otto, *The Idea of the Holy* (Oxford: Oxford University Press, 1958), 51.
47. Delbo, *Who Will Carry the Word?* 311.
48. Raphael, *The Female Face of God in Auschwitz*, 65.
49. Kristeva, *Powers of Horror*, 2.
50. Jerzy Kosinski *The Painted Bird* (New York: Grove, 1965), 55.
51. Kosinski, *The Painted Bird*, 152.
52. Kosinski, *The Painted Bird*, 154.
53. Delbo, *Who Will Carry the Word?* 277.
54. Kali Tal, "Speaking the Language of Pain: Vietnam War Literature in the Context of a Literature of Trauma," in *Fourteen Landing Zones: Approaches to Vietnam War Literature*, ed. Jason Philip (Iowa City: University of Iowa Press, 1991), 234.

Yehudit Dori Deston

When One Door Closes, Another Opens: The Demjanjuk Trials in Israel (1986–1993) and in Germany (2009–2011)

A QUARTER OF A CENTURY AFTER THE EICHMANN TRIAL, THE DEMJANJUK trial was only the second, and the final, time the State of Israel brought a suspected Nazi criminal to Israel to stand trial. At the beginning of 1976, information reached the Office of Special Investigations (OSI) within the U.S. Department of Justice that John Demjanjuk, a Ukrainian who had received American citizenship about a decade earlier, had served as a *Wachmann* (guard) in the Sobibor extermination camp in German-occupied Poland but did not report this on the citizenship application forms he submitted in 1951. The OSI sent Demjanjuk's photograph, along with his immigration application documents, to the Israeli Police, together with the names and photographs of another sixteen Ukrainians suspected of being *Wachmänner* (guards) in the Sobibor and Treblinka camps, so that survivors of those camps living in Israel could identify them. The Israeli Police called in survivors known to them from their investigation prior to the Eichmann trial, and to the great surprise of the investigators, a number of Treblinka survivors positively identified Demjanjuk as "Ivan the Terrible," the gas chamber operator from the Treblinka extermination camp who was known for his unusual cruelty. In contrast, survivors of Sobibor did not recognize Demjanjuk at all. The findings of the Israel Police investigation were transferred to the OSI and led to legal proceedings that concluded with the revocation of Demjanjuk's American citizenship.[1]

In 1983, the State of Israel filed a request to extradite Demjanjuk to its jurisdiction to be tried in Israel on charges of crimes against the Jewish people, crimes against humanity, war crimes, and crimes against persecuted persons, all under the provisions of the Nazis and Nazi Collaborators (Punishment) Law (1950). According to the indictment, all the offenses were attributed to Demjanjuk on the assumption that he was "Ivan the Terrible," the gas chamber operator at Treblinka. Demjanjuk's trial opened in 1987. The verdict, handed down a year later, declared that he committed the crimes attributed to him, and he was sentenced to death. An appeal against the district court verdict was filed in the Supreme Court and, during the six years that the appeal was conducted, new evidence was discovered regarding Demjanjuk. This included about forty affidavits submitted by former Treblinka guards, whose source was unknown, which claimed that the name of the gas chamber operator in Treblinka was Ivan Marchenko. Nine of the guards identified a photograph of Marchenko that did not resemble Demjanjuk at all. Likewise, some of the evidence indicated that Demjanjuk himself had served as a *Wachmann* in Sobibor as well as in the Regensburg and Flossenbürg camps, rather than in Treblinka.

This evidence led to the acquittal of the accused due to reasonable doubt. The court verdict closed with the words, "Wachmann Ivan Demjanjuk has been acquitted by us, due to doubt regarding his guilt of the heinous charges attributed to Ivan the Terrible of Treblinka. This was the proper course for judges who cannot examine the heart and the mind, but have only what the eyes see and read. The matter is closed—but not complete. The complete truth is not the prerogative of the human judge."[2] Following the Supreme Court's verdict, the attorney general decided against putting Demjanjuk on trial again on the charge of being a *Wachmann* in Sobibor.[3] Demjanjuk was expelled from Israel, returned to his home in Cleveland, and his American citizenship was reinstated.

Roughly a decade later, in 2002, Demjanjuk became the first person in history whose American citizenship was revoked twice. This time it was revoked because he had not declared that he'd served as a *Wachmann* in Sobibor on his citizenship application. In 2005, deportation orders were issued to expel Demjanjuk from U.S. jurisdiction, to Ukraine (the country of his birth), Poland (on whose soil the crimes were committed), or Germany. This time, however, there was no country willing to have him stand trial in its jurisdiction.[4] It was only in 2009, at the recommendation of the Central Office of the State Justice Administration for the Investigation for National Socialist Crimes ("Central Office"), that Germany issued an arrest warrant for Demjanjuk and requested his extradition in order to stand trial. Following a long legal battle, Demjanjuk was finally extradited to Germany.

His trial in the Munich Federal Court commenced in late 2009 on the charge of being an accessory to murder in the deaths of 28,060 Jews during the period when it was claimed he served as a *Wachmann* at Sobibor. On May 12, 2012, Demjanjuk was found guilty and sentenced to five years in prison.[5] While an appeal of his verdict was pending, Demjanjuk died at the age of ninety-two in a nursing home where he had been sent to await the decision in the appeal. Under the provisions of German law, the death of the defendant prior to the verdict being final led to the nullification of the verdict in the first instance, and as a result, from a technical standpoint, Demjanjuk died an innocent man.[6]

The Israeli and German legal proceedings in the Demjanjuk case were not "regular" criminal proceedings. The decision of the judicial authorities to conduct these proceedings stemmed not only from the traditional objectives present in any criminal proceeding but also from extralegal aims that are part and parcel of criminal proceedings dealing with Nazi war crimes.[7] These trials dealt not only with the question of the defendant's guilt or innocence but also with the nature of the historical memory of the Holocaust.[8] In making the decision to prosecute Demjanjuk, both Israel and Germany affirmed their intention to hold the Nazis and their collaborators accountable. This intention obviously had broader significance beyond conducting a proceeding in the case of a specific defendant.

This chapter compares the Israeli Demjanjuk trial and the German Demjanjuk trial by focusing on three of the crucial choices made by the Israeli and German legal authorities. First, the choice of the historical circumstances under which the crime was committed (Treblinka or Sobibor); second, the choice of the charge of indictment (whether a "crime against the Jewish people" or merely "accessory to murder"); and third, the choice of evidence to be presented to the court: survivor testimony, written documents, or historians' expert testimony. The chapter then demonstrates how these choices influenced the results of the proceedings and had direct implications for the prospect of conducting (in Germany's case), or not conducting (in Israel's case), additional legal proceedings against Nazi war criminals. It argues that the extralegal objectives of legal proceedings concerning Nazi crimes—

such as education, documentation, and commemoration—led the judicial authorities in Israel and Germany to make crucial choices that fundamentally affected the differences between the legal proceedings against Demjanjuk in each of the countries.

This chapter contributes to the existing historiography of Holocaust trials in Israel and Germany through a transnational analysis. Despite its historical significance, and although more than a quarter century has passed since its conclusion, the Demjanjuk Israeli trial has not been accorded its rightful place in legal and historical research.[9] This chapter draws on research into the Israeli Demjanjuk trial that makes use of newly unclassified archival material.[10] By presenting those findings, as well as by comparing similar aspects of the two proceedings in Israel and in Germany, the chapter shows the importance of extralegal objectives in conducting criminal proceedings against Nazi war criminals, and more specifically, it demonstrates the decisive influence of the legal outcomes of the proceedings on the prospect of realizing those objectives.

"IVAN THE TERRIBLE" FROM TREBLINKA OR AN ANONYMOUS *WACHMANN* FROM SOBIBOR?

The first choice to be discussed is the decision by Israel to try Demjanjuk for allegedly being "Ivan the Terrible" from Treblinka despite the historical documents, including his well-known *Trawniki* card, indicating that he had served as a guard in Sobibor.[11] The simple fact is that this decision was based on the testimonies of survivors who had clearly identified him in the initial police investigation. But beyond these mere facts lies a difference in outlook between Israel and Germany regarding the advantages and disadvantages of using criminal proceedings to bring atrocities to light. While Israel did not want to try just any Nazi war criminal, Germany was willing, seventy years after the war, to try even the last of the Nazi collaborators.

Some two decades after the enormous success of the Eichmann trial, Israel did not want to reduce its powerful impact by holding another trial, but this time of a minor, low-ranking Nazi war criminal. The Ministry of Justice, therefore, defined clear criteria for selecting potential files of Nazi war criminals to be tried in the Israeli courts: first, the availability of local witnesses able to testify as to the deeds of the defendant; second, the presence of clear evidence proving that the defendant took an active part in the mass murder of Jews, and did so with his own hands; and third, a good chance of indictment, as well as the potential for especially severe punishment.[12] Israel could not achieve all of these goals by conducting a criminal proceeding against an anonymous defendant whom no one could identify or testify in relation to the atrocities he had committed. These aims could only be achieved in the case of a well-known defendant, one personally responsible for the murder of many Jews, and by means of his trial, at least part of the story of the extermination of the Jews during the Holocaust could be told. In addition, Israel did not want to conduct a trial in which, even if the defendant were convicted, he would receive a minimal penalty of a few years of imprisonment after which he would be released and stay within the territory of the state. Only a very severe punishment, such as the death penalty, would meet the needs of the Israeli declarative dimension in prosecuting Nazis.

Demjanjuk was not the only candidate under consideration, but he was seen as the most suitable one. Another remarkable possibility was Valerian Trifa.[13] In a hearing conducted on January 24, 1983, in which the heads of the Israeli legal system took part, it was decided not to put in a request for Trifa's extradition, since the police were not in possession of evidence of his active participation in the murder of Jews. It was agreed by all that "an unsuccessful attempt to bring him to trial may end in a result opposite to the one desired, that is, clearing his name."[14] Three months later, on April 28, 1983, in an additional hearing conducted on the matter of Trifa, in which Israeli Ministry of Justice representatives and OSI directors participated, the concern was raised that even if they were able to overcome all the legal obstacles involved in bringing Trifa to trial, at the end of the day, the court would pronounce only a light sentence and after he was done serving his time, it would not be possible to expel Trifa from Israel's borders. This would lead to an absurd situation, in which a Nazi war criminal would be living in, of all places, Israel. Realizing this, the Israeli Ministry of Justice's representatives preferred the possibility of focusing on advancing with a criminal proceeding in the Demjanjuk case, which had high chances of success and seemed more promising. As they put it: "We feel it will better serve the interest of all in concentrating our efforts in bringing to trial a Nazi directly connected with murder—at least as a first test case—rather than a person accused of inciting to hatred of Jews."[15]

This was the reason why in the early 1980s only the Demjanjuk file was selected from among a variety of files presented to the Israeli Ministry of Justice by the OSI to be "the second trial after the Eichmann trial."[16] The Demjanjuk file was intended to be "a test case"[17] for the utility of extraditing and prosecuting other Nazi criminals in Israel. It had all the components of success. Ivan the Terrible, the operator of the gas chambers at Treblinka, was a well-known figure, there were survivors living in Israel who identified him, and he was likely to be sentenced to death, if convicted. It is very clear that if the Israeli prosecution had believed that he was "a less terrible Ivan"[18]—an anonymous guard from Sobibor—he would never have been put on trial in Israel at all.

On the other hand, in the German case, the prosecution displayed a new policy of bringing low-ranking collaborators to trial. This was the first time the German court prosecuted one of the thousands of Ukrainians who had served as *Wachmänner* in the concentration and extermination camps. The decision to prosecute Demjanjuk in Germany more than six decades after the war is conspicuous in its strangeness, especially in light of the acquittal of several high-ranking SS officials, including key officials in Operation Reinhard, during which the Treblinka and Sobibor death camps were established. Thus, in 1976 the Hamburg court acquitted Karl Streibel, commander of the Trawniki training camp where Demjanjuk had been stationed. In 1965 the Düsseldorf court acquitted Otto Horn, an SS man who was tried at the Treblinka trial, and who later testified as a witness on behalf of the prosecution both at the Demjanjuk denaturalization trial in the United States and at Demjanjuk's criminal trial in Israel.[19] Putting Demjanjuk on trial in Germany at the end of the first decade of the twenty-first century indicates, then, a trend in exact opposition to those acquittals: Demjanjuk was indicted despite his anonymity, despite his low status in the Nazi hierarchy, and despite the lack of evidence for the crimes he committed with his own hands. Through the Demjanjuk trial, Germany gave voice to a new message: the war criminals, down to the last of them, must be brought to justice.

GENOCIDE OR ACCESSORY TO MURDER

The second choice concerns the charges on which Demjanjuk was to be tried. The historical circumstances discussed above, on which each of the countries chose to focus, also had to correspond to a defined legal template. It was incumbent upon each country to determine the relevant criminal statute under which Demjanjuk would be indicted. The choice of legal category had a distinct effect on the results of each one of the proceedings, with reference both to the possibility of a conviction and the level of punishment. The choice to use the normative framework to prosecute Nazi war criminals extends beyond the Demjanjuk case and is related to historical legislative and ruling processes in each one of the countries.

In Israel, Demjanjuk stood trial under the provisions of the Nazis and Nazi Collaborators Law (Punishment) (1950).[20] The law includes a long list of offenses, some of which were adopted from the criminal code prevalent at the time, and some of which are unique to this law. The law's crowning glory, however, is the new criminal offense it created—"a crime against the Jewish people"—which Hannah Arendt strongly opposed in her famous critique of the Eichmann trial.[21] This crime is almost identical in content to the crime of genocide in the Genocide Convention, with one main difference: the victims in the Israeli law are not just any group of people, they are *the Jewish people*. In this manner, the law played a declarative and educational role, while at the same time legally validating the role of the State of Israel as the representative of the six million Jews who perished. As such, the Israeli law could not allow itself to demand any penalty lighter than the death sentence for a defendant convicted of committing this crime.[22] This, in fact, was the penalty Demjanjuk received when the Israeli district court convicted him at first of being Ivan the Terrible from Treblinka.

However, the acquittal of Demjanjuk due to reasonable doubt by the Israeli Supreme Court was inextricably linked to the death penalty. The mandatory death penalty leaves no discretion to the court in sentencing the defendant. The law did not take into account a range of defendants and the wide spectrum of the crimes, from robbery to the murder of thousands of Jews. Empirical research, which discusses the link between the threshold of proof required in criminal proceedings and the defendant's expected punishment, demonstrates that the harsher the punishment the defendant can expect if convicted of the crime, the higher the threshold of proof required for his conviction.[23] As a result, there is reason to believe that Demjanjuk was acquitted because of the death penalty hanging over his head. If the sentence for the crime had been less severe, it is possible that the Supreme Court would not have overturned the conviction. The declarative dimension of the Nazis and Nazi Collaborators Law, as it came to be expressed in the mandatory death penalty, thus worked to the detriment of the prosecution and made it difficult for the trial to end in a guilty verdict for the defendant.

In contrast, were someone to look into the indictment against Demjanjuk in Germany, they might be surprised to discover that it did not attribute similar crimes to the accused such as genocide, crimes against humanity, or war crimes—corresponding to the norms accepted in international law—but rather, accessory to murder alone; and, when Demjanjuk was convicted of the crime, the prosecution appealed for a sentence of only six years imprisonment. Whereas the Israeli legal system viewed Nazi crimes as crimes that were exceptional and which required special legal treatment, the German legal system employed standard legal instruments in relating to Nazi crimes and judged them according to the standards of regular crimes under the regular German criminal code. As Devin Pendas,[24] Rebecca Wittmann,[25] and Lawrence Douglas[26] have argued, from a conceptual perspective and procedural perspectives, this law was wholly inappropriate for dealing with the types of crimes committed by the Nazis.[27]

In West Germany, Nazi war criminals were brought to trial after 1955 under the provisions of the German criminal code. German law does not allow retroactive application of the crime of genocide,[28] which only became an offense in Germany after 1954.[29] Therefore, Nazi war criminals could only be brought to trial on the charge of murder, according to Articles 211 (*Mord*) and 212 (*Todschlag*) of the German criminal code. However, the statute of limitations for crimes of murder according to Article 212 is only fifteen years, and at present, it is no longer possible to make use of this charge.[30] There remained the option of trying a person on a charge of murder under specific aggravating circumstances, which has no statute of limitation.[31] But this crime, quite exceptionally, requires specific criminal intent on the part of the defendant and explicitly relates to the motive for committing the crime. German courts that tried Nazi war criminals on charges of murder under specific aggravating circumstances posed challenges when it came to proving guilt.[32] For example, according to German law, only someone who murdered or gave the order to murder out of an "inner conviction" (in the words of the German law) of the desirability of the victim's resulting death could be considered the main perpetrator of the crime of murder.

The legal solution was to accuse Nazi war criminals of the crime of accessory to murder (*Gehilfe*),[33] which demanded a lesser degree of *Mens Rea*. However, while the penalty for murder under specific aggravating circumstances is mandatory life imprisonment, the penalty for accessory to murder ranges from one to fifteen years of imprisonment. Thus, in the Frankfurt Auschwitz trials (1963–65), the court convicted most of the defendants who stood trial during that proceeding—among them Robert Mulka, the deputy commander of the Auschwitz camp—of accessory to murder alone. Similarly, about 90 percent of the *Einsatzgruppen* commanders and soldiers who were put on trial during the 1960s were convicted of the crime of accessory to murder alone and were sentenced to a few years of imprisonment. Nearly five decades after the Frankfurt Auschwitz trials, Demjanjuk was also indicted on charges of accessory to murder and sentenced to only five years of imprisonment, a punishment that has no parallel in Israeli law.

THE ROLE OF THE SURVIVOR-WITNESSES

The third and final choice to be discussed is the role of survivor-witnesses in the proceedings, and the significance attached to their oral testimonies as compared to written evidence. As is well known, the purpose of a criminal proceeding is to examine the degree of the defendant's guilt and to decide if he committed the deeds attributed to him. All the evidence presented to the court by the prosecution, including oral testimony, is meant to prove, in one way or another, the defendant's part in the criminal act. However, in a proceeding dealing with atrocity crimes, the testimonies of the victims of the crime have additional roles—to document and commemorate the historical story, to contribute to constructing a collective memory, and to educate the community.[34] This indeed was the role of Holocaust survivors in the Israeli trial as well as in the German trial. Nevertheless, there was a fundamental difference between the two proceedings. While in the Israeli Demjanjuk trial, the survivor witnesses had, first and foremost, a legal function—to identify the defendant and testify as to the crimes he committed—with the educational role being only secondary, in the

German trial, the only reason for hearing the survivors' testimonies was educational.

In his opening statement at the Israeli Demjanjuk trial, the prosecutor, Michael Shaked, said that the trial was one of the last opportunities, if not the final one, to hear the live testimony of Holocaust survivors who experienced the war crimes on their own flesh. According to him, as long as the prosecutorial evidence included the testimony of living survivors, it would be possible to conduct a criminal trial against Nazi war criminals. But the moment the last of the survivors is no longer alive to give testimony, "the topic will have to descend from the legal stage and move entirely over to the history stage."[35] For Shaked, survivor testimony is intrinsic to the criminal proceeding and without it, it is not possible to establish enough evidence for the purpose of bringing proceedings against war criminals. But beyond this evidentiary aspect, it was clear to the Israeli prosecution that survivor testimony had—as in the case of the Eichmann trial—a pedagogical role that is no less important than its legal role.

However, with Demjanjuk's acquittal in the Supreme Court, the survivors' testimonies during this trial sank into oblivion. Despite their immense historical value, no use was made of these testimonies in research, nor are they presented in Holocaust museums in Israel or around the world. Although the Israeli Supreme Court did not invalidate these witnesses' credibility and the evidentiary value of their testimonies, the legal conclusion of the proceeding, in effect, led to the nullification of their testimonies.[36]

In contrast to the central evidentiary role of survivors in the Israeli trial, in the German court there was no survivor present to point at the defendant and say, "This is the man." None of the survivor witnesses identified the defendant, either in the initial investigation or in court. In fact, when one of the survivor witnesses, Thomas Blatt, was asked in court if he could identify the defendant, he answered: "I can't remember the face of my own mother and father."[37] Since the survivors did not function as identifying witnesses, their testimonies did not contribute to the legal decision. Nevertheless, these testimonies were still heard in detail in court in order to fulfill the trial's educational and historical role of telling of the mass murder of the Jews in Sobibor from the victims' perspective. Indeed, these testimonies received widespread coverage in the press and were the focus of public attention at the trial. However, from the legal standpoint, the testimonies of the survivors at the German trial were only background testimonies, similar to the testimonies of many of the survivors at the Eichmann trial, who had never met Eichmann before in their lives.[38]

The German court based its ruling on written documents showing that Demjanjuk was stationed as a guard in Sobibor, but which were unable to point to any specific acts of murder committed by Demjanjuk himself. Contrary to Shaked's statement, the German Demjanjuk trial proved that it is possible to conduct a legal proceeding against Nazi war criminals even with the survivors being present and yet absent: they were present at the proceeding and even gave testimony, but they were not significant actors in the arena of legal decision.[39] Nevertheless, there is no doubt that the lack of the identification by the survivors harmed not only the strength of the evidentiary foundation laid before the court, but also the strength of the trial's pedagogical facets. While the Israeli district court relied, to a large extent, on the oral testimonies of the survivors, the German court preferred to base its verdicts on certificates or papers linked to the perpetrators and on the testimonies of historians and other legal experts.[40] In this sense, the German Demjanjuk trial brings us back to the starting point of the legal discussions regarding Nazi crimes, as was expressed at the Nuremburg trials. The main evidence at the heart of the trial was the historical documents and how the expert historians who testified interpreted these documents, while the survivor witnesses were positioned offstage, and their testimonies having become irrelevant to the legal proceedings despite their great historical value.

GERMANY AND ISRAEL: REVERSE MIRROR IMAGES

The different rulings of the legal proceedings in the Demjanjuk affair do not lead to a legal difficulty, since in each case Demjanjuk was accused of different crimes committed in different places. The interesting comparison between the proceedings is thus not the legal results but rather the different choices that both Israel and Germany made at the main crossroads in the proceedings. As this chapter has shown, the different choices made by the Israeli and German prosecution authorities and courts were the result of the different aims each country attributed to those proceedings. Moreover, these choices reflect the differing legal treatment of the Holocaust, as well as the broader context of the different politics of the memory of the Holocaust in each of those countries and the time period in which each of the trials was held.[41]

There is no doubt that the legal proceedings were presumed to contribute to shaping the collective memory of the Holocaust in each one of those countries, and at the same time, there was the expectation that the outcome of the proceeding would have a significant effect on the possibility of doing so. The capacity of the legal field, in general, and of the court, in particular, to shape collective memory is seen as potentially stronger than that of other fields (and institutions) of influence, such as politics, art, and religion, since the ceremonial dimension of the legal proceeding is compelling and conspicuous and because it derives its legitimacy to act from the State itself.[42] The courts' concern with writing history and shaping historical memory while deliberating the criminal responsibility of perpetrators of atrocities has grown significantly in recent decades, particularly in international legal forums.[43] In this respect, the court is perceived—rightly or wrongly—as a public institution with the capacity to do so, whether by placing witness-survivors on the stand or through legal verdicts written with the cognizance that they are to serve as declarative statements.[44]

Since the Israeli proceeding concluded with acquittal and not conviction, that trial was unsuccessful in its aim of shaping the collective memory of the Holocaust. Despite the great potential inherent in the survivors' testimonies and in the verdict of contributing to the memory of the Holocaust, both were relegated to the void of oblivion. In contrast, in Germany, since the trial concluded with the accused's conviction, which represented a highly significant legal innovation, the legal proceeding did succeed in bringing about a change in awareness regarding treatment of the Holocaust and its perpetrators in the courtroom.

These choices made by the Israeli and German prosecution authorities and courts thus had implications not only for the results of these trials, but also for the impetus to bring other Nazi war criminals to trial in each of these countries. The State of Israel has avoided initiating any further criminal proceedings against Nazi perpetrators following the Demjanjuk trial.[45] Conversely, Germany, which for more than six decades after the war did not invest the maximum effort in prosecuting and severely punishing Nazi war criminals—in part due to legal difficulties—has, since the Demjanjuk trial, renewed its efforts to bring war criminals to justice. In July 2015, the Lüneburg court convicted 93-year-old Oskar Gröning, known as the "Bookkeeper of Auschwitz," on charges of accessory to murder, and sentenced him to four years imprisonment. The German Supreme Court upheld his conviction in September 2016.[46] In June 2016, the Detmold court convicted 95-year-old Reinhold Hanning, a guard at Auschwitz, for the crime of accessory to murder and sentenced him to five years imprisonment. These two trials are two of close to thirty criminal proceedings that the German prosecution intends to conduct in the coming years.[47]

From the legal standpoint, all of these trials have been made possible due to the legal precedent established in the Demjanjuk case, stating that in order to find a person guilty of accessory to murder, it is sufficient to prove that he served as part of the workforce in an extermination camp. It is no longer necessary to prove the commission of a specific criminal act by the defendant.[48] More importantly, from the pedagogical perspective, the Demjanjuk case created a conceptual change in Germany, declaring that even those considered small cogs at the bottom of the Nazi hierarchy must be prosecuted, since even the last of the *Wachmänner* had a part in the extermination of the Jews during the Holocaust.

The two legal proceedings against Demjanjuk in Israel and in Germany serve as an important lesson about the limitations of criminal law and the legal system when facing the Nazi crimes. In Germany, the use of the state's criminal code posed considerable difficulties with respect to the possibility of prosecuting Nazi criminals for offenses that accurately reflected the magnitude of the crimes. The criminal code, which did not retroactively recognize the crime of genocide and even made it very difficult to try someone for the crime of murder, resulted in many Nazi criminals not being prosecuted at all, and others, who did stand trial, receiving shorter prison sentences than would have been expected. The German Demjanjuk trial can thus be seen as the beginning of a change with reference to legal treatment of the Holocaust. The nature and depth of the change wrought by the Demjanjuk trial, however, is not to be found in the normative prosecutorial framework, since, with reference to Nazi crimes, no change has been made to it since the 1960s. The kernel of change lies in understanding the potential of the legal proceeding to realize extralegal objectives in a given time and place.

For Germany, it was very clear that the Demjanjuk trial was one of the last Holocaust perpetrator trials, if not the last. The German court then used the Demjanjuk case to represent a profound change in shaping consciousness of the Holocaust in the public sphere, declaring an all-out war against the last of the Nazis and their collaborators. More than six decades after the crimes were committed, and with a large number of the perpetrators already set free or punished with minor penalties, it was much easier and had less significant implications for Germany to change its policy toward Holocaust perpetrators.[49] With such deliberate timing, it was clear that the main importance of the change was declarative and not practical. For the State of Israel, on the other hand, the Eichmann trial forged a model of Holocaust perpetrator trials. It followed all the criteria that the Nazi and Nazi Collaborators Law specified and fulfilled all the legal and the extralegal objectives of this kind of proceeding. The Eichmann trial continued to be the archetype when new options for prosecution become an issue in Israel in the early 1980s. Officially, the Demjanjuk case was intended to be "a test case" that would determine whether Israel would make additional extradition requests. But even more so, this trial was a test case of the feasibility of fulfilling extralegal objectives—such as commemoration, documentation, education, and the construction of a collective memory of the Holocaust—via a criminal proceeding, even in the case of the acquittal of the defendant. This test case failed. Demjanjuk's acquittal by the Israeli Supreme Court brought an end to the prospect of fulfilling these aims, and therefore discouraged those involved from taking further measures. Ever since, Israel has ceased to engage in any further efforts to bring other Nazi war criminals to trial. The Israeli Ministry of Justice was not willing to take another risk; it seems that the wound inflicted on the Israeli public in the aftermath of the Demjanjuk trial has not yet healed.

The Israeli legal system's big mistake was not that it prosecuted Demjanjuk on the charge of being Ivan the Terrible from Treblinka and not on the charge of him being "a less terrible Ivan" from Sobibor, as the Israeli defense attorney put it. It is not impossible that Demjanjuk was indeed Ivan the Terrible, the operator of the gas chambers in Treblinka, and at the same time, also a *Wachmann* in Sobibor. In point of fact, looking at historical circumstances, this is a plausible option.[50] The fundamental error was the mistaken link made between "historical truth" and "legal truth." Demjanjuk's legal acquittal said absolutely nothing about the question of his true role in the murder of Jews in Treblinka; the legal decision was limited to the question of what the trial could prove with respect to that. As in any legal proceeding, the court decision, by its nature, was limited to procedural rules and admissible evidence. In this case, however, which dealt with a historical question with broad implications for the memory of the Holocaust in Israel, the decision was also perceived as a factual decision: the pronouncement of "guilty" or "acquittal due to reasonable doubt" was transformed into "he is" or "he isn't" Ivan the Terrible. This flawed perception is instructive regarding the difficulty inherent in looking to a criminal proceeding to achieve historical, educational, and documentary aims. When Demjanjuk was acquitted at his trial, and the legal truth was misguidedly perceived as the sole historical truth, no other possibility for realizing extralegal aims related to memory of the Holocaust has materialized.

Thus, it seems that the use of extralegal aims as an inseparable part of the criminal proceeding against Demjanjuk led Israel and Germany to different legal outcomes and to different conclusions with respect to continuing to pursue Nazi criminals in court. The Demjanjuk affair, then, is instructive with reference to the key place held by the extralegal aims of legal proceedings concerned with Nazi crimes. As the discussion of the Demjanjuk trials showed, these aims contribute substantially to shaping the legal process and have implications for the way the outcome of the trial will be read and interpreted outside the legal arena.

NOTES

This chapter is based on parts of my doctoral thesis (the Hebrew University of Jerusalem, 2017). I am grateful to the doctoral thesis supervisors, Prof. Yfaat Weiss and Prof. Adam Hofri-Winogradow, for their valuable guidance and outstanding insights. I also wish to thank Miri Gur-Arye, Dan Michman, David Silberklang, Dan Porat, Rotem Giladi, Rivka Brot, Olga Frishman, Omri Ben-Zvi, Miriam Szamet, and Adi Livny for their useful comments on earlier drafts. The research leading to these results has received funding from the European Research Council (ERC) under the European Union's Seventh Framework Programe (FP7/2007-2013)/ERC Grant Agreement Number 340124: "JudgingHistories. Experience, Judgment, and Representation of World War II in an Age of Globalization," Principal Investigator: Prof. Dan Diner.

1. Crim. Case. 373/86 The State of Israel v. Ivan John Demjanjuk, PM 1988 (3) 116 ("The District Court Verdict"); Crim. Appeal 347/88: Ivan John Demjanjuk v. the State of Israel, PD 47(4) 221, par. 185 (1993) ("The Supreme Court Verdict").

2. The Supreme Court verdict, par. 471.

3. High C. Case 4442/93 Lapid Movement v. Attorney General (24.8.1993); High C. Case 4162/93 Federman v. Attorney General, PD 47(5) 309 (1993).

4. Lawrence Douglas, *The Right Wrong Man: John Demjanjuk and the Last Great Nazi War Crimes Trial* (Princeton, N.J.: Princeton University Press, 2016), 135.

5. Landgericht München II, 1 Ks 115 Js 12496/08, Urteil der 1. Strafkammer des Landgerichts München II als Schwurgericht in der Strafsache gegen Demjanjuk, John, wegen Beihilfe zum Mord, Munich 2011 ("The Federal Court Verdict").

6. Douglas, *The Right Wrong Man*, 257.

7. For a discussion on the extralegal objectives, see, among others, Mark Osiel, *Mass Atrocity, Collective Memory, and the Law* (New Brunswick, N.J.: Transaction, 1997); Lawrence Douglas, *The Memory of Judgment: Making Law and History in the Trials of the Holocaust* (New Haven, Conn.: Yale University Press, 2001), 3, 258; Lawrence Douglas, "The Didactic Trial: Filtering History and Memory into the Courtroom," in *Holocaust and Justice: Representation and Historiography of the Holocaust in Post-War Trials*, ed. David Bankier and Dan Michman (Jerusalem: Yad Vashem; New York: Berghahn Books, 2010), 11–22; Gerry J. Simpson, "Didactic and Dissident Histories in War Crimes Trials," *Alb. L. Rev.* 60 (1997): 801, 826; Donald Bloxham, *Genocide on Trial: War Crime Trials and the Formation of Holocaust History and Memory* (Oxford: Oxford University Press, 2001), 129–81; Leora Bilsky, *Transformative Justice: Israeli Identity on Trial* (Ann Arbor: University of Michigan Press, 2004), 3; Michael R. Marrus "History and the Holocaust in the Courtroom," in *Lessons and Legacies V: The Holocaust and Justice,* ed. Ronald Smelser (Evanston, Ill.: Northwestern University Press, 2002), 215–16; Richard Wilson, "Judging History: The Historical Record of the International Criminal Tribunal for the Former Yugoslavia," *Human Rights Quarterly* 27, no. 3 (2005): 908; and Ruti G. Teitel, *Transitional Justice* (Oxford: Oxford University Press, 2001), 73–4.

8. For a wider discussion on the legal and extralegal aims regarding the Eichmann trial, see, among others, Douglas, *The Memory of Judgment*; Osiel, *Mass Atrocity*; Bilsky, *Transformative Justice*; and Shoshana Felman, *The Juridical Unconscious: Trials and Traumas in the Twentieth Century* (Cambridge, Mass.: Harvard University Press, 2002). Regarding the Frankfurt Auschwitz trials, see Rebecca Wittmann, *Beyond Justice: The Auschwitz Trial*

(Cambridge, Mass.: Harvard University Press, 2005); and Devin O. Pendas, *The Frankfurt Auschwitz Trial, 1963–1965: Genocide, History, and the Limits of the Law* (Cambridge: Cambridge University Press, 2006). Regarding the Mauthausen trial, see Tomaz Jardim, *The Mauthausen Trial: American Military Justice in Germany* (Cambridge, Mass.: Harvard University Press, 2012). In addition, regarding the Nuremberg trials, see Bloxham, *Genocide on Trial*; and Kim Priemel, "Beyond the Saturation Point of Horror: The Holocaust at Nuremberg Revisited," in *The Trials of Nuremberg and Tokyo Revisited*, ed. Daniel Hedinger and Daniel Siemens (Munich: C.H. Beck, 2016), 522.

9. One key exception is Lawrence Douglas's book *The Right Wrong Man: John Demjanjuk and the Last Great Nazi War Crimes Trial* (2016), which focuses on the Demjanjuk German trial. For an earlier writing about the Demjanjuk Israeli trial see, among others, Tom Teicholz, *The Trial of Ivan the Terrible: State of Israel vs. John Demjanjuk* (New York: St. Martin's Press, 1990); Yoram Sheftel, *The Demjanjuk Affair: The Rise and Fall of a Show Trial* (Tel-Aviv: Adam, 1993) [in Hebrew]; Allan A. Ryan, *Quiet Neighbors: Prosecuting Nazi War Criminals in America* (San Diego, Calif.: Harcourt Brace Jovanovich, 1984), 94–141; Mordechai Kremnitzer, "The Demjanjuk Case," *Israel Yearbook on Human Rights* 24 (1994): 269–95; Douglas, *The Memory of Judgment*, 196–207; and Stephan Landsman, *Crimes of the Holocaust: The Law Confronts Hard Cases* (Philadelphia: University of Pennsylvania Press, 2005), 110–72.

10. The archival research is fully presented in Yehudit Dori Deston, "The Demjanjuk Trial: The End of Nazi Prosecution in Israel" (Ph.D. dissertation, Hebrew University of Jerusalem, 2017).

11. The "Trawniki card" is Demjanjuk's service record of his time at the Trawniki training camp. It included his photograph, his personal details, and his signature, as well as the dates and posts at which he served as a *Wachmann*. The document explicitly states that Demjanjuk was posted to service at Sobibor on March 27, 1943. There is no record on the document of its bearer serving in Treblinka. For a description of how the certificate was located in the Soviet Union and was brought to the Israeli court, see Ryan, *Quiet Neighbors*, 106–7; and Teicholz, *The Trial of Ivan the Terrible*, 55.

12. These criteria were mentioned in the Ministry of Justice's documents in a number of contexts, among them: the Israeli State Archives (ISA), the Ministry of Justice files, "Demjanjuk trial extradition" file, GL 21598/2 ("The extradition file"), a letter by Adv. Denis Goldman, to Moshe Gilboa, dated September 8, 1985; the extradition file, Protocol of meeting, January 24, 1982; ISA, the Ministry of Justice files, "District Court 1986" file, GL 21598/3, Goldman letter to the Ministry of Justice, dated March 20, 1986.

13. Valerian Trifa was an archbishop and leader of the "Iron Guard," a fascist, pro-Nazi group in Romania. On January 20, 1941, the day before

the pogrom perpetrated by the Iron Guard movement in Bucharest, Trifa made a speech on Radio Bucharest filled with incitement against the Jews, in which he called upon Romanian youth to come out in battle against the "international Judeo-Communist conspiracy." The brutal pogrom resulted in the murder of 120 Jews and hundreds of non-Jewish soldiers and citizens. Following the pogrom, Trifa and the Iron Guard's top command escaped to Germany, where he received shelter until the end of the war. At the end of the war, hiding his background, Trifa immigrated to the United States and received U.S. citizenship in 1957. Following an investigation and legal hearing, his citizenship was revoked in 1980. Later on, a deportation order was issued against him, but no country was willing to accept him into its borders. For a description of the legal proceedings conducted against Trifa in the United States, see Ryan, *Quiet Neighbors*, 218–45.

14. The extradition file, a document entitled "Nazi Criminals in the United States—A Discussion with the Minister of Justice on 24/1/83."

15. The extradition file, notes prepared ahead of the meeting on April 28, 1983. Eventually, Trifa immigrated in 1984 to Portugal, where he died three years later. See Efraim Zuroff, *Occupation: Nazi-Hunter—The Continuing Search for the Perpetrators of the Holocaust* (Hoboken, N.J.: Ktav Publishing House in association with the Simon Wiesenthal Center, 1994), 190.

16. These words were taken from Goldman's letter of September 8, 1985, which is mentioned above. In this letter, Goldman refers to the possibility of the extradition of the Ukrainian *Bohdan Koziy,* who immigrated to the United States in 1949 and who was suspected of killing Jews in Poland in 1942–43. In 1982, Koziy's American citizenship was revoked, and this was how the discussion arose about the State of Israel requesting his extradition. Goldman was opposed and declared: "*As terrible as the deeds attributed to Koziy may be, I do not believe that it will prove successful, after Eichmann, to hold a second trial of this kind. It is preferable to concentrate the meager resources we have at our disposal to advance more suitable trials, such as the trial we are hoping to conduct against the criminal Ivan Demjanjuk.*"

17. The Demjanjuk case was mentioned on several occasions as the first "test case" of the feasibility of prosecuting other Nazi criminals, in the context of whether the extradition request Israel was going to submit to the U.S. authorities would be granted; if it would, then later on, more extradition requests would follow. See, for example, the extradition file "Notes of meeting on January 24, 1982," 3; see also the quote above from a memorandum of April 28, 1983.

18. The Israeli defense attorney, *Yoram Sheftel,* used this phrase during the course of the appeal hearing in the Supreme Court to express his irritation at the possibility of Demjanjuk's conviction for being a *Wachmann* at

Sobibor, when most of the trial in the district court focused on him being "Ivan the Terrible" of Treblinka.

19. Otto Horn served in Treblinka from October 1942 to September 1943. In 1964 he was prosecuted at the Treblinka trial along with another ten SS men, and was the only one among them to be fully acquitted. Horn's judicial inquiry in the Demjanjuk trial was conducted in June 1987 at the Magistrate's Court located in the Tiergarten district of Berlin, in the presence of three Israeli judges. For his judicial inquiry, see ISA, Crim. Case 373/86, File Num. B- 22395/12.

20. The enactment of the Nazi and Nazi Collaborators (Punishment) Law (1951) was one of the outcomes of Israel's ratification of the Convention on the Prevention and Punishment of the Crime of Genocide [General Assembly resolution 260A (III) of December 9, 1948] (The Genocide Convention). In accordance with Article 5 of the Convention, the State of Israel enacted two laws which adopted the Convention's provisions into its lawbooks: The Crime of Genocide (Prevention and Punishment) Law, 1950, generally intended to prevent and deter commission of the offense in the future; and the second, The Nazi and Nazi Collaborators (Punishment) Law (1950), designed specifically to punish Nazi criminals.

21. Hannah Arendt, *Eichmann in Jerusalem: A Report on the Banality of Evil* (New York: Viking, 1963).

22. For a detailed discussion of the death penalty prescribed by the law as a mandatory sentence, see Dori Deston, "The Demjanjuk Trial," 219–59.

23. Phoebe C. Ellsworth and Lee Ross, "Public Opinion and Judicial Decision Making: An Example from Research on Capital Punishment," in *Capital Punishment in the United States*, ed. Hugo Adam Bedau and Chester M. Pierce (New York: AMS, 1976), 152, 169; Henrik Lando, "The Size of the Sanction Should Depend on the Weight of the Evidence," *Review of Law & Economics* 1, no. 2 (2005): 277; Ehud Guttel and Doron Teichman, "Criminal Sanctions in the Defense of the Innocent," *Mich. L. Rev.* 110 (2012): 597, 606; Talia Fisher, "Constitutionalism and the Criminal Law: Rethinking Criminal Trial Bifurcation," *U. Toronto L.J.* 61 (2011): 811, 819–30.

24. Pendas, *The Frankfurt Auschwitz Trial*, 53–79.

25. Wittmann, *Beyond Justice*, 7–9, 93.

26. Douglas, *The Memory of Judgment*, 179–93.

27. In this matter, Arendt's critique in the report she wrote on the Frankfurt Auschwitz trials is relevant: "What the old penal code had utterly failed to take into account was nothing less than the everyday reality of Nazi Germany in general and of Auschwitz in particular." See Hanna Arendt, "Auschwitz on Trial," in *Responsibility and Judgment*, ed., Jerome Kohn (New York: Schocken Books, 2003), 243.

28. Prosecuting war criminals using the charges of genocide or crimes against humanity was considered, according to the German criminal code, an *ex post facto*, which contrast Article 1 of the StGb: "An act may only be punished if criminal liability had been established by law before the act was committed." It also stood in contrast to Article 103(2) of the "Basic Law for the Federal Republic of Germany": "An act may be punished only if it was defined by a law as a criminal offense before the act was committed."

29. Article 220 of the StGb ("*Volkermord*").

30. Pendas, *The Frankfurt Auschwitz Trial*, 57; Wittmann, *Beyond Justice*, 8; Douglas, *The Memory of Judgment*, 189.

31. Concerning the statute of limitations for crimes of murder according to Article 211, it was following the German government's attempts to postpone the inevitable by extending the period of the statute of limitations to include crimes of murder, in order to create a possible path to prosecute war criminals, that in 1979 the statute of limitations for this crime was abolished. This was consistent with "The Convention on the Non-Applicability of Statutory Limitations to War Crimes and Crimes against Humanity," ratified by the UN in 1968 and which, in its Article 1, canceled the statute of limitations on war crimes and crimes against humanity as defined in the Nuremberg Charter. See Wittmann, *Beyond Justice*, 48–53.

32. Pendas, *The Frankfurt Auschwitz Trial*, 57–61; Douglas, *The Right Wrong Man*, 182–89.

33. Article 21(7) of the StGb defines *"Gehilfe"* as follows: "Any person who intentionally assists another in the intentional commission of an unlawful act."

34. Shoshana Felman, "Theaters of Justice: Arendt in Jerusalem, the Eichmann Trial, and the Redefinition of Legal Meaning in the Wake of the Holocaust," *Critical Inquiry* 27, no. 2 (2001): 201–38.

35. The Protocols of the Demjanjuk Trial, Jerusalem District Court, 127, Yad Vashem Archive, Tr.15/1–50.

36. In this context, it is worth noting that if one were to search for these testimonies, they can be found only in the protocols of the Demjanjuk trial, and there too, some of the testimonies are truncated or missing.

37. Lawrence Douglas, "Ivan the Recumbent, or Demjanjuk in Munich: Enduring the 'Last Great Nazi War-Crimes Trial,' " *Harper's Magazine*, November 30, 2009.

38. Since the majority of the survivors testifying in the Eichmann trial were unable to identify him, as is required in a criminal trial, it is clear that the objective of their testimony was not purely legal. Their testimonies were needed in order to provide the details of the execution of the Final Solution by the SS leaders, including Eichmann. See Rachel Auerbach, "Witnesses and Testimonies in the Eichmann Trial," *Yad Vashem Bulletin* (December

1961): 28, 35 [in Hebrew]; and Gideon Hausner, *Justice in Jerusalem* (Lohamei HaGhetaot: Beit Lohamei HaGhetaot, 1980), 294–96 [in Hebrew]. This was, naturally, accompanied by the trial planners' educational-historical aims—to raise public awareness in Israel and around the world of the Holocaust survivors' testimonies and to justify the existence of the State of Israel as a safe haven. See Hanna Yablonka, *The State of Israel vs. Adolf Eichmann* (Tel-Aviv: Miskal, 2001), 139 [in Hebrew].

39. In his analysis of D. D. Guttennplan's account of the Irving v. Lipstadt trial, which deals with the absence of the survivors' testimony in Holocaust trials, Tim Cole positions Guttennplan's understanding of the survivor's role as a "post-Eichmann trial sentiment." See Tim Cole, "The Holocaust and Its (Re)Telling: The Nature of Evidence at the Nuremburg and the Eichmann Trial," in *From the Protocols of the Elders of Zion to Holocaust Denial Trials: Challenging the Media, the Law and the Academy*, ed. Debra Kaufman, Gerald Herman, James Ross, and David Phillips (London, 2007), 56–66.

40. Johannes Houwnik ten Cate, "Looking Back on the Demjanjuk Trial in Munich," *Jerusalem Center for Public Affairs*, March 1, 2012, http://jcpa.org/article/looking-back-on-the-demjanjuk-trial-in-munich.

41. For a discussion of the potential of a legal proceeding to shape the collective memory, see, among others, Moshe Hirsch, *Invitation to the Sociology of International Law* (Oxford: Oxford University Press, 2015), 50; and Teitel, "Transitional Justice," 74.

42. Joachim J. Savelsberg and Ryan D. King, "Law and Collective Memory," *Annual Review of Law and Social Science* 3 (2007): 189–90.

43. Stuart Ford, "A Social Psychology Model of the Perceived Legitimacy of International Courts: Implications for the Success of Transitional Justice Mechanisms," *Vand. J. Transnat'l L.* 405 (2012): 45.

44. Costas Douzinas, "History Trials: Can Law Decide History?" *Annual Review of Law and Social Science* 8 (2012): 273, 278, 297.

45. Zuroff, *Occupation: Nazi-Hunter*, 210–11; Dori Deston, "The Demjanjuk Trial," 298–300.

46. BGH, (Beschluss 20.09.2016)—3 StR 49/16—Landgericht (LG) Lüneburg.

47. Efraim Zuroff, *Worldwide Investigation and Prosecution of Nazi War Criminals (April 1, 2014—March 31, 2015), an Annual Status Report* (Simon Wiesenthal Center—Israel Office, December 2015).

48. The Federal Court Verdict, Art. DI2. In all of the trials of Nazi criminals in West Germany, proving that the accused committed murder or abuse was a condition without which there could be no proof of guilt. In its deliberations in an appeal of the verdict handed down in the Frankfurt Auschwitz trial in 1969, the German court determined the rule of "func-

tional liability" while rejecting the assumption that anyone who had been involved in the extermination process in the camp was considered to have participated in murder. In this context, it was determined that in order to convict an accused of being an accessory to murder, the prosecution must prove that he committed a specific criminal act (*Einzeltat*). This precedent blocked the possibility of bringing the guards at the concentration and death camps to trial, since the prosecution would have come up against many difficulties in proving that they murdered with their own hands, in part because there were not many survivors (in Germany, and in general) who were able to identify those guards. See Douglas, *The Right Wrong Man*, 147.

49. At the conclusion of his book *The Right Wrong Man*, 256, Douglas argues that "the claim that change came only when it was safe for it to do so ignores the power of law to shape a contested social reality." According to Douglas, the legal breakthrough in the Demjanjuk case in Germany was made possible at that time owing to two factors: the first was the development of historical research which confirmed the legal determination that every ordinary *Wachmann* was an accessory to murder, and that Demjanjuk's decision to serve as a *Wachmann* had been voluntary. The second factor was the groundbreaking interpretation of the Central Office that attributing individual responsibility to the individual for committing the crimes, even if it was not demonstrated that he had murdered with his own hands. Indeed, both the German Central Office and the work of the OSI jurists and historians were most crucial contributions to the outcome of the Demjanjuk trial in Germany. At the same time, in my view, the change cannot be exclusively attributed only to these factors. The change in legal perception could have, theoretically, developed years earlier just as well. Also, historical research on the role of the *Wachmänner* in committing murder in the death camps had been partially available at least a decade earlier. The change in Germany's attitude was thus not only legal or historical, but first and foremost a change in consciousness. This change was also facilitated by the personnel change in the judges presiding over the trials of Nazi criminals in the 1950s and 1960s who, in the past, had been members of the Nazi Party themselves. But, even more so, in my opinion, was the distance in time from the events which, naturally, led to the death of many of the survivors, as well as to the deaths of many of the perpetrators, and brought with it the realization that this was the last chance to rectify the historical distortion.

50. The Jerusalem District Court related to this possibility when, during the summation portion of the trial, it received statements from a *Wachmann* from Sobibor named Danilchenko in which Demjanjuk's name was mentioned as having served together with him in Sobibor. The court determined that based on the testimonies of historians it had heard, *Wachmänner* serving in several of the Operation Reinhard camps was a common occur-

rence, which also emerged from, among other things, the details recorded in their service records. As the district court determined, from a chronological standpoint, it was definitely possible that Demjanjuk had served as a *Wachmann* in Treblinka from July 1942 to March 1943 and was then transferred to service in Sobibor, as noted in his Trawniki card. Actually, in spite of Demjanjuk's conviction in the German court for the offense of having served as a *Wachmann* in Sobibor, until today, two of the judges in the Jerusalem District Court case still believe that he was Ivan the Terrible from Treblinka. See The District Court Verdict, 232–34; Author interview with Justice Dorner, Jerusalem (October 7, 2013); Author interview with Justice Tal, Jerusalem (October 1, 2013).

II. S·U·R·V·I·V·A·L S·T·R·A·T·E·G·I·E·S A·N·D O·B·S·T·R·U·C·T·I·O·N·S

Susanna Schrafstetter

The Geographies of Living Underground: Escape Routes and Hiding Spaces of Fugitive Jews in Germany, 1939–1945

BETWEEN 1941 AND 1945, AN ESTIMATED 10,000–15,000 GERMAN JEWS ATtempted to escape deportation by going into hiding. No more than 5,000 of them survived.[1] Supported by non-Jewish helpers, they sought shelter in apartments and attics, cellars, bombed-out ruins, forests, cemeteries, stables, and boats, to name but a few categories of hiding places. Most of these escapes took place in Berlin, which was home to 40 percent of the 164,000 Jews still remaining in Germany in fall 1941 when the deportations began.[2] Not all of the fugitive Jews remained in the city. The Berlin Jews, like fugitive Jews from other parts of Germany, were extremely mobile, traveling the country in search of refuge.

This chapter seeks to illuminate several aspects of this relatively understudied "escape history" by focusing in particular on mobility and the geography of escape. It traces escape routes, analyzes escape patterns, and explores the circumstances of hiding, asking why certain big cities and rural areas were attractive for Jews in hiding, while others were not. A close analysis of Jews from Berlin, Frankfurt, and Munich shows varying local and regional patterns and conditions of hiding. Both Berlin and sections of rural Bavaria were preferred places of refuge among fugitive Jews, although they offered very different advantages. While many of those who came to Bavaria became more stationary and did not change hideouts as frequently as did fugitive Jews in Berlin, others were constantly on the move. Some tried to cross borders, others found shelter in multiple locations separated by great distances, and some even dared to go on vacation.

As the example of Berlin shows, the geography of escape was not located solely in fixed hiding places. Jews in hiding called themselves "submarines" (*U-Boote*), a term which implied mobility. Many "submerged" Jews resurfaced from time to time to travel somewhere by train. Sometimes the very act of traveling was a form of hiding, as for example when submarines rode trams from one end of the line to the other in order to kill time or to sleep.[3] Many Jews in hiding traveled frequently, and some wrote about their travel experiences. This phenomenon was not confined to Germany. Jewish submarines all across Europe traveled in order to avoid capture, among them Jews in Italy trying to reach Switzerland and Dutch Jews leaving the major cities to hide in rural areas, to mention just two examples.[4]

This chapter contributes to existing literature on hidden Jews in the Holocaust in two main ways. First, it examines mobility and travel as a survival tactic of Jewish submarines in Nazi Germany. While individual stories about Jews in hiding who traveled appear in the literature,[5] the overall importance and frequency of this phenomenon has been neglected. This chapter, therefore, is an initial effort to map travel patterns and routes across Germany and beyond the borders of the Reich. Second, the chapter examines Germany as a space within which some regions were more conducive to hiding than others. Where in Germany did fugitive Jews seek shelter? Which areas might they have avoided? While there is a substantial body of literature about Jews hiding specifically in Berlin (where by far the largest number of Jews lived in illegality), and some about some other areas of Germany,[6] questions about regional differences have not been sufficiently addressed.[7] Much of the existing literature has focused on Germans who gave help to fugitive Jews,[8] diverting attention from the experiences of the Jewish submarines.[9] Marten Düring, for example, has examined the composition of a number of networks of helpers in Berlin. By examining the social relations among numerous individual helpers, Düring was able to map the connections among individual helpers and their networks.[10]

With its focus on space and mobility, this chapter furthermore aims to connect the literature about fugitive Jews to the study of the spatial aspects of the Holocaust. Within the broader European context, the studies *Solidarity and Help for Jews during the NS-Period* and the work of Bob Moore analyzing rescue and hiding operations in France, the Netherlands, Belgium, and Denmark are central.[11] Moore has shown how conditions for rescue and survival could be very different in areas of close proximity within the Netherlands.[12] The number of helpers in the Walloon region of Belgium and in Brussels was substantially higher than in the Flemish-speaking provinces.[13]

Moore's comparative focus is particularly instructive as it demonstrates the atypicality of the situation of Anne Frank and her family. Unlike the Frank family, most submarines in the Netherlands did not stay in one place for prolonged periods of time.[14] Neither did Jews in illegality in other parts of occupied Europe.[15] But much work on both the micro and macro levels remains to be done. For example, with the exception of Vienna, the situation in Austria more broadly has received little attention.[16] The history of hiding is, in important respects, a transnational and mobile history of embodied geographies, a field of Holocaust research that has recently started to receive a good deal of attention and has provided inspiration for this chapter.[17] Although the current chapter cannot claim to be based on innovative methodologies such as geo-visualization, it does expand this field in two ways. First, by examining regional and local differences, it is the first work to attempt to develop a geography of hiding in Nazi Germany, analyzing spatial patterns of hiding. Second, by considering the dynamic nature of hiding, it adds to existing research about mobility and travel among Jews living in illegality, particularly Tim Cole's *Holocaust Landscapes*, which discusses these experiences and places from a broader European perspective.[18]

This chapter is based on numerous memoirs and diaries, on primary sources such as postwar compensation claims files, postwar trials, and victims' testimonies, and on files from a database of known fugitive Jews and their helpers housed at the *Gedenkstätte Deutscher Widerstand* (*The German Resistance Memorial Center*) in Berlin.[19] This database contains a large number of cases, but often only incomplete information is available, and new cases are continuously being added. If neither a Jew in hiding nor a helper had left written testimony, cases are difficult to find, especially if the person was caught and deported, or if the person disappeared in one place and resurfaced in another at the end of the war. Some regions of Germany remain blind spots when it comes to research about Jews in hiding.[20] Hence, the conclusions presented here are preliminary and based on limited data, but some clear patterns will be shown. Many submarines were highly mobile, some traveled out of necessity, and some did so to escape "the overwhelming sense of imprisonment"[21] induced by life in hiding, at least temporarily. Within Germany, Berlin and rural upper Bavaria were both preferred hiding spaces for Jews on the run, for reasons that will be explained below. However, other areas of Germany still warrant examination. In this respect, this chapter raises as many questions as it answers. It does so in the hope of providing ideas for potential approaches to future interdisciplinary and, especially, spatially conceptualized research on the subject.

ESCAPE ROUTES TO AND FROM BERLIN

The escape patterns of fugitive Jews did not reflect free choices or preferences. Access to individual helpers or networks of helpers often determined one's ability to flee. Whether a fugitive had managed to gain false papers and travel safely was a key factor. The specific, immediate circumstances of flight played an important role. Some fugitive Jews had time to plan carefully for life underground, while others fled at the last moment with nothing more than the clothes on their back. Yet even these individuals made their own decisions about helpers and escape routes. Isabel Enzenbach has rightly pointed out that "in many cases not only the initiative to flee, but also the planning and coordination of activities that were necessary for survival" lay with the submarines themselves.[22]

This point is evident in several specific cases. Erna and Aaron Segal and their two children went into hiding together in Berlin in 1942. The family—as did many others—then split up and the individual family members stayed with numerous different helpers in and around the city, rotating frequently in their use of the hiding places available to them until the end of the war in 1945.[23] Erna Segal had planned very carefully in advance whom she would contact for help once underground, and once they were living in illegality, it was mainly Erna who made the decisions about other persons that should be approached for help.[24] In contrast to the Segal family's strategy of staying in Berlin and its environs, Max and Ines Krakauer decided, against the advice of their helpers, to travel from Berlin to Stuttgart, although they lacked false papers.[25] Assessing the needs and risks, fugitives decided in favor of certain options and against others. One result of these decisions was that some areas of Germany became preferred destinations for fugitive Jews, while others did not.

Max and Ines Krakauer as well as Erna Segal and her family were among the 5,000–7,000 Berlin Jews who went into hiding.[26] Conditions for going underground in Berlin were different than in the rest of Germany. The Jewish population of Berlin was large in comparison to the number of Jews left in other cities, and for this reason, it was more difficult to concentrate them into "Jew houses" (*Judenhäuser*) or makeshift camps (*Judenlager*), as was the case in many other German cities.[27] This meant that Jews were less isolated from the non-Jewish population than in other cities. Friendly neighborly relations between Jews and non-Jews often remained intact.[28] Berlin's Jews who decided to flee from the deportations may have found it easier to organize help from non-Jews than did the Jews in other cities. At first, the Gestapo Berlin had sent out letters to Jews who were about to be deported, informing them of the date of their deportation. As more and more Jews avoided their deportation by committing suicide or going into hiding, the Gestapo came to pick up those scheduled for deportation at their homes without prior warning.[29] By fall 1942, Gestapo men were cordoning off entire blocks of streets in search of Jews.[30] However, a couple of thousand Jews still managed to go underground and evade deportations.

The ongoing deportations notwithstanding, large numbers of Jews working as forced laborers remained in Berlin until February 1943. For this reason, the mass deportations in Berlin were completed much later than in other cities. The timing is important, as Beate Kosmala and others have pointed out.[31] In Frankfurt, for example, the mass deportations had been completed by September 1942.[32] At this point, only Jews in mixed marriages remained in Frankfurt. By February 1943, many of the remaining Jews in Berlin understood what "resettlement to the east" really meant.[33] Often all of their relatives had already been deported, and they had nothing to lose.[34] In addition, news of the Battle of Stalingrad had proven that Germany was not invincible.[35] When the last remaining Jews—except for those living in mixed marriages—were rounded up for deportation in connection with the so-called factory raids (*Fabrikaktion*) in late February 1943, more than 4,000 fled,[36] joining other Berlin Jews who had already gone underground. At this point, the remaining Jews were arrested at their workplace (hence "factory raids") without prior notice. However, many had been warned in advance, in most cases by colleagues and superiors at work.[37] Given their large numbers, efforts to capture fugitive Jews in Berlin were more intensive than elsewhere in Germany. In addition to frequent raids and inspections, so-called Jewish searchers—*Greifer*—were employed to track down and betray Jews living in illegality.[38] Typically, these *Greifer* were captured Jewish fugitives who had been promised exemption from deportation if they betrayed other Jews. They operated mainly in Berlin and on a smaller scale in Vienna.[39]

Despite these dangers, the majority of Berlin submarines remained in the city and its surrounding areas to the end of the war.[40] This is all the more interesting, as many of the Berlin Jews were recent arrivals who had moved to the city in the late 1930s in the hope that life under persecution would be less severe within a large Jewish community.[41] We know little about whether the recent arrivals in Berlin sought and received help from acquaintances in the locations they had left behind. Else Krell, who had moved from Munich to Berlin in 1939, benefited from helpers in rural Bavaria who held her belongings and sent her food parcels and ration cards, although she did not contact her family or friends in Munich.[42]

In Berlin, one of the least-Nazified areas of the country, submarines could rely on friends and acquaintances, who gradually expanded their assistance as the deportations progressed. This was one of the ways in which networks of helpers emerged. Ruth Andreas-Friedrich began collecting ration cards and food, and as the situation of her friends became more and more difficult, she and her family expanded their assistance activities.[43] Members of the Confessing Church made the transition from legal to illegal forms of assistance with counterfeit papers, ration cards, and hiding spaces.[44] So did Countess Lagi von Ballestrem and her mother Hanna Solf, who had helped Jews to emigrate before they began to provide shelter to Jewish friends going underground. They formed part of a network that became known as the *Solf-Kreis* (Solf circle).[45] The addresses of helpers circulated among Jewish forced laborers who worked in factories.[46] Ilse Rewald remembered how "on January 11, 1943, a winter day with a temperature of 20 below zero and a cutting easterly wind, I go to the family P., which I don't know personally at all. I've heard about their humanity and unhesitating readiness to help only through friends."[47] During the "factory raids," some Berliners were spontaneously moved to help after witnessing the brutality of the roundups as thousands of Jews were dragged onto trucks.[48] But given the danger of raids, *Greifer*, and denunciations, hideouts had to be changed frequently in order to avoid betrayal or discovery. Edith Rosenthal eventually used seventy different hiding places in Berlin.[49] Some submarines moved every few days.[50]

As Claudia Schoppmann and Beate Kosmala have pointed out, a majority of submarines were women, and women played an important role as helpers. Among the Jewish fugitives, around 60 percent were women. They could move about much more freely in a wartime society than men of draft age.[51] The latter were subject to frequent controls on the streets. In addition, more women than men were left in Germany in 1941 in the first place.[52] Examining the numbers for Berlin, Richard Lutjens has suggested that "proportionately more men than women went into hiding, but that more men were arrested," resulting in a higher percentage of female survivors.[53] Among the helpers, women were in a majority as well. This should not come as a surprise, since many men had been drafted and the wartime society was one of women.[54] Claudia Schoppmann has shown that many of them acted spontaneously and on their own initiative, and did not inform their absent husbands about their decisions.[55] According to Schoppmann, female helpers could act much more inconspicuously than men, and the Gestapo did not expect middle-aged women to be involved in resistance activity.[56]

Berlin was the only place in Germany where fugitive Jews were widely understood to be part of the fabric of society. The thriving black market catered to the needs of all Berliners, including the thousands of Jews who lived underground. Accommodation, ration cards, clothing, counterfeit papers, and weapons could be bought on the black market, as could the services of guides specializing in smuggling fugitive Jews across the German-Swiss border. Lothar Orbach, for example, bought a gun and paid for it with money he had made in a casino.[57] Other Jews invested in counterfeit papers. These options were hardly available in other regions of Germany, where the numbers of Jewish submarines were small and certain goods or services were in shorter supply or not available at all.

The anonymity, diversity, and sheer size of the Reich capital made it attractive to submarines. Marie Jalowicz Simon ventured out of Berlin to the city of Magdeburg, where she immediately realized that she stood out. "I had never attracted attention in Berlin," she explained. "My voice, my appearance, and my behavior all made it obvious that I was a local woman. I could mingle proudly and freely with all the other inhabitants of the city. As soon as I arrived in Magdeburg, however, I stood out as a stranger. I drew an important conclusion for future reference: if I wanted to live underground without hiding all the time, I could do so only in Berlin."[58] Berlin also provided opportunities to work and earn money. Margot Friedlander became part of a group of black marketeers. Selling food and other illegal goods, she could afford to rent a tiny room in a village in Brandenburg, just outside of Berlin, where she lived when Allied bombing raids became frequent.[59] Some fugitive Jews, like Hans Rosenthal and Zvi Aviram, sought shelter at the edge of the metropolis in the famous *Laubenkolonien*—areas where city dwellers had garden allotments[60]—while others found temporary refuge in rural areas of Brandenburg and Pomerania. Members of the latter group often ventured back into the city after a few weeks, as prolonged stays might render them suspicious. "Each time I stay for a few days or a week out in the country, and then I return to Berlin," Margot Friedlander wrote. "I can't stay all the time in the small village. I have to play the role of the young, exhausted girl from the city who seeks protection from the air raids."[61] According to Richard Lutjens, this way of moving back and forth between Berlin and a hiding place in the countryside was a common strategy.[62]

While many depended on friends and acquaintances to shuttle them from one hideout to the next, renting temporarily from a helper whose interest was primarily financial was also an option. For a while, Lothar Orbach lived with an old petty criminal who made his money cheating in poker games.[63] Others bought bug-ridden beds in miserable working-class housing. To be a *Taucher* in Berlin often meant to "submerge" (*eintauchen*) into spaces that had previously been unfamiliar to fugitive Jews.[64] Reflecting on her time in hiding, Marie Jalowicz Simon wrote that she "began thinking about social questions. After all, I was living in circumstances that I could never have dreamed of."[65] "Remarkably adaptable" is the expression that Lothar Orbach used for a fellow *Taucher*, his friend Erika, who shared a room with Kitty, a brothel madam.[66] This kind of adaptability was essential in dangerous situations, as was a quick wit.

Many of the younger submarines were not only prepared to take risks, but also later reflected positively on their period of living underground. Jizchak Schwersenz explained: "It was a strange feeling. As Jews, we were not allowed to move around in the city for years. Now, living in illegality, we could use mass transportation, go into restaurants and cafes, experience the hustle and bustle of the big city. In the face of all fears and worries, that was also exciting."[67] Going underground had made them mobile again. Many submarines of all ages found brief periods of relaxation in cinemas and concerts, even though police raids were frequent around those venues. Jizchak Schwersenz often went to the opera to distract himself. It also had the advantage that opera-lovers typically lined up outside the ticket office on the evening before performances. Schwersenz could join the line and spend the night there, chatting, sleeping, and buying tickets in the morning.[68] One of his friends remarked that she had never visited and enjoyed as many opera performances as during her time in hiding.[69] Many submarines longed to get away from their miserable lives for more than a few hours. Some of them even had the audacity to go on a vacation. Lothar Orbach and his mother took a vacation in Rahnsdorf, a popular resort on the Müggelsee, outside of Berlin, where they could stay with the aunt of Lothar's friend Anton, a Polish military deserter.[70] Orbach had insisted on the vacation despite his mother's concerns. He wanted to get out of the city, despite the fact that the beach at the lake was notorious for frequent inspections. He also used the opportunity for a brief sexual encounter with the bored wife of a Nazi Party functionary on holiday with her five children, but without her husband.[71] The young woman saw in Lothar Orbach a chance for revenge, as her husband had been involved in an affair with his secretary. Orbach saw her and her children as an opportunity to blend in more fully with the vacationers at the Müggelsee. Suntanned and well-fed as he and his mother appeared when they returned to Berlin, they did not look at all like Jews on the run.

Ludwig Brummer's friend Karlchen had deserted from his military unit and, on the occasion, had stolen several blank paybooks, furlough books, and rubber stamps with Wehrmacht seals. He was therefore able to provide himself and his friend Ludwig Brummer, a fugitive Jew, with new identities. A real daredevil, Karlchen went on a skiing vacation, pretending that he and his friends were participating in a *Wehrmacht* ski course in Bavaria. He obtained an old military uniform for Brummer. Then the two of them, along with Karlchen's girlfriend and a second young woman, went skiing in Bavaria. "That I, of all people, had to sleep under a portrait of Hitler in the Bodenschneid cabin was the height of comedy," Brummer later recalled.[72] On the way back, they stopped in Munich, where they posed for pictures as soldiers with their girlfriends. Brummer did not reminisce about the details of the train voyage, but he clearly found the whole masquerade hilarious. Those who witnessed it, such as the fellow passengers on the train, probably regarded Brummer and his friends as perfectly normal young people. If they suspected something, they kept quiet.

The examples of Lothar Orbach and Ludwig Brummer show that submarines traveled not just out of necessity but sometimes voluntarily. Occasionally, they succumbed to the desire to escape or seek distraction from the worries of daily existence. Interestingly, both had friends who were hard-nosed military deserters, displaying in their behavior a complete disregard for official rules and authority. But it was not just young men who took such risks. Marianne Ellenbogen participated in a camping vacation organized by her helpers, members of *Der Bund, Gemeinschaft für sozialistisches Leben*,[73] a small "Lebensreform" movement that also provided aid to fugitive Jews.[74] Ellenbogen's biographer, Mark Roseman, has expressed surprise that she would do something as "lighthearted" as going on a camping vacation while living underground.[75] There were other such cases. Else Behrend Rosenfeld traveled to Strassburg for a mini-vacation from her hiding place in Freiburg.[76] Most submarines however, undertook travel only out of necessity, either when they had to change hiding places or when they tried to escape to another country.

CROSSING BORDERS

Between 1933 and 1945, 2,592 Germans reached Switzerland. Among them were 1,404 Jews.[77] However, these numbers may include German Jews who tried to cross the border into Switzerland from Austria or from other European countries. For example, Sally and Hanna Goldschmidt from Frankfurt reached Basel via Strassburg and Mulhouse.[78] In addition, it is unclear how many may have tried and failed. Therefore, it is difficult to determine exact numbers. The canton of Schaffhausen counted ninety-five Jewish refugees between 1942 and 1945.[79] This section of the border was considered to be the easiest for illegal crossings. The river Rhine did not run along the border, which meant that refuges did not have to swim the river, and the border line, zigzagging back and forth, was not continuously secured with barbed wire.[80] For this reason, this section of the border between Schaffhausen and Baden was the most popular for both Jewish and non-Jewish refugees.[81] Another area in which the topography facilitated illegal border crossings was around the German town of Singen.[82]

Because the Jews from Baden, the region closest to the German-Swiss border, were among the first to be deported, they had practically no chance to escape their sudden transfer to France in the fall of 1940. Consequently, German Jews who wanted to escape to Switzerland were not familiar with the border region and were dependent on the help of local non-Jewish Germans.[83] Hence, it is not surprising that many submarines living far away from the border seem to never have entertained that option, but focused instead on organizing their lives in illegality within Germany.[84]

The dangers of undertaking a journey to the border region and crossing into Switzerland were manifold. In the first place, one had to find a reliable guide. Because of the high demand in Berlin, numerous swindlers offered their services in exchange for substantial sums of money, only to disappear as soon as they had received payment, or, even worse, they denounced their Jewish victims to the Gestapo. Zvi Aviram and his friend Gad Beck almost signed up for a trip that turned out to be a deadly trap: "Our friend related a hair-raising experience. She and her husband learned of an escape possibility in which Jews, concealed in boxes of munitions hidden among Wehrmacht vehicles, would be shipped to the Swiss border. The couple scraped all of their money together to ride on such a transport. But on the night of the escape, they arrived too late at the agreed-upon meeting place in the forest near Oranienburg and were able to see only the taillights of the vehicles driving away. The couple desperately attempted to catch up to the vehicles on their bicycles, but then watched as the vehicles drove through the entrance gate to the concentration camp Sachsenhausen."[85]

In a number of instances, successful escapes to Switzerland were organized through networks of helpers that connected Berlin with the Swiss border. These connections formed gradually in response to the demand for guides that had emerged in Berlin.[86] One of the most successful networks centered around Luise Meier and Josef Höfler. Operating in Berlin, Meier had established contact with Höfler, who lived close to the border, and had excellent knowledge of the terrain.[87] Meier brought individual Jews to the border town of Singen, where Höfler would receive them and show them the way into Switzerland.[88] Else Krell and her daughter, Margot Murzynski, were among the submarines who made contact with Meier in Berlin. To be able to pay the substantial amount of money that Höfler demanded for his help, Krell had to recover her remaining possessions, which were stored with a non-Jewish friend in Bavaria. Considering it less risky for Margot, a fifteen-year-old girl, to make the trip, Else sent Margot from Berlin to Bavaria to pick up jewelry and valuables.[89] Once on their journey from Berlin to the town of Singen on the Swiss border, Krell and her daughter tried to blend in by initiating conversations with the other travelers in their train compartment. Krell successfully played the role of a chatty middle-aged woman traveling with her daughter to visit a family grave. Pouring out her made-up family history to a man she suspected to be a Gestapo agent, she bored the man to the point where he was desperate to leave, in the process convincing him that this chatterbox could not possibly be an illegal Jew.[90] The story of Krell and her daughter Margot illustrates that audacity, acting skills, and quick thinking were essential on these train rides. It also demonstrates that sometimes a major journey needed to be taken in order to organize the financial resources required to pay for a guide across the border. Lotte Strauss, another Berlin "submarine" heading for the Swiss border, was fortunate inasmuch as her train was overcrowded and there were no inspections, but she almost missed her connection in Stuttgart, which would have caused her to miss her contact at the border.[91] With the help of Höfler, Strauss, Krell, and her daughter made it across the border. Overall, the network of Meier and Höfler managed to guide twenty-eight Jews to Switzerland before one of the fugitives was captured and Meier and Höfler were arrested.[92] Another group of helpers around the Berlin artist Franz Heckendorf and Wilhelm Martin, an innkeeper at the border town of Altenburg in Baden, led at least twenty Jews across the border.[93]

Other Jews were less lucky. Among them was Hildegard Dannenbaum, a young Jewish woman from Berlin who had booked a week at the Kölner Haus, a rustic mountain retreat close to the Swiss border that was popular with vacationers. Dannenbaum arrived shaken and exhausted because she had spent the train ride in the company of SS men aggressively courting her. At the Kölner Haus she learned that she had to share her room with a stranger. Matters got worse, as she was supposed to meet her guide there, but he had changed his mind and was now unwilling to lead her into Switzerland. After a week, she traveled back to Berlin.[94] Gertrud Zuelzer traveled from Berlin to Bavaria, where she stayed in hiding for several weeks with the family of Hilger van Scherpenberg in Hohenpeissenberg, Upper Bavaria. The time in Bavaria was intended as a stepping-stone en route to Austria, from where she and her friend Helene Marwitz tried to reach Switzerland. They were caught by German border police, arrested, and deported. Only Zuelzer survived.[95]

It may well have been the case that flights into Switzerland were more successfully organized from Berlin than from Bavaria. In Berlin, the network around Luise Meier, with contacts to guides living right at the border, had developed because so many Berliners were looking for escape routes.[96] The Berlin artist Franz Heckendorf had traveled to the Swiss border to scout out an escape route for his Jewish friends. During his exploratory journey, he made the acquaintance of the Altenburg innkeeper Wilhelm Martin. Once Martin had been successful in guiding the first person across the Swiss border, other Berlin Jews sought help from Heckendorf.[97] Franco Battel noted that the overwhelming number of German Jews who arrived at the border in the Schaffhausen region came from Berlin.[98] Else Behrend Rosenfeld, who fled the deportations in Munich, went to Berlin because she and her helpers in Munich had decided that they lacked the contacts to organize a successful escape from Munich to Switzerland. In Berlin, she met people who were able to put her in touch with Luise Meier.[99] This is not to say that successful escapes from Switzerland could not be organized from other parts of Germany. But those undertaken from Munich by Jews who were unable to prearrange assistance from a local guide were unsuccessful.[100] In Berlin, one of the main dangers was falling victim to fraudsters.[101] A comprehensive analysis of flights and flight attempts of Jews from Germany to Switzerland in the years 1941–45 is still missing.

While the overwhelming majority of those submarines who tried to leave Germany headed for the Swiss border, some sought out other destinations. Only a small number of isolated cases are known, but there may have been more. German submarines who may have been captured "traveling" in occupied Europe would most likely not have survived, thus leaving behind no evidence of their escape journey. Supported by members of the Swedish community in Berlin and by some Berliners, a few submarines escaped on commercial trains to Sweden.[102] Ezra Ben Gershôm (formerly Ben Ernst Friedmann) made it from Berlin to Vienna, on to Budapest, and ultimately all the way to

Palestine.[103] In the hope of reaching Palestine, Marie Jalowicz Simon got as far as Bulgaria. In Berlin, she had fallen in love with a Bulgarian civil worker, Dimitr Petrov Tchakalov, and, having obtained reasonably well-made fake papers, she left Berlin together with Tchakalov in September 1942.[104] Once they reached Sofia, she realized that it would be too difficult to continue her journey. Eventually, she was arrested by Bulgarian policemen. She was lucky, however, as a German official in the German embassy in Sofia issued her travel documents back to Berlin, probably understanding her situation. However, on the way back, which included travel on a vessel up the Danube, she had a couple of narrow escapes.[105]

ODYSSEYS: TRAVELING FROM NORTHERN GERMANY TO THE SOUTH

While some submarines from northern Germany used southern Bavaria as a base en route to Switzerland, others came south as part of a multi-stop odyssey in search of a remote hiding place far away from home. As travelers, they blended in with a steadily growing number of Germans fleeing bombing raids in the cities. In some places in rural Bavaria as early as 1942, the number of evacuees from the cities was so high that conflicts between locals and evacuees arose.[106] For the individual Jews who sought shelter far away from home, their decisions may have been based on a number of factors: the location of individuals who were willing to help, whether they were widely known at their place of residence, whether they were experienced travelers, and whether they were familiar with other parts of Germany.

As soon as they had obtained false papers, Eva Guttmann and her daughter Steffi fled Berlin for Bavaria. Guttmann resided with Princess Victoria von Bentheim, who ran a boarding house in Mittenwald near Garmisch-Partenkirchen. Eventually, following a denunciation by one of the other guests, the Princess took her to a remote farmhouse owned by her family in rural Württemberg. A combination of personal connections in Mittenwald and a desire to keep a low profile under an assumed identity far from home had led Guttmann to the south of Germany. Her case shows that some fugitives were always on the run. From Berlin, she went to Bavaria, then moved on to the Tyrol, where she was denounced. She fled and went back to Berlin for a while, then went to Bad Godesberg, and next to Bonn, where she worked as a maid. She left Bad Godesberg to return to Mittenwald, and from there she fled again to Württemberg. Her daughter, Steffi, separated from her shortly after their arrival in Mittenwald. Steffi seems to have impersonated her assumed identity better than her mother. Living and working in Oberammergau, she was seen as a fanatical Nazi by neighbors and colleagues.[107]

Steffi and Eva Guttmann were not the only Berlin Jews who traveled hundreds of miles as illegals. Among them were fugitives who received help from circles of the Confessing Church, which had networks of supporters across the country. Max and Ines Krakauer spent several months in various parsonages in Pomerania before they arrived in Württemberg, where they received help from members of the Württembergische "Parsonage Chain" (*Pfarrhauskette*), a network of Lutheran clergy in the region.[108] Hermann Pineas left Berlin for Vienna and then alternated between hiding places in Vienna, Linz, and St. Pölten. Later, he found refuge in Schwenningen with the pastor Margarete Hoffer, who was a central member of the *Pfarrhauskette*.[109] His last stop was Memmingen in southern Bavaria, where he signed up for the *freiwilliger Ehrendienst*, voluntary service in the war economy, which he hoped would provide effective cover. He was fortunate, as he was assigned to a tool-manufacturing company that needed a traveling representative. Traveling thus became his form of hiding, as he was sent on work assignments to Detmold, Essen, and Berlin, to name just three of his destinations.[110] He maintained his travels until April 21, 1945. Marianne Ellenbogen undertook "probably more than 50" train trips between her various hideouts, which extended from cities in the Ruhrgebiet to Göttingen, Braunschweig, and Beverstedt, a small town near Bremen.[111] She always dressed well, traveled first class, and if she spotted high-ranking Nazis on the train, she would join them in their compartment.[112]

Jewish submarines were obviously frightened while traveling on trains, but they had an opportunity to listen to conversations among their fellow Germans and overhear important information. Lotte Strauss was surprised at how openly people in her compartment spoke about the aerial bombings and the likelihood that they would increase and affect larger and larger areas of Germany.[113] Already by 1943, Germans were not exactly optimistic about the "final victory" and discussed the deteriorating military situation quite openly. Max Krakauer's interlocutors also talked about the Allied bombing campaigns, but they were somewhat more cautious: "everybody appeared to understand that they would be risking their necks with every suspicious comment, but nevertheless the secret grumblings could not be ignored."[114] Krakauer learned about Mussolini's fall from power on a train. The news spread from one compartment to the next, instilling him with hope in his desperate situation.[115]

RURAL BAVARIA AND THE TYROL AS A HIDING SPACE

A sizeable number of submarines sought out locations in southern Upper Bavaria and northern Tyrol for short- or long-term shelter. Their specific numbers are difficult to determine as there are only vague references in a number of cases, but more than thirty individuals could be traced. Among them were fugitive Jews from Berlin and other parts of northern Germany, as well as Jews from Munich, the Bavarian capital. Nearly all fugitive Jews from Munich left the city for remote areas of either Upper or Lower Bavaria, in contrast to the submarines in Berlin who decided to hide in an urban environment. In Frankfurt, like in Munich, many submarines sought to leave the city as soon as possible.[116] Fugitives from Frankfurt were sometimes brought to the Swiss border or to other regions of the *Reich*.[117] Among the longest journeys undertaken from Frankfurt was that of Margarete Knewitz, who reached the remote estate of Ovelgönne near Hamburg via Memmingen, Stuttgart, and Marburg, to name just a few of her stops.[118] In Hamburg, some Jews used the bombing raids of July 1943 as an opportunity to disappear and leave the city.[119] Unfortunately, there is hardly any information on cities like Cologne or Stuttgart, but there seems to be a pattern that submarines tended to leave major cities—except for Berlin. The capital attracted Jewish refugees from other cities such as Munich. In Munich and Frankfurt, Jews in hiding were a tiny minority isolated from each other. Unlike in Berlin, there was no black market that catered to their needs, and no sense of solidarity and encouragement provided by the presence of other fugitives. The countryside did not offer these benefits either, but at least there was more food, fewer bombs, a low population density, and remoteness.[120]

Valerie Wolffenstein had come from Berlin to Bavaria under an assumed identity. For Wolffenstein, her time in a remote village near Traunstein meant relaxing in beautiful natural surroundings and enjoying good food.[121] Johanna Wörner from Munich hid herself in the town of Traunstein.[122] Some submarines sought out completely isolated farms, especially if they came from the city of Munich and had no false papers, which was the norm. Hugo Holzmann hid in Goben, a village consisting of two farmhouses, miles from anywhere, and Albertine Gimpel was sheltered in a solitary manor house near Traunstein.[123] Whenever a car approached, Gimpel fled through the back door into the adjacent dense forest. This was often necessary because her host, the writer Fritz Reck-Malleczewen, was under the supervision of the Gestapo. But his widow kept Gimpel in the house even after her husband had been murdered in Dachau.[124]

Long periods of time in one hideout, rather than frequent changes of accommodation, were the norm in rural Bavaria. It is not always clear whether this was the result of a lack of options or a sense of relative security. Annie Kraus lived from August 1943 to the end of the war in the village inn of Therese Fritz in Schattwald in the Tyrol.[125] Before that, she had stayed for several weeks in Durach in the Allgäu region of Bavaria. She looked for a different hiding place while she lived in Schattwald, but failed to find something more suitable. Living in Schattwald, a village of 300 inhabitants, her presence must have been noticed, and one must wonder if the locals suspected something. In any event, she was not betrayed.[126] Living in the town of Ruhpolding, Elise Probst, a local Jewish widow who had lost her non-Jewish husband in 1936, did not have to be hidden at all. The family that ran the village inn provided her with room and board. The situation only became dangerous when the SS established a makeshift military hospital in the inn late in the war. From that point onward, Probst was properly hidden.[127] This is all the more remarkable because Probst was the stepmother of Christoph Probst, a member of the White Rose student resistance group who had been sentenced to death and executed in February 1943.[128]

These examples raise the question of whether the rural Bavarian or Austrian population was less prone to denounce suspicious individuals than Germans in other regions. Clinging, as many of them did, to traditional Catholic values, they did exhibit greater resilience to Nazi ideology than the inhabitants of more thoroughly Nazified regions. John Delaney has posited such an argument with regard to the relatively humane treatment of Polish forced laborers in rural Catholic Bavaria.[129] It is clear that in many cases, Christian piety and solidarity with a fellow Christian did play a role. Some of these hidden Jews such as Annie Kraus and Valerie Wolffenstein were "non-Aryan Christians," the term used to describe Germans who were Christian by religion but Jewish according to Nazi race laws. Among the helpers were priests, such as Anton Fischer in Durach in the Allgäu, who hid Annie Kraus.[130] Many of the helpers were not locals but rather unconventional individuals who had taken residence in Bavaria, such as the writer Fritz Reck-Malleczewen and the Princess von Bentheim, who believed that she had to atone for her original support of Nazism by saving a Jew.[131] Payments did most likely play a role (although this is rarely mentioned openly), and so did the fact that most of those who were hidden were women or children. Compared to the rural areas around Berlin, Upper Bavaria was less densely populated,[132] and less Nazified overall, but there were dramatic local differences.[133] What Berlin and rural Upper Bavaria had in common was a relatively low level of Nazification and a relatively high presence of hidden Jews, although on the local level inside Upper Bavaria, this correlation did not always apply.

Denunciations and arrests of Jewish submarines happened even in closely knit communities of rural Bavaria.[134] Elise Probst, mentioned above, was denounced once, although for reasons that remain unclear, the denunciation did not lead to her arrest.[135] It is evident that the overwhelming number of cases of hiding in rural Bavaria happened in the Catholic south (or nearby Catholic Tyrol) rather than in Protestant Franconia.[136] The Franconian towns that in the past had been home to a much higher number of Jews than Upper and Lower Bavaria did not appear to have been destinations for hiding. The Oestreicher family, who had fled Hamburg after the Allied bombing campaign in the summer of 1943, made it to the Franconian town of Hof. There, the family felt very uncomfortable because of the high level of Nazification. They went back and found shelter on a farm near Hamburg.[137] Many Jews had fled Franconia in the 1930s and had moved to big cities. Returning to formerly familiar turf and making use of old acquaintances was not a hiding strategy for Franconian Jews. Southern Bavaria and northern Tyrol, however, provided refuge to a sizeable number of refugees. For them, a multitude of factors may have played a role, including proximity to the Swiss border, stable food supplies, the geographic remoteness of the region, and positive memories of past vacations. Traveling to, from, and within southern Bavaria (and the Tyrol) was a substantial part of an underground traffic of German Jews who were on the run during the war.

CONCLUSIONS

This chapter has offered a starting point for mapping the movements of Jews who went into hiding in Germany, highlighting both the dynamic nature of the process and regional particularities, with—for example—greater mobility among Jews hiding in Berlin compared to Bavaria. The reasons why Jewish submarines traveled were manifold. There were the obvious reasons of changing hiding places, and of trying to reach and cross a national border to safety. In some cases, traveling frequently for a job became the main form of cover. A few fugitives escaped from deportations and camps. Robert Eisenstädt managed to flee from Majdanek in 1942 and returned to Frankfurt.[138] Others took "vacations" from the confines of crammed hiding spaces, visited relatives, or had to travel to retrieve valuables and money stored with friends. Submarines of all ages traveled, sometimes in groups, but more often as individuals. Generally, women attracted less suspicion than men, but some of the most astounding journeys were undertaken by men, as the example of Eisenstädt shows. Further research will be necessary, however, to reconstruct in detail the escape routes and chronologies of fugitive Jews across German territory. One promising approach is offered by the work that has been done on the numerous illegal border crossings from the Rhineland into Belgium and the Netherlands during the years 1939–40, before the start of the mass deportations from Germany.[139] Additional systematic research into international escape routes and transnational networks of aid would also be desirable. Although their numbers were relatively small, submarines crossed not only into Switzerland but also reached more remote destinations. And many Jews from Germany went into hiding in foreign countries following complex and often well-established routes of flight and emigration. One such example would be German Jews who fled to Italy and, upon receiving expulsion orders from that country in 1938, crossed into France illegally before going into hiding.[140] Ultimately, several factors determined the escape routes of Jews fighting for survival. These included circumstances and timing, the location and nature of hiding spaces, the geographical characteristics of escape routes, the transnational mobility of the individual, and the role of guides. The Jewish submarines in Germany are therefore part of a larger and complex picture of Jews in hiding across occupied Europe.

NOTES

1. Numbers according to Claudia Schoppmann, "Rettung von Juden: Ein kaum beachteter Widerstand von Frauen," in *Solidarität und Hilfe für Juden während der NS Zeit*, vol. 5: *Überleben im Untergrund: Hilfe für Juden in Deutschland*, ed. Beate Kosmala and Claudia Schoppmann (Berlin: Metropol, 2002), 114; and Marnix Croes and Beate Kosmala, "Facing Deportation in Germany and the Netherlands: Survival in Hiding," in *Facing the Catastrophe: Jews and Non-Jews in Europe during World War II*, ed. Georgi Verbeeck and Beate Kosmala (Oxford: Berg, 2011), 97.

2. Numbers according to Croes, Kosmala, "Facing Deportation," 101.

3. See, for example, Jizchak Schwersenz, "Verstecke der Großstadt," in *Mit falschem Pass und fremden Namen: Junge Menschen im Holocaust*, ed. Harald Roth (Gerlingen: Bleicher, 2002), 35.

4. Bob Moore, *Survivors: Jewish Self-Help, and Rescue in Nazi-Occupied Western Europe* (Oxford: Oxford University Press, 2010); Silvano Longhi, *Exil und Identität: Die italienischen Juden in der Schweiz, 1943–1945* (Berlin: de Gruyter, 2017).

5. See, for example, Mark Roseman, *A Past in Hiding: Memory and Survival in Nazi Germany* (New York: Metropolitan Books, 2001); and Andreas Mix, "Hilfe im katholischen Milieu: Das Überleben der Konvertitin Annie Kraus," in *Überleben im Dritten Reich: Juden im Untergrund und ihre Helfer*, ed. Wolfgang Benz (Munich: Beck, 2003), 131–42.

6. Marten Düring, *Verdeckte soziale Netzwerke im Nationalsozialismus* (Berlin: de Gruyter, 2015); Susanne Beer, *Die Banalität des Guten: Hilfeleistungen für jüdische Verfolgte* (Berlin: Metropol, 2018); Richard Lutjens, *Submerged on the Surface: The Not-So-Hidden Jews of Nazi Berlin 1941–1945* (New York: Berghahn, 2019); Richard Lutjens, "Jews in Hiding in Nazi Berlin, 1941–1945: A Demographic Survey," *Holocaust and Genocide Studies* 31 (2017): 268–97; Richard Lutjens, "Vom Untertauchen: 'U-Boote' und Berliner Alltag 1941–1945," in *Alltag im Holocaust: Jüdisches Leben im Großdeutschen Reich 1941–1945*, ed. Andrea Löw, Doris Bergen, and Anna Hajkova (Munich: Oldenbourg, 2013), 49–63; Marion Kaplan, *Between Dignity and Despair: Jewish Life in Nazi Germany* (New York: Oxford University Press, 1998). For Munich, see Susanna Schrafstetter, *Flucht und Versteck: Untergetauchte Juden in München—Verfolgungserfahrung und Nachkriegsalltag* (Göttingen: Wallstein, 2015). For Frankfurt, see Petra Bonavita, *Mit falschem Pass und Zyankali: Retter und Gerettete aus Frankfurt am Main in der NS-Zeit* (Stuttgart: Schmetterling, 2009); Heike Drummer, *Gegen den*

Strom: Solidarität und Hilfe für verfolgte Juden in Frankfurt und Hessen, ed. Fritz Backhaus and Monica Kingreen (Frankfurt: Jüdisches Museum, 2012). For Hamburg, see Beate Meyer, "A conto Zukunft: Hilfe und Rettung für untergetauchte Hamburger Juden," *Zeitschrift des Vereins für hamburgische Geschichte* 88 (2002): 205–33; and Ulrike Hoppe, ed., "*. . . und nicht zuletzt Ihre stille Courage": Hilfe für Verfolgte in Hamburg, 1933–1945* (Hamburg: Edition Wartenau, 2010).

7. To some extent, regional differences have been addressed in Schrafstetter, *Flucht und Versteck*.

8. For example, Wolfgang Benz, ed., *Überleben im Dritten Reich: Juden im Untergrund und ihre Helfer* (Munich: Beck, 2003); Kosmala and Schoppmann, *Überleben im Untergrund*; Arno Lustiger, *Rettungswiderstand: Über die Judenretter in Europa während der NS-Zeit* (Göttingen: Wallstein, 2011).

9. Much of the literature focuses on the "*stille Helden*" (silent heroes), as the helpers are called in Germany because they did not talk about their help after the war. For example, see Inge Deutschkron, *Sie blieben im Schatten: Ein Denkmal für "stille Helden"* (Kevelaer: Butzon & Bercker, 2012).

10. Düring, *Verdeckte soziale Netzwerke*.

11. The research project *Solidarität und Hilfe für Juden während der NS-Zeit* (Solidarity and Help for Jews during the NS-Period) at the Zentrum für Antisemitismusforschung Berlin resulted in the publication of seven volumes dealing with aid and rescue of Jews in Germany and Europe. The following volumes edited by Wolfgang Benz and Juliane Wetzel cover aid across Europe: Wolfgang Benz and Juliane Wetzel, eds., *Solidarität und Hilfe für Juden während der NS-Zeit: Regionalstudien 1: Polen, Rumänien, Griechenland, Luxemburg Norwegen, Schweiz* (Berlin: Metropol, 1996); *Regionalstudien 2: Ukraine, Frankreich, Böhmen und Mähren, Österreich, Lettland, Litauen, Estland* (Berlin: Metropol, 1998); *Regionalstudien 3: Dänemark, Niederlande, Spanien, Portugal, Ungarn, Albanien, Weißrußland* (Berlin: Metropol, 1999); *Regionalstudien 4: Slowakei, Bulgarien, Serbien, Kroatien mit Bosnien und Herzegowina, Belgien, Italien* (Berlin: Metropol, 2004). See also Moore, *Survivors*. In addition, the following anthology discusses the rescue and hiding of Jews across Europe from a comparative perspective: Dan Michman, ed., *Hiding, Sheltering and Borrowing Identities: Avenues of Rescue during the Holocaust* (Jerusalem: Yad Vashem, 2017).

12. Moore, *Survivors*, 243–45.

13. Moore, *Survivors*, 205.

14. Moore, *Survivors*, 4–5.

15. In eastern Europe, more stationary forms of hiding seem to have been common, for example, in underground bunkers in Poland. But as Gunnar Paulsson has shown for Warsaw, there was some mobility of Jews in

hiding. Gunnar S. Paulsson, *Secret City: The Hidden Jews of Warsaw, 1940–1945* (New Haven, Conn.: Yale University Press, 2002).

16. On Vienna, see Brigitte Ungar-Klein, *Schattenexistenz. Jüdische U-Boote in Wien, 1938–1945* (Vienna: Picus, 2019); Brigitte Ungar-Klein, "'Don't Go—You Will Stay With Me!': Hidden Jews in Vienna and Their Supporters," in *Hiding, Sheltering and Borrowing Identities*, ed. Michman, 195–205; Traude Litzka, *Kirchliche Hilfe für verfolgte Juden und Jüdinnen im nationalsozialistischen Wien* (Münster: LIT, 2011). On Austria more broadly, see Angelika Königseder, "Österreich—ein Land der Täter?" in *Solidarität und Hilfe für Juden während der NS-Zeit, Regionalstudien 2*, ed. Benz and Wetzel, 173–229.

17. Anne Kelly Knowles, Tim Cole, and Alberto Giordano, eds., *Geographies of the Holocaust* (Bloomington: Indiana University Press, 2014); Tim Cole, *Holocaust Landscapes* (London: Bloomsbury, 2016).

18. See Cole, *Holocaust Landscapes*, particularly chapter 5.

19. The database has been compiled as part of the research project Solidarität and Hilfe für Juden während der NS-Zeit situated at the Zentrum für Antisemitismusforschung in Berlin. It contains dossiers about known helpers of Jews in hiding and the Jews who went into hiding. Since 2005, the database has been based at the Gedenkstätte Deutscher Widerstand. I would like to thank Dr. Beate Kosmala for granting me access to some of the dossiers in the database.

20. One important example is the city of Breslau, which was home to a large Jewish community in 1933. Katharina Friedla's study, *Juden in Breslau—Wrocław 1933–1949: Überlebensstrategien, Selbstbehauptung und Verfolgungserfahrungen* (Cologne: Böhlau, 2015), does not address flights from deportation in any detail.

21. Cole, *Holocaust Landscapes*, 149.

22. Isabel Enzenbach, "Zur Problematik des Begriffs 'Retter,'" in *Überleben im Untergrund*, ed. Kosmala and Schoppmann, 243.

23. On the Segal family, see Düring, *Soziale Netzwerke*, 150–64.

24. Düring, *Soziale Netzwerke*, 152, 157.

25. Max Krakauer, *Lichter im Dunkel* (Stuttgart: Behrendt, 1947), 59.

26. An estimated 5,000-7,000 Berlin Jews went into hiding. Croes and Kosmala, "Facing Deportation," 115. Most recently, Richard Lutjens has made the case for a figure of "approximately 6,500." Lutjens, "Jews in Hiding," 268.

27. The situation in Berlin was complicated by the ambitious plans for the reconstruction of Berlin as the capital of the Reich, which necessitated the relocation of numerous non-Jewish Berliners. The deportation of the Berlin Jews would provide apartments for those non-Jewish Berliners. See

Susanne Willems, *Der entsiedelte Jude: Albert Speers Wohnungsmarktpolitik für den Berliner Hauptstadtbau* (Berlin: Hentrich, 2000).

28. Wolf Gruner, "Die Berliner und die NS-Judenverfolgung: Eine mikrohistorische Studie individueller Handlungen und sozialer Beziehungen," in *Berlin im Nationalsozialismus: Politik und Gesellschaft 1933–1945*, ed. Rüdiger Hachtmann, Thomas Schaarschmidt, and Winfried Süß, *Beiträge zur Geschichte des Nationalsozialismus* 27 (Göttingen: Wallstein, 2011), 79.

29. Doris Tausendfreund, *Erzwungener Verrat: Jüdische "Greifer" im Dienst der Gestapo 1943–1945* (Berlin: Metropol, 2006), 43.

30. Tausendfreund, *Erzwungener Verrat*, 45.

31. Beate Kosmala, "Zwischen Ahnen und Wissen: Flucht vor der Deportation (1941–1943)," in *Die Deportation der Juden aus Deutschland: Pläne—Praxis—Reaktionen, 1938–1945*, ed. Birthe Kundrus and Beate Meyer (Göttingen: Wallstein, 2004), 158.

32. Monica Kingreen, "Gewaltsam verschleppt aus Frankfurt: Die Deportationen der Juden in den Jahren 1941–1945," in *"Nach der Kristallnacht": Jüdisches Leben und antijüdische Politik in Frankfurt am Main 1938–1945*, ed. Monica Kingreen (Frankfurt: Campus-Verlag, 1999), 383.

33. Kosmala, "Zwischen Ahnen," 156–58.

34. Kaplan, *Between Dignity and Despair*, 202.

35. Claudia Schoppmann, "Die 'Fabrikaktion' in Berlin: Hilfe für untergetauchte Juden als Form humanitären Widerstandes," *Zeitschrift für Geschichtswissenschaft* 53 (2005): 143.

36. Estimates on how many Jews fled the "factory raids" differ and range from 4,000 to 5,000. See Lutjens, *Submerged on the Surface*, 211–12, and Schoppmann, "Fabrikaktion," 142.

37. Schoppmann, "Fabrikaktion," 139.

38. On the *Greifer*, see Tausendfreund, *Erzwungener Verrat*. For individual cases of Jewish collaborators in western Europe, see Moore, *Survivors*, 345–55.

39. Tausendfreund, *Erzwungener Verrat*, 252–58.

40. Angela Borgstedt, "'Bruderring' und 'Lucknerkreis': Rettung im deutschen Südwesten," in *Überleben im Untergrund*, ed. Kosmala and Schoppmann, 192.

41. Croes and Kosmala, "Facing Deportation," 101.

42. Else Krell, *Wir rannten um unser Leben: Illegalität und Flucht aus Berlin 1943*, ed. Claudia Schoppmann (Berlin: Metropol, 2015), 125–26, 154–55.

43. Ruth Andreas Friedrich, *Der Schattenmann: Tagebuchaufzeichnungen 1938–1945* (Berlin: Suhrkamp, 1947); Düring, *Soziale Netzwerke*, 103–9.

44. Ursula Büttner, "Die anderen Christen: Ihr Einsatz für verfolgte Juden und 'Nichtarier' im nationalsozialistischen Deutschland," in *Überleben im Untergrund*, ed. Kosmala and Schoppmann, 135.

45. Andreas Mix, "Hilfe im katholischen Milieu: Das Überleben der Konvertitin Annie Kraus," in *Überleben im Dritten Reich*, ed. Benz, 133.

46. Margot Friedlander with Malin Schwerdtfeger, *"Try to Make Your Life": A Jewish Girl Hiding in Nazi Berlin*, trans. William Gilcher (Potomac, Md.: Bea Press, 2014), 110.

47. Ilse Rewald, *Berliner, die uns halfen, die Hitlerdiktatur zu überleben: Vortrag an der Gedenk-und Bildungsstätte Stauffenbergstraße am 14. März 1975* (Berlin: Gedenkstätte Deutscher Widerstand, 1975), 6.

48. Schoppmann, "Fabrikaktion," 143.

49. Christine Zahn, "Von einem Quartier zum nächsten: Eine Odyssee im Berliner Untergrund," in *Überleben im Dritten Reich*, ed. Benz, 229.

50. Wolfgang Benz, "Überleben im Untergrund 1943–1945," in *Die Juden in Deutschland 1933–1945: Leben unter nationalsozialistischer Herrschaft*, ed. Wolfgang Benz (Munich: Oldenbourg, 1988), 665, 677–78.

51. Croes and Kosmala, "Facing Deportation," 119; Schoppmann, "Rettung von Juden," 109–26.

52. Croes and Kosmala, "Facing Deportation," 117.

53. Lutjens, "Jews in Hiding," 283.

54. Croes and Kosmala, "Facing Deportation," 122.

55. Schoppmann, "Rettung von Juden," 122.

56. Schoppmann, "Rettung von Juden," 126.

57. Larry (Lothar) Orbach and Vivien Orbach-Smith, *Soaring Underground* (Berlin: Kowalke, 1998), 133.

58. Marie Jalowicz Simon, *Underground in Berlin: A Young Woman's Extraordinary Tale of Survival*, trans. Anthea Bell (London: Clerkenwell, 2015), 213.

59. Friedlander, *"Try to Make Your Life,"* 163–64.

60. Hans Rosenthal, *Zwei Leben in Deutschland* (Bergisch-Gladbach: Lübbe, 1982), 62; Zvi Aviram, *Mit dem Mut der Verzweiflung: Mein Widerstand im Berliner Untergrund 1943–1945*, ed. Beate Kosmala and Patrick Siegele (Berlin: Metropol, 2015), 63–64.

61. Friedlander, *"Try to Make Your Life,"* 164–65.

62. Lutjens, "Jews in Hiding," 274.

63. Orbach, *Soaring Underground*, 156–67.

64. Kaplan, *Between Dignity and Despair*, 201–2.

65. Jalowicz Simon, *Underground in Berlin*, 102.

66. Orbach, *Soaring Underground*, 185.

67. Schwersenz, "Verstecke der Großstadt," 35–36.

68. Schwersenz, "Verstecke der Großstadt," 37.

69. Schwersenz, "Verstecke der Großstadt," 37.

70. Orbach, *Soaring Underground*, 268–69.

71. Orbach, *Soaring Underground*, 273–82.

72. Ludwig Brummer, "My Illegal Life in Germany: The Final Solution: Illegal Life and Escapes," Eyewitness Accounts, Archives of the Wiener Library London, Archives unbound. Online: http://go.galegroup.com/gdsc/retrieve.do?inPS=true&prodId=GDSC&userGroupName=1euro&tabID=T001&searchId=R1&searchType=AdvancedSearchForm&contentSet=GALE&docId=GALE|SC5106929888&resultListType=RESULT_LIST&docType=GALE&viewtype=Manuscript&currentPosition=3&sort=DA-ASC-SORT

73. Roseman, *A Past in Hiding*, 298–300.

74. On the Bund, see Mark Roseman, "Gerettete Geschichte: Der Bund, Gemeinschaft für sozialistisches Leben im Dritten Reich," *Mittelweg 36, Zeitschrift des Hamburger Instituts für Sozialforschung* 16 (2007/08): 100–121, on the Bund's role in the rescue of Jews see Mark Roseman, *Lives Reclaimed: A Story of Rescue and Resistance in Nazi Germany* (New York: Metropolitan Books, 2019).

75. Roseman, *A Past in Hiding*, 300.

76. Else Behrend Rosenfeld and Siegfried Rosenfeld, *Leben in zwei Welten: Tagebücher eines jüdischen Paares in Deutschland und im Exil*, ed. Erich Kasberger and Marita Krauss (Munich: Volk Verlag, 2011), 245.

77. Numbers from Kurt Schilde, "Grenzüberschreitende Flucht und Fluchthilfe (1941–1945): Ereignisse, Interessen und Motive," in *Überleben im Untergrund*, ed. Kosmala and Schoppmann, 154.

78. Bonavita, *Mit falschem Pass*, 58.

79. Franco Battel, *"Wo es hell ist, dort ist die Schweiz." Flüchtlinge und Fluchthilfe an der Schaffhauser Grenze zur Zeit des Nationalsozialismus* (Zürich: Chronos, 2000), 171.

80. Battel, *Schweiz*, 53–54.

81. Battel, *Schweiz*, 53.

82. Schilde, "Flucht und Fluchthilfe," 153.

83. Claudia Schoppmann, "Das Fluchthilfenetz um Luise Meier und Josef Höfler," in *Wir rannten um unser Leben*, ed. Schoppmann, 198. On the deportation of the Baden Jews to France, see Erhard Wiehn, *Camp de Gurs: Zur Deportation der Juden aus Südwestdeutschland 1940* (Konstanz: Hartung-Gorre, 2010).

84. See, for example, Valerie Wolffenstein and Andrea Wolffenstein, *Erinnerungen von Valerie Wolffenstein bis 1945, Andrea Wolffenstein 1938 bis 1945* (1979).

85. Aviram, *Mut der Verzweiflung*, 130.

86. Claudia Schoppmann, "Fluchtziel Schweiz. Das Hilfsnetz um Luise Meier und Josef Höfler," in *Überleben im Dritten Reich*, ed. Benz, 206.

87. Schoppmann, "Fluchtziel," 208. On Höfler and Meier, see Schoppmann, "Fluchtziel"; Schoppmann, "Fluchthilfenetz," 196–224; and Battel, *Schweiz*, 204–15.

88. Schoppmann, "Fluchtziel," 209, 211.

89. Krell, *Wir rannten um unser Leben*, 154–56.

90. Krell, *Wir rannten um unser Leben*, 163–65.

91. Lotte Strauss, *Über den grünen Hügel: Erinnerungen an Deutschland* (Berlin: Metropol, 1997), 153.

92. Schoppmann, "Fluchtziel," 205.

93. It is unclear how many Jews were rescued by Heckendorf and Martin. Battel provides a figure of "nearly 20" Jews, while Schilde estimates that "between 20 and 80" Jews were saved. Battel, *Schweiz*, 199; Schilde, "Flucht und Fluchthilfe," 157–58.

94. Alison Owings, *Frauen: German Women Recall the Third Reich* (New Brunswick, N.J.: Rutgers University Press, 1995), 382–85.

95. Max Bloch, "Gertrud und Magarete Zuelzer. Zwei Schwestern im Holocaust," *Aschkenas* 24 (2014): 204–6.

96. Schoppmann, "Fluchtziel," 205–19; Schoppmann, "Fluchthilfenetz," 204–12.

97. Battel, *Schweiz*, 197–99.

98. Battel, *Schweiz*, 201.

99. Rosenfeld, *Leben in zwei Welten*, 250.

100. Schrafstetter, *Flucht und Versteck*, 143.

101. On this point see also Krell, *Wir rannten um unser Leben*, 148–49. For a discussion of Jews in hiding falling victim to theft, robbery, fraud and blackmail: Susanna Schrafstetter, "'Life in Illegality Cost an Extortionate Amount of Money.' Ordinary Germans and German Jews Hiding from Deportation," in *The Holocaust and European Societies: Social Processes and Social Dynamics*, ed. Andrea Löw and Frank Bajohr (London: Palgrave, 2016), 69–85.

102. Maria Gräfin von Maltzan, *Schlage die Trommel und fürchte dich nicht: Erinnerungen* (Frankfurt: Ullstein, 1986), 161–62. See also Lutjens, *Submerged on the Surface*, 108–13.

103. Ezra Ben Gershôm, *David: Aufzeichnungen eines Überlebenden* (Frankfurt: Fischer, 1993), 323–29.

104. Jalowicz Simon, *Underground in Berlin*, 102–3, 116–25.

105. Jalowicz Simon, *Underground in Berlin*, 131–36.

106. Katja Klee, *Im Luftschutzkeller des Reiches: Evakuierte in Bay-*

ern 1939–1953: Politik, soziale Lage, Erfahrungen (Munich: Oldenbourg, 1999), 80.

107. Gedenkstätte Deutscher Widerstand (GDW), Datenbank Stille Helden, dossier Eva und Stefanie Guttmann.

108. Krakauer, *Lichter im Dunkel.*

109. Benz, "Überleben im Untergrund," 678–80.

110. Benz, "Überleben im Untergrund," 681–84.

111. Roseman, *A Past in Hiding*, 273.

112. Roseman, *A Past in Hiding*, 276–77.

113. Strauss, *Hügel*, 153.

114. Krakauer, *Lichter im Dunkel*, 62.

115. Krakauer, *Lichter im Dunkel*, 50.

116. See Bonavita, *Mit falschem Pass.*

117. Bonavita, *Mit falschem Pass*, 21–22, 24–25, 30–33, 58.

118. Bonavita, *Mit falschem Pass*, 30–33.

119. Meyer, "A conto Zukunft," 218–23.

120. Witold Mędykowski has emphasized the importance of the countryside as hiding space for Polish Jews; see Witold Mędykowski, "Modes of Survival, Techniques of Hiding, and Relations with the Local Population: The Polish Case," in *Hiding, Sheltering and Borrowing Identities*, ed. Michman, 45–50.

121. Wolffenstein and Wolffenstein, *Erinnerungen*, 140.

122. Archive of the International Tracing Service, 2.1.1.1/70288875.

123. Schrafstetter, *Flucht und Versteck*, 94, 165.

124. Schrafstetter, *Flucht und Versteck*, 94–96.

125. Mix, "Hilfe im katholischen Milieu," 137.

126. Mix, "Hilfe im katholischen Milieu," 137–38.

127. Weisse Rose Stiftung, http://www.weisse-rose-stiftung.de/fkt_standard2.php?aktion=ls&ma=cs&c_id=mamura&id=11190008&page=1&topic=077&mod=10&lang=de.

128. On the White Rose, see Detlef Bald, *Die "Weisse Rose": Von der Front in den Widerstand* (Berlin: Aufbau-Taschenbuch-Verlag, 2004).

129. John Delaney, "Rassistische gegen traditionelle Werte: Priester, Bauern und polnische Zwangsarbeiter im ländlichen Bayern," in *Rüstung, Kriegswirtschaft und Zwangsarbeit im "Dritten Reich,"* ed. Andreas Heusler, Mark Spoerer, and Helmuth Trischler (Munich: Oldenbourg, 2010), 163–78.

130. Mix, "Hilfe im katholischen Milieu," 137.

131. GDW, Datenbank Stille Helden, dossier Eva und Stefanie Guttmann.

132. *Statistisches Jahrbuch des Deutschen Reiches*, Vol. 1943, 62:10 and 65:13. Districts (*Landkreise*) in Brandenburg on average had around 60,000 inhabitants, in Upper Bavaria around 40,000; in Lower Bavaria even fewer.

133. Compare, for example, the election results for March 1933 in the regions of Garmisch, Traunstein, and Rosenheim. In Garmisch, the Nazis gained 50.5 percent, in Rosenheim 39.8 percent, and in Traunstein 29.5 percent. Peter Miesbeck, *Bürgertum und Nationalsozialismus in Rosenheim: Studien zur politischen Tradition* (Rosenheim: Hist. Verein, 1994), 551.

134. Schrafstetter, *Flucht und Versteck*, 159.

135. Bayerisches Landesentschädigungsamt, EG 6534, Antrag B, 15 Oct. 1949.

136. For a couple of exceptions, see Charlotte Knobloch with Raphael Seligmann, *In Deutschland angekommen: Erinnerungen* (Munich: Deutsche Verlags-Anstalt, 2012); and Monika Schmittner, *Verfolgung und Widerstand am bayerischen Untermain, 1933–1945* (Aschaffenburg: Alibri, 2002), 228–35.

137. Ulrike Sparr, "'Wahrscheinlich ist es viel leichter, das Opfer zu sein als der Unterdrücker': Margarethe Oestreicher und ihre Familie," in *". . . und nicht zuletzt Ihre stille Courage,"* ed. Hoppe, 101–2.

138. Bonavita, *Mit falschem Pass*, 17.

139. Günther Ginzel, *". . . das durfte keiner wissen!" Hilfe für Verfolgte im Rheinland von 1933 bis 1945: Gespräche, Dokumente, Texte* (Cologne: Rheinland-Verlag, 1995), 1–17, 23–24, 83–91, 119–25, 223–32.

140. For such a case, see Bayerisches Hauptstaatsarchiv, LEA 29429. On the border crossings from Italy to France, see Klaus Voigt, *Zuflucht auf Widerruf: Exil in Italien 1933–1945*, vol. 1 (Stuttgart: Klett-Cotta, 1989), 298–312.

Dalia Ofer

Bella Hazan Ya'ari: A Member of the Jewish Resistance in Pursuit of Self and a Future

THIS CHAPTER FOCUSES ON THE EXPERIENCES OF BELLA HAZAN, A courier of the Dror Zionist underground movement during World War II. I will follow her choices and actions as a member of the Dror Zionist youth movement who joined the resistance and undertook dangerous missions, and analyze the impact of these missions on her understanding of the means and meaning of Jewish resistance.[1] The shifts in her actions will be major points of interest when looking for the tipping points that demonstrate an awareness, self-understanding, and identity that may explain her decision-making processes.

I follow the methodology of microhistory—a detailed examination of the life of my protagonist, contextualizing it, on the one hand, to the larger Jewish reality under German occupation in Poland and Lithuania, and on the other, to the major goals of the Jewish underground movement of armed resistance and the self-understanding of its members.[2] Examining Bella Hazan's biography before the war, under the German occupation of Poland, life in German-occupied Vilna, and her incarceration in Auschwitz affords an opportunity to trace the evolving emphasis on, and the meaning of, resistance. Hazan's resistance gradually embodied a larger scope of actions and intentions relating to both the public and private spheres. The ideals of the Zionist youth movement were major factors in shaping Hazan's new understanding. However, only her involvement in armed resistance in the ghettos, together with what she experienced in the Auschwitz death camp, fashioned her particular understanding of resistance. This emerges clearly from her activities and the narrative of her memoirs.

Bella Hazan Ya'ari survived the war and immigrated to Palestine in 1945, lived in Israel, and raised her family. She died in Jerusalem on January 18, 2004. When she arrived in Palestine, she was invited to talk about her war experiences in public meetings and was extensively interviewed in the Hebrew press. As she was among the first members of the resistance movement to reach Palestine, the desire to listen to her recollections and learn about her personal experiences was immense. The ensuing talks and publicity took a great toll on Hazan's well-being. She needed to recuperate and was sent to a rest home in Kibbutz Giva't Brener, where she wrote her memoirs. Her first sentence, "The sun shines and the slaughterer slaughters," is a paraphrase of a famous verse by the great Hebrew-language poet Chaim Bialik in the poem "On the Slaughter," written following the pogrom of 1905 in Russia. Hazan wrote continuously, driven by the images of lost friends and horrors and nightmares until the "pen fell from my palm." She wrote in Hebrew, which she had learned in her Tarbut school (Hebrew language school) before the war. Her handwriting is clear, yet not once one could sense the storms that engulfed her while writing. After a few weeks she completed her writing and handed the three notebooks to the secretariat of the kibbutz, and eventually it was handed to the Ghetto Fighters Archive. Hazan's memoir is the major source which informs my analysis of her story.[3]

Before outlining the tipping points in Hazan's biography, a short explanation of the concept of tipping points is needed. Lenore Weitzman and I used this term in our essay "The Sequential Development of Jewish Women's Coping Strategies in the Ghettos during the Holocaust: A New Theoretical Framework."[4] It served as an interpretive concept to explain radical changes in ghetto women inmates' responses to critical information and perilous situations in the ghetto. It may serve better as an analysis of women's responses, since many women in the prewar years were mostly active in the private sphere, while in wartime they were obliged to extend their activities to the public sphere and often had to use unfamiliar tactics to defend their spouses and provide for their families. Observing the reactions of women of different ages across ghettos, we realized that many went through a sequential process. First they reacted to the occupation and move to the ghetto with the knowledge they had attained through tradition, education, and their own life experience. When the situation became more difficult, women acquired new techniques to fulfill their basic obligations and moved to spheres of action not intended earlier. At a certain point, some women realized the extreme situation and followed a revolutionary path they would never have imagined before. Women in the armed resistance, women who slipped in and out of the ghetto, and those who lived under false identities may be counted in this category. The tipping point occurred when they lost a loved one, heard about mass killings, or realized how ghetto life was causing massive death and desperation.

BELLA HAZAN, 1922–1940

Bella Hazan Ya'ari was born in December 1922 in Rozyszcze (Rozhishche), a small village in the Volhynia district of Poland. Hazan's father died when she was very young and her mother, who had to care for herself and her eight children, opened a grocery store. She made a great effort to give her children a sound Jewish education and they all went to Tarbut schools. Hazan was later sent to the ORT vocational school in the nearby city of Kobel to learn a vocation. In the summers, she participated in Dror Hehalutz seminars and summer camps. Her older sister Hayah immigrated to Palestine, and her mother encouraged both Bella and her younger sister to do the same.[5]

In the summer of 1939, Hazan was sent by the Zionist youth movement to a defense (*haganah*) course conducted in Zielonka, near Warsaw. There she made the acquaintance of two prominent members of Hehalutz's head office: Frumka Plotnicka and Zivia Lubetkin.[6] Upon completing the course, Hazan did not return to her home, which led to a conflict with her mother, who for a number of months maintained no contact with her. Hazan began serving as a combat instructor at the kibbutz *hakhsharah* (training program) in Bedzin.[7]

Hazan did not spend much time in Bedzin. Shortly after the war broke out and the area was cut off from Poland, Hazan, together with a group of other Dror members, intended to cross the border with the aim of moving to Vilna, which had been declared a free city. After a complicated journey, she crossed the San River to Russian-occupied eastern Poland and was detained for a few weeks by the Soviets. When released, and before continuing to Vilna in December 1939, she came to Rozyszcze to meet with her mother and siblings. It was a short, very emotional visit. This time her mother did not stop her from leaving. She was hoping, like Bella herself, that from Vilna, Bella would immigrate to Palestine and join her sister. This was the last time that Bella Hazan saw her family. They were all murdered by the Nazis.

At that time Vilna hosted over 2,000 young members of various Zionist youth organizations who reached the city after the beginning of the war, all hoping to get immigration certificates to Palestine. After reaching Vilna and until the Nazi occupation, Hazan was involved in her Shaḥariyya kibbutz *hakhsharah* activities and worked to earn a living. These activities needed more courage and creativity after the Soviet takeover in June 1940 and her work became partially illegal. Together with other Zionist youth members, she worked in agriculture and conducted a collective home on the farms. They kept hoping to be able to immigrate. Since the borders to different parts of eastern Europe under Soviet rule were more or less open, many tried to take advantage of the situation and move to places from where they hoped to leave Europe, such as Romania. Though most did not succeed, the few who did manage to immigrate through the Soviet Union kindled the hopes of the others.[8] Many lost their lives on the way, but not all this information reached the youth movement in Vilna.[9]

Reflections

A reading of Hazan's narrative of the first weeks of the German occupation of Poland suggests a first turning point in her response to the war. Following the early days of the war, when a flood of refugees on the roads and bombing by the German air force spread horror and devastation, Hazan thought that a leading group of youth would stay to keep their kibbutz home in Bedzin while the rest of the group should move to safety. The members of the group considered themselves a kibbutz *hakhsharah*, a community preparing itself for communal life, and they would fulfill together the mission of immigration to Palestine. However, the occupation and the mass flight of people from the town spurred the young members to leave. In Hazan's own words: "The members left crying, nobody wanted to leave our home [the house where the group lived together], everyone struggled with his inner soul. The consolation was that perhaps we shall be able to continue together as a kibbutz. The four walls of our dining room and our bedrooms joined us together forever."[10] This attempt failed. The advance of the Germans was so fast that no place seemed safe. The Dror group returned to Bedzin with the hope that they would rebuild their communal home and renew their activities. In reality, they had no means of acquiring basic supplies and could not find work. Lack of food and the cold autumn days without heating drove them to seek another way out. Information about concentrations of *ḥalutzim* (young pioneers who intended to immigrate to Palestine) in Vilna, which was a free city, fired their imagination, and the decision was made to try this path.

We can conclude that leaving the "home" of the kibbutz in Bedzin was a first turning point, but still within the framework of the Zionist youth movement's ideology. Hazan was one of the leading figures in the kibbutz *hakhsharah* and demonstrated awareness regarding the need to alter their course of action, though still in line with the central goals of the youth movement. While the war disrupted regular routines, it did not shake the foundations of their ideology. The impetus to leave Poland became stronger and Palestine seemed even more desirable since it reflected the traditional approach of the Zionist youth movements: that the future of the youth was not among the Jewish community in the diaspora, but in Palestine. Therefore, they should leave their communities and families without hesitation. The war, they believed, would end shortly.

We may ask whether they were preoccupied with the thought that they had deserted friends and youngsters in the youth movement who were unable to move to Vilna. Hazan's narrative does not reflect on this issue. In the chaotic first weeks of the war, leaders of a number of youth movements escaped from German-occupied Poland, among them Zivia Lubetkin and Yitzhak Zuckerman of the Dror movement. Some returned after a few months to the towns where they had been leaders, and others did not. Hazan, though not a central leader at that point, was among the second group.[11]

On the way to Vilna, Hazan and her friends encountered the uncertain and fluid situation of the first months of occupation. They had to conceal their Jewish identity to travel on trains and could not speak freely among themselves. They reached Przemysl, on the San River, a town divided between the Germans and Soviets. The eastern bank was the border of Soviet occupation. They managed to cross the river to the east side where they were detained by the Soviet military. Such "illegal" activities were not part of the routine of Hazan and her friends. However, they were somewhat familiar with these activities as part of the legacy of illegal border crossing by Zionist youth movements. Flight across borders in the attempt to reach Palestine without legal papers had in the past been part of the experience of Zionist youth movements.[12]

Released from the harsh prison before her male friends, Hazan used her youth and beauty to impress the Soviet guards and the interrogator.[13] She spoke with them using the little Russian she knew and told them of her mother's devotion to communism and that she had taught them some Russian. Her fearless behavior was not part of her past experience, but demonstrated a type of daring when faced with dangerous situations, and perhaps also some naïveté. Would it hint at her future capabilities? We may appreciate at this point Hazan's ability to change modes, to make a turn and adopt another personality as a way of overcoming an obstacle.

Hazan's description of her short visit with and farewell from her mother and the sisters who still lived with her mother is telling. Her mother had been angry when, at the end of the defense course in summer 1939, Bella went to Będzin instead of returning home to assist in supporting the family. She broke off all contact with Bella. Now, in December 1939, they met under different conditions. Bella did not come to stay and support her mother despite the war and the Soviet occupation. Her mother understood this but was sad at the same time. The possibility that Bella would immigrate now seemed the best option, and she hoped that Bella would prepare the ground for her sisters and herself to immigrate to Palestine.

However, this short meeting demonstrated that both Bella and her mother, like most Jews, were unable to perceive the real threat of the war. Hazan left her mother and her siblings with an elusive promise to prepare a home for them in Palestine, where her older sister was already residing. This, too, was essentially how young Zionists viewed their immigration to Palestine when faced with leaving their families. In retrospect she wrote painfully: "This was the last time I saw my family."[14]

Bella's narrative of the first months in Vilna, until the German occupation, demonstrated again a rather traditional reaction to unforeseen difficulties. She had to find her place among Dror members, she experienced disappointment as immigration did not materialize, and it was difficult to make a living in the commune. The Soviet occupation of Vilna in June 1940 confronted Hazan and the Zionists with new difficulties, as the Soviets banned all Zionist activities. The need to conceal their work and visions called for manipulations to which they had previously been unaccustomed. Still, an analysis of her narrative concerning their conduct and lifestyle demonstrated that Hazan and her friends realized the turn in the course of events, but planned to find a way to continue with their educational and other activities. They stuck to the goal of immigration. One should bear in mind that some knowledge of the negative approach of the Soviets toward Zionism and about clandestine youth activities there in the early 1920s was part of the legacy of those Zionists who had left the Soviet Union.

BELLA HAZAN, 1941–1942

After the German occupation of Vilna in June 1941, Hazan experienced the first raid on Jews. Special Lithuanian militias and Einsatzkommando 9 entered Jewish homes robbing, abusing, and murdering people. The kidnapping of men for forced labor became the rule of the day and many did not return; information about their murder followed.[15] In her memoirs, Hazan mentioned that a group of movement members was taken for forced labor and never returned. A few days later she and her friends learned how they were murdered. Information about the mass killings accumulated, and the descriptions were beyond imagination. Fear increased when in August women and children were also taken to be murdered and the dread of total destruction of the Jews was in the air. Until the establishment of the ghetto on September 6, some 20,000 of Vilna's 70,000 Jews were murdered.

Hazan and her friends moved into the ghetto with all the other Jews and tried to manage their lives as a group. At this point, the idea arose of crossing over to the Aryan side of the city for short periods of time—hours or days—in order to get information and provide commodities for the members. Hazan's non-Jewish appearance and her being a stranger in the city were an advantage. This was the very first step in her direct underground activities. She also worked in the ghetto hospital and experienced hiding from deportation and listening to stories of victims of Nazi violence. From September through December 1941, the mass murder of Jews was carried out at Ponar. Of the 50,000 Jews who moved to the ghetto, some 20,000 were murdered. The 30,000 Jews who remained in the ghetto were the remnants of the 70,000 Jews of the city in June 1941.[16]

The Zionist youth movements endeavored to fathom the meaning of the mass murder. Was it a local situation, in which the Germans were retaliating against the Jews who were under Soviet rule, or was it a more comprehensive plan to annihilate the Jews? It was at this point that an underground movement began to form. In order to understand the broader situation, contacts with other Jewish communities under occupation were crucial. The main goal was to spread information about the mass killings in Vilna, to find out what was happening in other cities, and to find a safer haven for members of the movement. Hazan volunteered to serve as a liaison between the various chapters of the movement. She was able to obtain the passport of a Polish acquaintance, Bronislawa (Bronia) Limanowska, and after changing the photo Hazan assumed this name for the duration of the war. She purchased a crucifix and a small Christian prayer book and passed as a young Polish woman who had lost her family in the war.

After leaving the Vilna ghetto in October 1941 she moved to Grodno (Horodna), which became her base for a few months. Grodno lay at the crossroads between Vilna, Bialystok, and Warsaw, all in different zones of occupation. It was therefore important to have a base in Grodno, but it was also very difficult to move between the different zones without proper permits. Hazan found employment as an interpreter for the Gestapo and received a formal work permit, which enabled her to obtain official Polish identity papers and replace the forged ones. She rented a room with a Russian woman (who would not recognize her poor Polish) and acted like a Catholic Pole, going to church on Sundays with a fellow worker, a young Polish woman. These actions enabled her to be relatively mobile; with endless manipulations she obtained permits to visit Vilna and Bialystok and thus provide information about them. In Grodno she made contact with a member of her Dror movement, providing information on the mass killings in Vilna and in the surrounding Jewish towns.[17]

The situation in Grodno was relatively stable when Hazan arrived. Confinement to ghettos occurred on November 1–2, 1941, much later than in other towns in the area. The first months after the establishment of the ghettos were not marked by any dramatic events or mass killings. Hazan managed to get special permission from her boss to enter the ghetto, where she met with members of Hehalutz and with officials of the Judenrat and its head, Dr. David Braver. She told them of the slaughter of the Jews in the Vilna ghetto and asked them to prepare to receive movement members from Vilna in Grodno, where the situation seemed safer. In a video interview, she lamented that Braver did not believe that the information she provided was true.[18]

Since her first mission to Grodno and until spring 1942, Hazan maintained contact between the movement in Vilna and the chapters in Lida, Grodno, and Bialystok, providing information and relaying movement bulletins, money, and weapons. In March 1942 she decided to leave Grodno for Bialystok, where a large number of her Dror movement members had managed to establish a base. I will not narrate all of the daring activities of Bella Hazan, such as her many trips from Grodno to Vilna and Bialystok, which required immense courage and a capacity to manipulate the situation on the spot. These actions included buying tickets for trains and visiting Jewish towns that she found without Jews—including her hometown and her home, now occupied by non-Jews. I will only relate her mission in April 1942 that ended in imprisonment.

While in Bialystok, Hazan was asked to transport two handguns to the movement's kibbutz at Czerniakow (near Warsaw) and to discover what had happened to another emissary, Lonka Kozybrodska, who had been sent on a mission to Warsaw and never returned. At the border crossing at the Malkinia (Malkinia Gorna) railway station, Hazan was checked, taken off the train, and arrested. After initial questioning and beating, she was taken to the Gestapo headquarters in Warsaw for interrogation on suspicion that, under her false Polish identity, she belonged to the Polish underground, the Armija Krajowa (Home Army). Although severely tortured, she did not disclose her true identity and her mission. From there she was transferred to the notorious Pawiak prison, and was held for five months. There she met her friend and fellow courier Lonka Kozybrodska, who had also been imprisoned as a Pole, and from then on the two were never separated until Lonka died in Bella Hazan's arms in Auschwitz.[19]

Reflections

It is obvious that the risks Bella Hazan took upon herself when she became a courier were immense, and perhaps she was unable to envision the direction her life would take while carrying out her missions. What motivated her to undertake this work? In my assessment of her memoirs, the tipping point was the experience of the mass killings during the first weeks of occupation. It touched her directly when members of her group who were taken for forced labor did not return. Later, news of their murder reached Hazan and her friends.

She narrates the Soviet period as a difficult time for the movement, which lacked leadership and did not know how to react to the yoke of the Soviets. She tells about the efforts of members to illegally cross borders and the lack of news of what happened to them: "It was a difficult time for the movement and the pioneers. But we remembered the few days that we were under German occupation and we understood the difference between the Germans and the Russians. Under Soviet occupation, we could work and we even spoke Hebrew."[20] A few sentences later she relates rumors about the fate of the Jews in Poland under German occupation: "The rumors were very bad. We knew that the Germans hate us and do not give us the right to exist. But it was difficult to believe. We knew that this was the truth, since we were able to grasp what they were during the first days when they bombed Bedzin. Very painful was the news about our brethren under German occupation and we were unable to help them, since the Germans secured the borders and it was impossible to cross."[21]

When the Soviets retreated in the face of the German invasion of the Soviet Union, Hazan, together with a number of friends in the movement, tried to escape to the east. They were unsuccessful because the roads were filled with fleeing multitudes and the German air force bombed the roads and the rail lines. They returned to Vilna and found that their home had been taken over by the Germans. The realization that the rumors were true hit Bella Hazan when the kidnapping and killing started. At this point, it was clear to her and her friends that the horrendous fate of the Jews was at their doorstep. They tried to avoid being outside when the risk of kidnapping was high; nevertheless, as mentioned above, a few young men from the movement were taken for forced labor and never came back. After a few days, the news arrived that all the men had been murdered. In Hazan's narrative this information receives prominence, testifying to how heavily the news of their death weighed upon her. "Then we understood that death is awaiting us too, only we did not know what form it would take."[22] I dare say that this was Hazan's tipping point. Now she realized that there was no longer any prospect of immigrating to Palestine unless the war came to an end. She moved into the Vilna ghetto with all the other Jews and felt trapped.

Looking at Bella Hazan's actions at this stage, we can sense her restlessness in the search for an activity that would confront the new situation. Thus, from the first days in the ghetto, in addition to her work in the hospital, she felt that she had to leave the ghetto, move in the city as a non-Jew, and smuggle food into the ghetto. The leaders of the Dror youth movement in Vilna, Mordekhai Tennenbojm Tamaroff and Zvi Mersik, debated how to interpret the mass killings in Vilna. The need to find and provide information about the mass killings became crucial for any planning of further actions.

At this point the role of the couriers became crucial, and Hazan with her non-Jewish good looks volunteered to become one. I explain this step as part of the tipping point mentioned before. However, one should take into account that taking the decision did not mean that Bella fully understood the difficulties that awaited her. On the other hand, her experience of the German occupation and of the restrictions on travel meant that she was aware of the obstacles ahead.

Bella's life from October 1941 to the day she was caught by the Gestapo and imprisoned was radically different from anything she had previously experienced. She had already demonstrated the ability to readily understand complex situations and move ahead without losing sight of the main goal. She showed dedication to her friends and to the mission they had pursued on the difficult road to Vilna. She disguised her identity, acted alone, pretended endlessly, and was on constant alert. Over and above courage, her role called for the ability to act with a thousand faces. On one level, she was a young girl to be pitied after the death of her family, while on another level she was a daring and innovative emissary confronting the disbelief of the Jewish leadership in Grodno or keeping a poker face before the Poles who occupied her parents' home after the murder of her mother and siblings. Though she had to act with the pretense of self-assurance, beyond all these lay the great fear of being discovered or handed over to the Germans.

If we ask ourselves how Bella Hazan understood the goals of the resistance when she started out on her mission, we must remember the evolution of the resistance idea within the youth movement. Its leaders and members debated how to interpret the deportations and mass killings. In the fall of 1941, as I mentioned above, the resistance and the underground tried to collect information in order to establish a strategy of survival and rescue by comparing the situation in different ghettos and move the youth to a safer ghetto, Bialystok or Grodno, for example.

Hazan's first missions in October and November 1941 were to collect and transmit information. When she was in Grodno, she encouraged the young people there to keep the movement going and to prepare places for members from Vilna. She informed the Jewish council in the ghetto of the radical events in Vilna and demanded that they assist movement members who would flee to Grodno. As noted, in December 1941 she returned to Vilna for one week and experienced a raid on the ghetto after tens of thousands of its population had already been murdered. At the beginning of 1942, back in Grodno, she met again with Tenenbojm Tamaroff, who informed her of the development of the resistance movement and the underground. This was after the famous call by Abba Kovner and Tamaroff to the Jewish youth "not to go like sheep to the slaughter." In her memoirs she makes no mention of this call.

During the months in which Hazan served as a courier, the objectives of the underground movement slowly took shape as the youth movements progressed toward physical and armed resistance with the goal to confront and disrupt the deportations. A few more events may shed light on the turns through which Hazan went as she absorbed the idea of active and armed resistance. Her cooperation with two other couriers, Tema Schniederman and Lonka Kozybrodska, who traveled to Warsaw and other places in the General Government, and the seminar conducted by Frumka Plotnicka in Bialystok in March 1942, revealed the new directions in the goals and activities of the movement. Hazan's dedication was reinforced after going on a mission to Volhynia and visiting her hometown, where she realized that none of her family remained and Poles were living happily in her home without changing its furniture and settings. When apprehended by the Germans in Malkinia, Hazan was carrying weapons for the underground in Warsaw.

BELLA HAZAN, 1942–1945

Bella Hazan, whose Jewish identity was never revealed, was suspected of being a Polish underground activist and was tortured by the Gestapo, first in Malkinia and then for many days in the Gestapo headquarters in Warsaw before she was transferred to the notorious Pawiak prison in the city. Badly wounded and confined in isolation in a dark cell for six weeks, she was unable to look at light. She was moved to the prison hospital for a number of days and then transferred to the Polish women's ward. During her interrogation, she learned that Lonka Kozybrodska was also interned in Pawiak, and that a photo of them together with Tema Schniederman, which was found on Kozybrodska, had led to her capture. Knowing that she might meet Kozybrodska was a comfort to Hazan. During the months they spent in Pawiak and until Kozybrodska's death in Auschwitz, they were together, both in the guise of Poles.

In Pawiak, Hazan had to maintain good relations with the Polish prisoners, bear their antisemitic comments, and limit conversation with her dear friend Lonka Kozybrodska to when they were allowed to walk in the prison yard. In the close confines of the prison cell, the antisemitic remarks voiced by the Polish inmates were even more troubling than those she heard when traveling on the trains or during her work in Grodno. Many of them were made against the background of the deportations from the Warsaw ghetto, which the window of their cell faced.

Hazan and Kozybrodska witnessed the terrible abuse of Jewish prisoners in Pawiak. They identified a sixteen-year-old girl, Shoshana Grzenda, who was imprisoned in Pawiak for distributing bulletins of their Dror movement. Hazan used the latrine to make contact with her and assisted in some desperate hours after a night of horrific cruelty. She recruited the Polish woman doctor Choparska, who was a communist, to treat Shoshana.[23] She was careful not to show the Polish prisoners that she had contacts with Jews. In one moment of weakness and great fear, when the Russians bombed Warsaw, she revealed her real origins to an imprisoned Polish painter. She was never betrayed.

The five months in Pawiak were a horror. The constant fear of unexpected torture, random selections for executions, listening to the screams from the Warsaw ghetto during the months of the mass deportations to Treblinka, and the need to disguise her identity, all added up to unbearably long and troubled days. The greatest anxiety was that she would die and her real identity would be concealed forever. In November 1942, fifty-three prisoners were sent from Pawiak to Auschwitz, among them Hazan and Kozybrodska.

The time Hazan spent in Auschwitz-Birkenau can be divided into two major periods: from November 13, 1942, the day of her arrival at the camp, to April 13, 1943, when Lonka Kozybrodska died; and from then to the death marches starting on January 18, 1945.[24] I will mention only some of Hazan's experiences in Auschwitz-Birkenau in order to characterize her years in the camp. In the first period Hazan, like many other inmates, was under the shock of the reality of Birkenau. She worked mostly outside the camp, performing difficult physical labor in the bitter cold of the fall and early winter of 1942/43. She suffered from the harassment of the guards, but somehow preferred being outside the camp in the fields for a few hours. Although the revelation of Birkenau's horrors was painful, being together with her dear friend Lonka Kozybrodska created a sense of mutual responsibility and a sharing of providence and pains. Kozybrodska, who was fluent in a number of European languages, worked as a translator in an office and waited for Hazan's return with her work brigade. Meeting Lonka each day, after the long and difficult hours in the fields, gave her great mental and emotional support. This relationship and sharing were the powers that fueled Hazan's energy and ability to survive. With Lonka Kozybrodska she felt as if she continued her contact with the movement, and this sense of belonging helped her to endure the difficult daily routine of the camp.

In late January 1943, Hazan fell ill with typhus and was hospitalized in the *Revier* (the infirmary) for six weeks. Slowly, she was able to get back on her feet. She did not go back to her previous work brigade, but for a while remained in the infirmary in a semi-official status as an assistant.[25] While Hazan was in the hospital, Lonka Kozybrodska contracted typhus, and for some weeks they shared a bunk in the hospital. Lonka's condition deteriorated, and toward the end of March she died. This was a terrible blow for Hazan, who felt lonely and isolated and was on the verge of despair. Yet, during the last days in which Hazan took care of her friend in the infirmary, with great effort Kozybrodska whispered and urged Hazan to keep going, endure the suffering, and survive. Conceal your Jewishness and keep your Polish identity, she murmured, and you will survive. You have to hold on to the thread of life that I lost so that you will tell about us.[26] These last words were the beam of light that kept Bella Hazan going. She had a mission. It was Hazan's and Kozybrodska's mission that she had to realize—to survive and transmit the knowledge of Nazi horrors and their efforts to resist.

The most difficult period for Hazan was in Auschwitz-Birkenau, lasting for almost two years between April 1943 and January 1945. Her experiences during these twenty-two months tested both her physical and mental ability to carry on and her dedication to survive and tell her own and Lonka Kozybrodska's story. Hazan worked part of the time in labor squads outside Birkenau and for a few months was transported to Babice, one of Auschwitz's subcamps, where she worked in agriculture. She ended up as a nurse in the hospital in Birkenau and in a special barrack for prisoners who had come down with scabies. In the final month, she worked as a nurse in the hospital in Auschwitz I.[27]

The months she worked outside Birkenau were challenging, but she felt more at ease outside the compound. The time she was imprisoned in Babice was relatively easier. The prisoners worked in agriculture, and the physical conditions and food were better than in Birkenau. Hazan liked the work outside and in particular in agriculture, which provided her with some time for quiet reflection. However, she was punished by her direct commander and transferred back to Birkenau and attached to a squad that was allocated to digging tunnels. The work was physically arduous, the women were harassed by the German guards, and two women were raped and killed. The women were terrified and screamed when a third girl was dragged away to be raped. They were punished severely with four days in confinement in standing cells. On another occasion, when the prisoners sang the Polish anthem, an angry German guard shot to stop the singing and wounded Hazan and one other woman.

After these incidents, Hazan pleaded with a Polish physician who treated her injury to employ her as a nurse in the hospital in Birkenau. After several weeks of serving as an ordinary nurse, the doctor appointed Hazan to temporarily replace the nurse responsible for the cleanliness of the hospital barrack. She feared the responsibility but was unable to refuse. She comforted herself by the thought that in this position she could provide more assistance to the Jewish patients.[28] At this stage, the condition of the hospitals in Birkenau had improved. Water supply reached the hospital and it was easier to keep the barracks clean. The number of sick prisoners increased, however.[29] Medicines and extra food were smuggled into the infirmary by prisoners who were members of the Polish underground.[30]

Returning as a nurse to the hospital confronted Hazan with the suffering of the Jewish patients, who were separated from the others and intentionally neglected by many of the Polish nurses. She volunteered to work with the Jews despite the concern that she would be identified as a Jew or a Jew-lover. Later she volunteered to work in a special barrack where sick inmates with scabies were gathered and poorly treated. Only a few nurses were willing to work there. Hazan was gratified that she was able to support the sick Jews, and she sought ways to supplement their nutrition and keep their bunks clean. She wrote that she often heard the prisoners express amazement at "the good Polish nurse," and in her heart she yearned to remove the mask and identify herself.[31]

Throughout these months Hazan sought a confidante, as she felt very lonely after the death of Kozybrodska. To get close to a Jewish inmate would raise suspicion and was dangerous for both the Jewish inmate and Hazan. Nevertheless, she persisted. During the long months of 1943 and 1944 she managed to establish good contacts with a number of young Jewish inmates who were members of the Zionist youth movements, and with a few who had even been active in the Jewish resistance before being imprisoned in Auschwitz. With a few of these inmates she shared her Jewish identity and even developed close relationships. This was a source of comfort and eased the difficult daily routine.[32] Because she was incarcerated as a political prisoner, her Polish inmates believed that she was part of the camp's Polish underground and interpreted her solitude as resulting from that. This generated respect for her and her activities. During the last month she was transferred to the hospital in Auschwitz 1. The Polish doctor whom she knew from Birkenau proposed her as head of the block (*Blokowa, Blockältest*), since the doctor was unable to work with the Jewish nurse who filled that role. Hazan was hesitant but could not refuse, and she suffered from the ill treatment of the kapo Edit, a Slovak Jewess, who was suspicious of her being Jewish. [33]

Reflections

From her very first days in Auschwitz, Hazan, together with Lonka Kozybrodska, demonstrated much resourcefulness in confronting the camp routine that was intended to eradicate the humanity of the inmates. After a period of working outside in the cold during the fall and winter of 1942/43, they overcame their fear and approached the head of the block, suggesting that advantage be taken of their skills. Lonka Kozybrodska offered her knowledge of languages, and Hazan her experience as a nurse. It was a daring approach, and partly successful. Kozybrodska was sent to work in an office, while Hazan tried to serve in the hospital but could not stand the difficult conditions and ill treatment by the German doctors, so she returned to the squad working in the field.

Hospitalized after contracting typhus, she recovered, but since she was weak she remained in the hospital to assist and be with Lonka Kozybrodska, who had come down with both typhus and dysentery. The great turn was the death of Lonka. For Hazan this was a tipping point; she was left alone, but with a mission and a great sense that she must dedicate her survival to the memory of Lonka Kozybrodska. After the death of Lonka, Hazan was unable to continue her work in the hospital and instead worked outdoors. She was able to cope with the brutal and inhuman environment, negotiate the endless dangers, and at the same time search for opportunities to extend her activities beyond herself and her own survival. She needed, however, to share her pain and hopes. Although her former activities as a courier between the ghettos and life in Grodno had taught her to be alone, it was the belief that she would reach the ghetto and meet her friends that gave her strength.

Hazan found a person with whom to connect in order to overcome her unbearable loneliness. Hilda was a young Jewish musician who played in the band (orchestra) of Birkenau.[34] Its music accompanied the prisoners when they marched to work and returned to the camp. Before deportation, she had been in a Zionist youth group and a member of a collective. All this information was revealed to Hazan when she met Hilda in person. This happened following eye contact as Hazan listened to a sad melody the band played for the German camp administration. Moved by the music, she had tears in her eyes, which Hilda noticed. Hazan took the initiative, approached Hilda, and asked to meet her in person. To her amazement, Hilda agreed. Hazan's narrative about their meeting demonstrates how she longed for and was anxious to meet the girl. The fear of having her Jewish identity discovered loomed over her all the time. Therefore, she felt that it was dangerous for her, as a Pole, to invite and converse with a Jew, and she feared the consequences if this was discovered by her Polish inmates. "There was something about this young girl that attracted my attention. I suddenly had an urge to talk to her, but how? For that was forbidden. Despite that, motivated by an uncontrollable impulse, I decided to try. I invited her to my block at six p.m. 'Come for a talk.' Once again she wondered why a Polish woman should ask her to come see her. To my great joy, she agreed to come. Very tense, I waited for the appointed hour; the girl came and sat down on my bed." [35]

This meeting and what she learned about Hilda and her friends was the next tipping point. Hilda was not just a Jewish girl to talk to; she was the person with whom Hazan could bond. She embodied the ideals and friendship that Hazan longed for. Hilda introduced her to a group of Zionist youth movement girls interned in Birkenau who managed to keep together and cherish their friendship and mutual responsibility.[36] Hazan wanted to be part of this group but it was too dangerous, as it endangered her ability to keep her promise to Korzybrodska. Thus, she behaved like an invisible onlooker, except to an isolated few. A Hebrew tune or a word in Hebrew were the hints she used to identify herself, enabling her to build support.

Hazan was now emotionally conflicted between loneliness and a sense of belonging while being physically apart. She trod a narrow path as a Pole who tried to draw near to Jews, serving them in the hospital, while also concealing her Jewish identity. The maintenance of this concealed identity, to find ways to assist Jewish inmates while posing as a Pole, and—under great danger—to act to save children from gassing, all reveal her new understanding of the meaning of resistance in Birkenau. From reading about her actions and relationships with both Poles and Jews in the camp, it was clear that Hazan's self-perception was that of a Jewish underground activist. Her Polish inmates admired her, convinced that she was a Polish underground member. She wrote about her need to be alone, to write the letters of the Hebrew alphabet and Hebrew names on small pieces of paper so as not to forget the language. The Poles thought she was writing for the Polish underground bulletin in the camp.

Moreover, she exploited her relatively unrestricted ability to sneak in extra food from the kitchen for the Jewish and non-Jewish sick in the hospital barracks. She hid the very ill when an inspection was conducted in order to avoid sending them to the gas chamber. The first time she performed such a daring deed was to save Lonka Kozybrodska when she was ill with typhus, but she also did this with other inmates.

CONCLUSIONS

Bella Hazan gradually adopted a broader understanding of resistance through her role as a member of a youth movement. Each expansion was the building of events that created the turning points. Her understanding of resistance went together with that of the movement up to a certain point, but the Auschwitz experience impelled her to go further. She went beyond the movement toward the wider range of fellow Jews and the suffering of others. Her particular Jewish perspective was a dominant factor, and the anti-Jewish conversations she heard among the Poles simultaneously reinforced her sense of being Jewish and fostered her anger toward the Poles. Even in the worst experience of Auschwitz she adopted the role of the future witness: to tell her and Lonka Kozybrodska's story and to fulfill the ideal of the movement and immigrate to Palestine.

On the face of it, the path followed by Bella Hazan as a member of the Jewish resistance seems to be almost linear. Yet it is not. On one level, it followed the stages through which her Dror youth movement passed during the war and under Nazi occupation. On another level—paradoxically, precisely in Auschwitz—while building on the legacy of the Dror youth movement, she implemented the idea of resistance in a broader contextualized interpretation, as an individual who turned the limitations under which she acted into a constant pursuit to assist her fellow inmates, to endure the camp, and, finally, to envision a future.

NOTES

I would like to thank and acknowledge the assistance of Prof. Yoel Ya'ari, the son of Bella Hazan, whom I interviewed for this research. His support and assistance in finding more sources and documents contributed immensely to my knowledge. He also read and commented on the draft of this paper.

1. Dror-Hehalutz was a Zionist socialist youth movement established in Poland in the late 1920s whose members came mostly from lower-class proletarian families. The movement prepared its members for immigration to Palestine and life in a kibbutz. Eli Tzur, "Dror," in *The YIVO Encyclopedia of Jews in Eastern Europe*, ed. Gershon David Hundert (New Haven, Conn.: Yale University Press, 2008), 1:429–30 (henceforth *YIVO Encyclopedia*). For a detailed history of the movement in Poland, see Israel Oppenheim, *The*

Hehalutz Movement in Poland 1917–1929 [in Hebrew] (Jerusalem: Magnes, 1982); and Israel Oppenheimer, *The Hehalutz Movement in Poland 1929–1939* [in Hebrew] (Sede Boker: Ben Gurion Institute, 1997).

2. For a fine example of recent microhistorical research on the Holocaust, see Claire Zalc and Tal Bruttmann, eds., *Microhistories of the Holocaust* (New York: Berghahn Books, 2017), 1–16.

3. The information about Bella Hazan is based on her memoirs. The original manuscript is in the Ghetto Fighters Archive, 442/1 (henceforth Hazan, manuscript). It was published and somewhat edited (mostly language corrections) years later as *Bronislava Was My Name: On a Mission and Imprisoned, 1939–1945* [in Hebrew] (Tel Aviv: Hakibbutz Hameuḥad, 1991); video interview, YVA (Yad Vashem Archives), JT 36II; oral interview YVA 0.33 298. I had long conversations with her son Yoel Ya'ari, who is a professor at the Hebrew University of Jerusalem. I also had many conversations with Bella Hazan Ya'ari herself in the retirement home where she spent the last years of her life, about her life in Israel and her war experiences. For a brief biography, see Sara Bender, "Bella Ya'ari Hazan," in *Jewish Women: A Comprehensive Historical Encyclopedia*, ed. Paula Hyman and Dalia Ofer (Jerusalem: Shalvi, 2007).

4. In *Women and the Holocaust: New Perspectives and Challenges*, ed. Andrea Peto, Louise Hecht, and Karolina Krasuska (Warsaw: Wydawnictwo Instytut Badán Literackich PAN, 2015), 27–63.

5. Tarbut was a network of Jewish schools that taught in the Hebrew language, and which were secular and Zionist in their ideology. The schools were established in eastern Europe starting in the early years of the twentieth century and flourished in Poland, Lithuania, Latvia, and Romania between the two World Wars. Adina Bar-El, "Tarbut," *YIVO Encyclopedia*, 2:1841–43. On ORT schools, see *YIVO Encyclopedia*, 2:1291–92.

6. Bella Gutterman, *Fighting for Her People: Zivia Lubetkin, 1914–1978* (Jerusalem: Yad Vashem, 2014); Naomi Shimshi, "Frumka Plotnicka," in *Third Person, Singular: Biographies of Youth Movement Activists during the Holocaust,* ed. Avihu Ronen and Yehoyakim Cochavi [in Hebrew] (Tel Aviv: Moreshet, [1994]), 165–220.

7. On Bedzin and the underground youth movements, see Avihu Ronen, *Condemned to Life: The Diaries and Life of Chajka Klinger* [in Hebrew] (Haifa: University of Haifa, 2011).

8. Hazan's descriptions of Vilna are more detailed in her handwritten memoirs, where she devoted a few pages to their work, living conditions, the relations between members of the different youth movements, and also to the advance of the Soviets. See Hazan, manuscript, 10–12

9. On stealing across the borders and the youth movements in Vilna, see Rivka Perlish, *The Pioneering Zionist Youth Movements in Nazi Occupied*

Poland [in Hebrew] (Tel Aviv: Hakibbutz Hameuḥad, 1988), 43–105; for Hazan's account of her crossing, see Hazan, *Bronislava Was My Name*, 38.

10. Hazan manuscript, 2

11. On the issue of youth movement leaders who left occupied Poland and then returned, see Gutterman, *Fighting for Her People*, 73–119.

12. For an extensive description of illegal immigration, see Dalia Ofer, *Escaping the Holocaust: Illegal Immigration to the Land of Israel, 1939–1944* (New York: Oxford University Press, 1990).

13. Hazan wrote at length on the difficult conditions in the prison. See Hazan, manuscript, 6–8.

14. Hazan, manuscript, 10.

15. For the direct orders to Einsatzkommando 9 to increase the killings, see Peter Longerich, *Holocaust: The Nazi Persecution and Murder of the Jews* (Oxford: Oxford University Press, 2010), 198–99.

16. On the situation in Vilna during the first months of occupation, the killing and deportations to Ponar, and the origins of the resistance movement, see Yitzhak Arad, *Ghetto in Flames: The Struggle and Destruction of the Jews of Vilna during the Holocaust* (Jerusalem: Yad Vashem, 1980); and Dina Porat, *The Fall of a Sparrow: The Life and Times of Abba Kovner* (Stanford, Calif.: Stanford University Press, 2010). On Bialystok, see Sara Bender, *The Jews in Bialystok during World War II and the Holocaust* (Waltham, Mass.: Brandeis University Press, 2008).

17. On the Grodno ghetto, see Tikva Patal-Knaani, *Grodno Is Not the Same: The Jewish Community in Grodno and Its Vicinity during the Second World War and the Holocaust 1939–1943* [in Hebrew] (Jerusalem: Yad Vashem, 2001); on Hazan's activities in Grodno, see 230–32.

18. YVA, JT 36II.

19. Sara Bender, "Lonka Kozybrodska," in *Jewish Women*, ed. Hyman and Ofer.

20. Hazan, manuscript, 10.

21. Hazan, manuscript, 10.

22. Hazan, manuscript, 11.

23. Shoshana Grzenda-Kliger was in Pawiak in July 1942 and was later sent to Majdanek and Gross-Rosen, where she was liberated and thereafter immigrated to Palestine. See Hazan, manuscript, 29. A testimony of Shoshana Grzenda-Kliger was published in *The Ghetto Fighters Book*, ed. Yitzhak Zuckerman and Moshe Bassok [in Hebrew] (Tel Aviv: Hakibbutz Hameuchad, 1956), 572–76.

24. The sequence of events in Auschwitz is not dated in Hazan's memoirs, and therefore we are unable to give precise dates for the sub-periods of her stay there. These dates were confirmed by consulting other sources.

25. For hospitals and medicine in Auschwitz-Birkenau, see Irena

Strzelecka, "Hospitals," in *The Anatomy of the Auschwitz Death Camp*, ed. Yisrael Gutman and Michael Berenbaum (Bloomington: Indiana University Press, 1994), 379–92. See also Strzelecka, "The Hospitals at Auschwitz Concentration Camp," in *Auschwitz 1940–1945: Central Issues in the History of the Camp*, vol. 2: *The Prisoners, Their Life and Work* (Oswiecim: Auschwitz-Birkenau State Museum, 2000), 291–346. Scholarly books do not use the word *Revier* but "hospital" or "infirmary."

26. Hazan, manuscript, 36; Hazan, *Bronislava Was My Name*, 92.

27. It is impossible to give exact dates or times since she did not write dates in her memoirs. I tried to identify the dates in the context of the events she was narrating and place them in the history of the camp as presented in research. Her mention of Christmas or Hanukkah provided a benchmark.

28. Hazan, manuscript, 44.

29. Danuta Czech, "The Auschwitz Prisoner Administration," in *The Anatomy of the Auschwitz Death Camp*, ed. Yisrael Gutman and Michael Berenbaum (Bloomington: Indiana University Press, 1994), 363–78; Hazan, manuscript, 42–43; Hazan, *Bronislava Was My Name*, 100–101.

30. Hazan, manuscript, 42–43. Hazan refers to the assistance of Polish underground members in transferring food and medicine to the inmates in the hospital. On the supplies provided by the Polish underground in Auschwitz, see Hermann Langbein, "The Auschwitz Underground," in *The Anatomy of the Auschwitz Death Camp*, ed. Yisrael Gutman and Michael Berenbaum (Bloomington: Indiana University Press, 1994), 485–502.

31. These events are not recorded in sequence but appear in Hazan, manuscript, 40–44; Hazan, *Bronislava Was My Name*, 99–108.

32. For a group of Jewish Polish girls in Birkenau who were members of a Zionist youth movement, some of whom participated in the Jewish uprising in Warsaw, see the testimony of Masha Benger Fisher, Ghetto Fighters Archive (GFA) 1541. See also Havka Folman-Raban, *They Are Still with Me* (Loḥamei ha-gettaot: Ghetto Fighters' Museum, 2001), 168

33. Hazan, manuscript, 54–56. See also Raya Kagan, *Hell's Office Women* (Tel Aviv, 1947), 132, 135; in these two pages she tells about Hazan as a Polish nurse whose Jewish identity was known to her.

34. On the women's orchestra in Birkenau, see Czech, "The Auschwitz Prisoner Administration," 366–67.

35. Hazan, manuscript, 94.

36. Anna Heilman, *Never Far Away: The Auschwitz Chronicles of Anna Heilman*, ed. Sheldon Schwartz (Calgary: University of Calgary Press, 2001), 126. Heilman tells about a group of young Jewish women prisoners who were part of the Jewish underground before being interned in Auschwitz. In Auschwitz they continued to maintain contact and met in the evening when possible. She wrote about a Jewish young woman who was identified

as a Pole: "Though this group consisted only of Jewish girls, there was one girl who wore a red triangle on her number, identifying her as a Pole. She was Jewish but had succeeded in maintaining her false identity as a non-Jew. This girl was either directly involved with the Polish Underground or was close enough to them to have gained their confidence." This may very well relate to Hazan, though her name is not mentioned.

Lorena Avila, Nancy Nicholls, and Yael Siman

Migration Narratives of Holocaust Survivors in Chile, Colombia, and Mexico

LATIN AMERICA BECAME AN IMPORTANT REFUGE FOR JEWISH survivors in the second half of the 1930s.[1] It has been estimated that around 100,000 Jews emigrated to this region between the rise of Nazism and the end of the war.[2] This number is only slightly lower than the 113,260 Jewish refugees who emigrated to the United States, and higher than the 66,500 refugees who arrived in British Palestine during the same period. This phenomenon has not been ignored in the literature. Studies on the migration of Jewish survivors to Latin America include pioneer works on rescue and refuge by Haim Avni,[3] alongside a number of other Latin Americanist and Holocaust scholars.[4] However, in this body of scholarship, countries such as Colombia,[5] Costa Rica, Ecuador,[6] and Venezuela receive less attention or remain marginal.[7] Moreover, this literature has focused on the immigration policies of Latin American governments, only indirectly studying the survivors as subjects—and not simply objects—of this transnational history.[8] This reflects a broader absence, with transnational histories of the Holocaust remaining underexplored until very recently.[9]

This chapter is an exploratory study of a sample of Jewish survivors who sought refuge in Latin America. It seeks to contribute to Latin American Jewish migration studies during and after the Holocaust. It asks, how do Holocaust survivors who immigrated to Latin America remember their experiences? How do they narrate their departures, journeys, and arrivals from Europe to Latin America?[10] What did these experiences signify to them? What did they think, feel, and imagine as they traveled to Chile, Colombia, and Mexico? How did the particular moment and national context of their arrival influence their migration experiences? We seek both to establish certain "facts" about these transnational movements as well as detect "emotional responses, political views and the very subjectivity of existence."[11] This is survivors' history from below based on multiple individual subjectivities. Adopting this approach, this chapter argues that immigration to Latin America represented a new episode in the mobility trajectories of Holocaust survivors. Departing, journeying, and arriving from Europe to Latin America were physical and emotional experiences. In contrast to other Latin American countries, most survivors found—in Chile, Colombia, and Mexico—symbolic and concrete places for recreating rootedness, fixity, and territoriality, even if those countries had not been their ideal destination for immigration.[12] Only Colombia remained partly a transit destination for sojourner survivors. In their experiences of migration to the region, the Holocaust became a mobile reference point as it traveled with survivors across geographies and sociocultural spaces, but it remained fixed in their imaginaries, with shifting interpretative resonances resulting from the particular national contexts in the region.

SOURCES AND METHODS

This chapter uses a mixed-methods approach that combines oral history with tools used for analyzing big data in order to map the trajectories of ninety Holocaust survivors who immigrated to Chile, Colombia, and Mexico. Our study analyzes the content and narratives of migration in audiovisual testimonies from three digital collections:[13] the USC Shoah Foundation's Visual History Archive (VHA), *Voces de la Shoá Memoria Viva*, and the Fortunoff video archive.[14] We selected the testimonies based on country destination (thirty for each country), combining different criteria to generate diversity in the sample: in terms of gender, place of residence before displacement, and Holocaust experience. Other factors such as age or year of immigration to Latin America were random. Most of the testimonies are in Spanish. Colombia stood out in our sample because of its higher rate of later emigration from that country, mainly to the United States (50 percent of the interviewee sample who initially emigrated to Colombia). For purposes of comparison, we also included a small number of testimonies of survivors who subsequently emigrated from Chile and Mexico to other destinations.

For the purposes of identifying our sample, we worked with a broad definition of a "Holocaust survivor" to include every European Jew who came under the threat of Nazism, either concretely or potentially, between 1933 and 1945. Thus, the category of survivor includes Jews who were sent to ghettos and to concentration and death camps, but also those who survived in hiding, had a false identity, fled to other territories, or became political refugees.[15] Almost every type of Holocaust experience is represented in our sample (figure 7.1).

The survivors had diverse socio-demographic and cultural profiles: they came from different European countries and different cities and towns, although we find that Chile had a larger number of survivors from Germany, while Polish Jews had a larger representation in both Colombia and Mexico (figure 7.2). Our sample includes an equal number of women and men. Children and adolescents had a greater presence, except in the case of Colombia. Most survivors arrived in the region between 1946 and 1950, although a larger number of German Jews immigrated to Chile between 1933 and 1939.

Based on this sample of ninety testimonies, we created mobility plots.[16] Circular migration plots are "effective, engaging and beautiful visualizations that are more appropriate to flow data than any of the existing graphical representations."[17] These represent group trajectories of survivors from the more representative countries in our sample (Germany and Poland). Another set of plots represents the individual trajectories of nine survivors who came from Germany and Poland to Chile, Colombia and Mexico at different times. In the case of Colombia, the three individuals immigrated to different destinations in the same country, illustrating the singularity of the Colombian migration experience. The initial point in the individual plots is the first place of displacement, while the last point is the place of residence where the survivor gave the testimony. Every intermediate stay (but not very brief stops) mentioned by the survivors is included.[18] Group and individual plots illustrate the intense mobility trajectories of Holocaust survivors as told by them. As scholars have shown previously, the plots visualize the Holocaust as a "profoundly geographical phenomenon" that occurred both collectively and individually.[19] In this sense, migration can be seen as part of a mobility continuum even if interrupted by spaces of "fixity"[20] such as ghettos or camps.

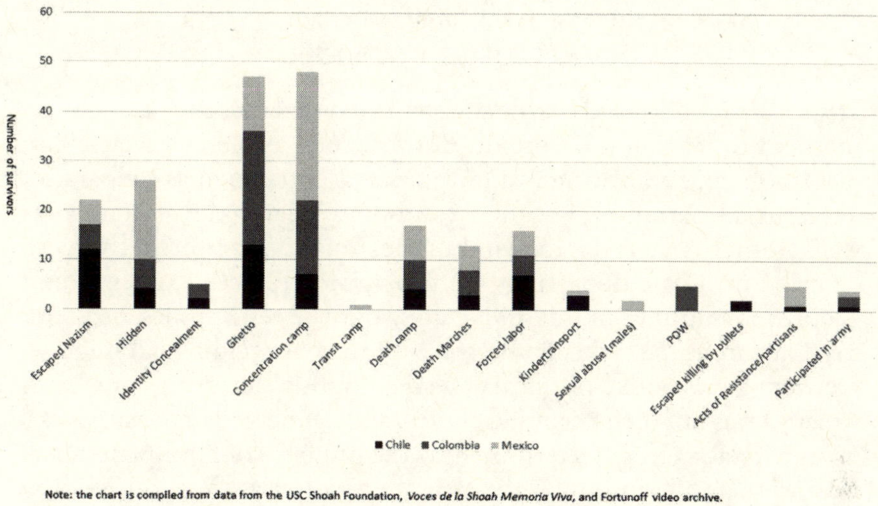

Fig 7.1. Experiences of Holocaust survivors in Latin America. Courtesy of the authors.

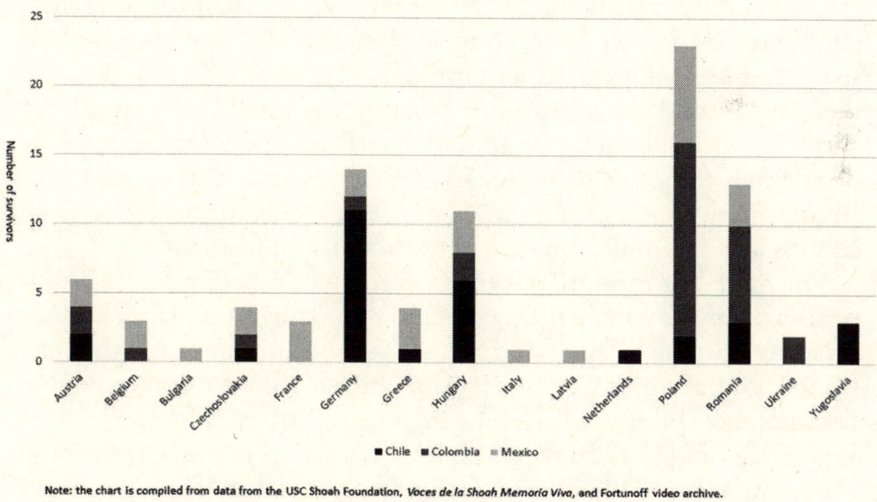

Fig 7.2. Place of birth of Holocaust survivors in Latin America. Courtesy of the authors.

DEPARTURES FROM EUROPE TO LATIN AMERICA: LEAVING AND DECIDING WHERE TO GO

Departure is conceived in this chapter in a broad sense. It refers to the moment of leaving the ports in Europe, such as Genoa, Marseilles, or Lisbon, and transiting to new points of entry such as Valparaíso, Veracruz, or Barranquilla. Some testimonies refer to the difficult farewells from friends and family in European stations or ports. They also describe nostalgic departures from particular places, cultures, and deeply biographical and familiar sites. But the testimonies also refer to departure as the difficult and costly process of deciding to emigrate. Departing was both a physical and an emotional act. For many, Latin America was not their preferred choice, and it emerged in the survivors' imaginary as a refuge determined by the presence of family members already there or simply by the availability of visas. Marion Mostny remembers that when her parents decided to emigrate from Germany in 1939, Shanghai was a possible destination, given that some German Jewish families had already emigrated there. On the contrary, Chile was totally unknown.[21] Ultimately, her father decided to emigrate to Chile, without giving clear reasons to Marion about his choice.

For survivors, emigration implied recovering their social agency, although they had not lost it completely even in desperate and oppressive situations. The particular narrative form in which they describe their desires and choices (in first person: "I wanted" or "I decided") contrasts with the one used to describe their experience of mobility during the Holocaust ("they led us," "they took us," "they moved us"). But deciding to leave and emigrate in a genocidal or post-genocidal context was a complex process of push-and-pull factors.[22]

In their testimonies, survivors mention Nazism and antisemitism as the two main factors leading to their emigration from Europe (mentioned twenty times). Even those who initially thought they would not be subjects of persecution changed their mind following *Kristallnacht* (1938) and the ensuing imprisonment of thousands of Jewish men in concentration camps. Personal or family decisions to emigrate from Germany coincided with a period in Chile of greater flexibility, as the administration of Pedro Aguirre Cerda of the Popular Front (1938–41) called for humanitarian considerations to change the government's immigration policy toward Jews and refugees of the Spanish Civil War.[23] This contrasts with the policy of his predecessor, President Arturo Alessandri of the Liberal Party (1932–38), and with the restrictive immigration policies of Colombia and Mexico. Indeed, Jewish immigrants escaping Nazism came to Chile in greater numbers from 1938 on.

Survivors who emigrated after the war mention postwar antisemitism less frequently (eleven times) than those who emigrated during the Nazi years. Those who do mention it were mainly the ones who had returned to their homes in Poland, Romania, and France. The threat of advancing communism or its actual presence is mentioned more frequently than any other factor after the war (twenty times) by survivors in countries under Soviet influence: Bulgaria, Czechoslovakia, Poland, and Hungary. They express a fear of living again under a "terrorist" or "totalitarian" state. Some survivors say that communist regimes were hostile to their "bourgeois" status, not to their Jewish identity.[24] Other factors mentioned, although less frequently, include loss of family and Europe in ruins.

The retention of family networks emerges most frequently in the survivors' testimonies as pull factors: sixty-three survivors mentioned their desire to reunite with their families in Latin American countries. Indeed, their family members in Chile, Colombia, and Mexico applied for visas, became sponsors, and contacted local politicians or lawyers. But even with their families' efforts, survivors had to wait or emigrate elsewhere before they could travel to countries such as Mexico. Some survivors underscore that it was "impossible" to obtain an entry visa to Mexico even after the war. Survivors in Chile and Colombia remember facing difficulties—long periods of waiting—but they do not mention that getting a visa was a problematic matter. Latin American countries as ideal or good places to go is only mentioned eight times in the sample as the reason to emigrate. This contrasts with the reasons that led survivors to emigrate to Israel (Zionism) or the United States (a land of opportunities), but also to Argentina. Less frequently mentioned are reasons such as knowing *Ladino* (Judeo-Spanish), having a Spanish passport, being able to emigrate to the United States from Mexico, knowing other Polish Jews in Colombia, getting a visa at a bargain price in Chile, finding work, or marrying a local Jew.

Migration was also facilitated by ethnic and institutional transnational networks. Like other diasporas, the Jewish case was characterized by the intersection between family chains and institutional networks. Ethnic Jewish networks provided jobs, affidavits, and labor contracts.

In some instances, family networks worked privately and independently from international humanitarian organizations, but in other cases, a plethora of Jewish international organizations were involved: the World Jewish Congress,[25] HIAS (Hebrew Sheltering and Immigrant Aid Society of America), ICA (Jewish Colonization Association), EMIGDIRECT (*Vereinigtes Kommittee für Jüdische Auswanderung/Berlin*), HICEM,[26] and Joint.[27] These institutions often collaborated with non-Jewish organizations like the International Red Cross, American Friends Service, UNRRA, and IRO. But in the testimonies, international organizations are mentioned infrequently, with only HIAS and Joint standing out. The invisibility of international Jewish and non-Jewish organizations may be related to the young age of most survivors. Most likely they were not aware of the complex emigration procedures undertaken behind the scenes by their parents, while family members became highly visible helpers and hosts in their new destinations.

Moving from the more qualitative analysis of the testimonies to collective or individual plotting, a number of patterns can be seen in the sample of testimonies that was studied. First, there is a suggestion of distinct flows, with a clear preference for Chile as a destination among the German Jews in our sample. Figure 7.3(a) shows that the largest number of Jews from the sample who were residing in Germany when the Nazis took power emigrated to Chile between 1933 and 1939, especially in 1939 before the beginning of the war. While Jews from Germany also emigrated to Colombia and Mexico in this period, they did so in smaller numbers. Figure 7.3(b) shows that, throughout the war, only a small number traveled to Mexico. As previously stated, this may be related to the temporary opening of Chile's immigration doors. However, this variance may also be related to the small size of our sample and is a pattern worth exploring with a larger population. Figure 7.3(c) shows that after 1945, Jews originating in Germany emigrated to the three countries following similar patterns in the 1933–39 period.

These collective patterns can be seen in more detailed mapping of the trajectories of individual German Jews. Figure 7.4 shows that three survivors emigrated from Germany to Chile between 1933 and 1939. Gunter Seelman was in his hometown (Aachen, Germany) but, fearing Nazism, moved with his family to the Netherlands. He then emigrated to Concepción, Chile. Walter Borchheim, born in Breslau, moved with his parents to Berlin in 1932 and, alarmed by antisemitism,

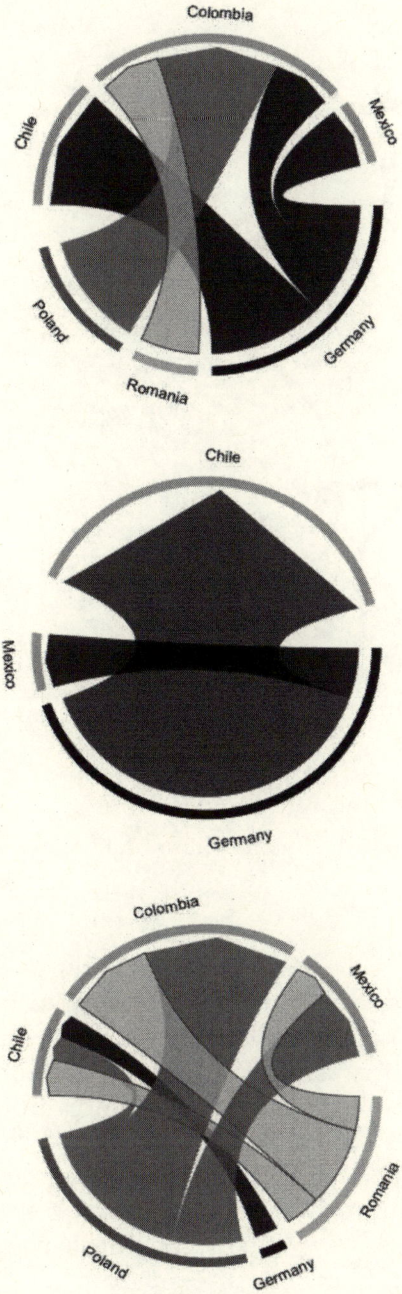

(a) Prewar (before 1939)

(b) During the war (1939–1945)

(c) Postwar (after 1945)

Fig 7.3. Main countries of emigration and immigration per period. Courtesy of the authors.

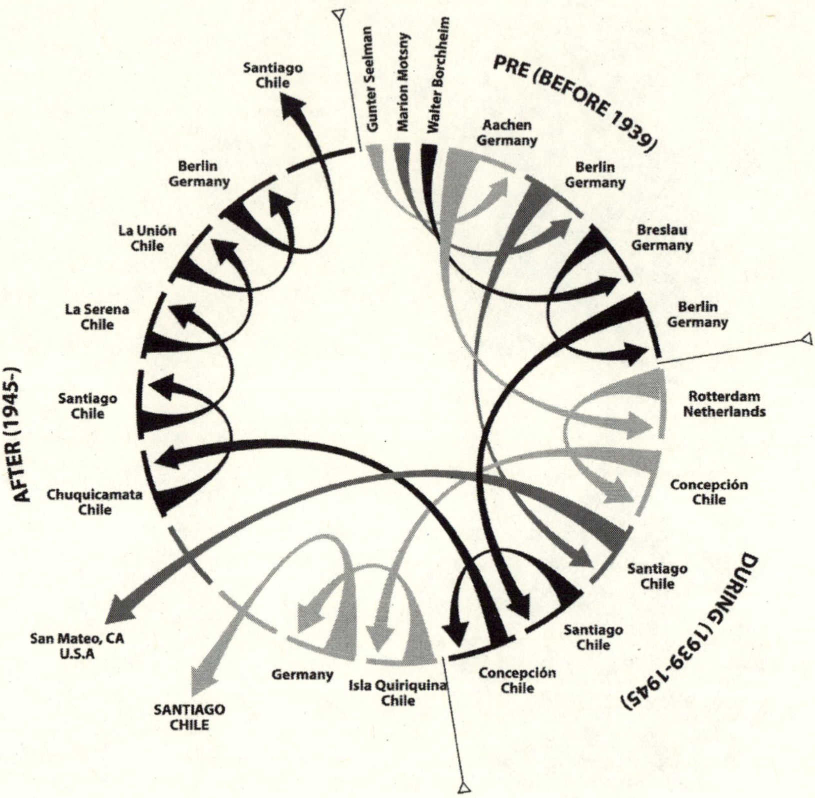

Fig 7.4. Trajectories of Holocaust survivors who immigrated to Chile. Courtesy of the authors.

emigrated to Chile before the war. Marion Mostny lived in Berlin until May 1939, when her parents decided to emigrate due to antisemitism; they traveled to Santiago. German survivors who emigrated to Chile had few or no intermediate stays between their point of departure and their destination. Gary Simonsohn's arrived in Colombia from Germany with his mother years after they lost trace of his father, who emigrated first to survive Gestapo persecution. Because of their personal connections, Gary was placed in an orphanage in Berlin together with his mother who pretended to be a worker in the same orphanage. Gary emigrated in 1938, arriving in Buenaventura, the main Pacific port in Colombia, but then moved to Bogotá (figure 7.5).

Alternatively to the German Jewish emigration flows to Chile,

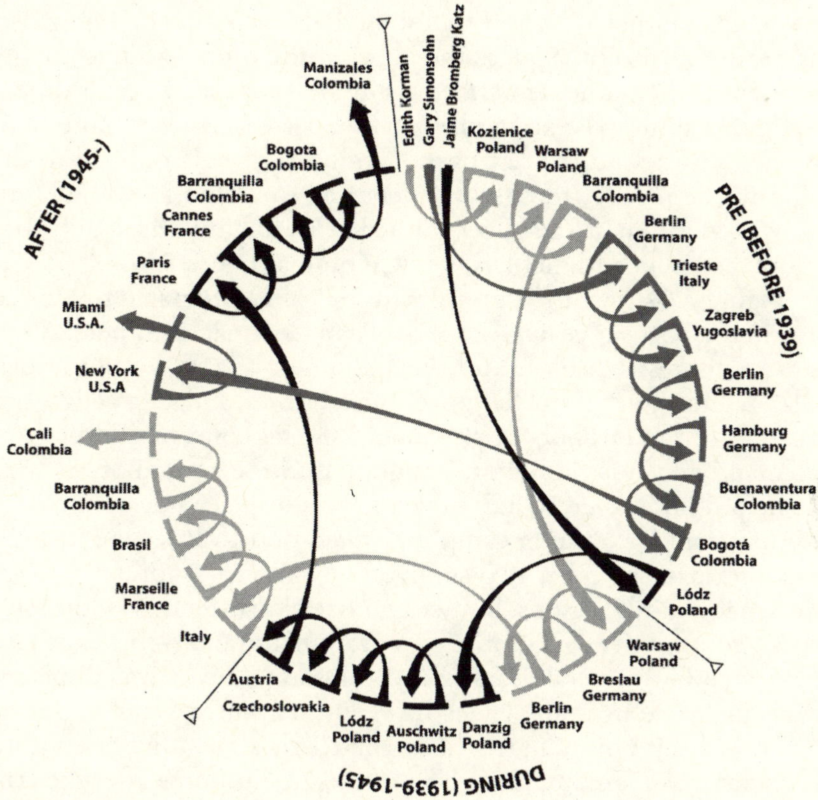

Fig 7.5. Trajectories of Holocaust survivors who immigrated to Colombia. Courtesy of the authors.

there appears to be a different geography to Polish and Romanian Jewish emigration patterns to Latin America. Figure 7.3 shows that Jews from Poland and Romania arrived in Colombia between 1933 and 1939, but they stopped immigrating during the war period. Survivors from Romania and Poland emigrated to all three countries—Colombia, Chile, and Mexico—in the postwar period, but in larger numbers to Colombia. A very small number of survivors from Poland emigrated to Chile after 1945. This may relate not only to the possibility of getting visas, but also to the ethno-national communities in each country. Due to good timing and family connections, Edith Korman emigrated from Poland to Barranquilla, Colombia, before the war. However, her mother's poor health led her family to return to Poland and they were able to restore their livelihood despite growing antisemitism. In 1939, as the political situation was increasingly threatening, her father emigrated again to Colombia, but this time it would take him two years to fill out the paperwork and send the visas. By then, Edith and the rest of the family had been confined to the Warsaw ghetto. Her mother was deported to Treblinka while Edith survived in the ghetto and later worked in Berlin under a false identity before reuniting with her father in Colombia (figure 7.5).

Figure 7.6 shows that survivors from Poland emigrated to Mexico only in the postwar years, even if they had close relatives there. Abraham Avigdor was displaced for the first time when the Nazis invaded Poland. During the war he moved seven times, hid in a cellar, and was sent to the Drohobycz ghetto and several concentration camps in Poland and Austria. Before emigrating to the United States with the help of his father, Avigdor lived in two displaced persons camps in Austria and a training camp for emigration to Palestine in Italy. In contrast to the other two survivors, Avigdor did not emigrate to Mexico for family reasons. Rather, an invitation extended by the local Jewish community to his father—a prominent rabbi—brought him to Mexico City several years later. Bronislaw Zajbert was displaced from his home in Lòdz when the Nazis arrived in his city, but he stayed with his family in the Lòdz ghetto for almost five years until its liberation in January 1945. He returned to his home after the war, emigrated first to Caracas, Venezuela, and only several years later to Mexico. Elena Zondowicz, originally from Vilna, was displaced with her family following the outbreak of war. She remembers the "tragic" decision of her father attempting to sell his possessions while having visas for Mexico, but not being allowed to cross the Russian border. Forced to return to Vilna, Elena was hidden by a Catholic family in a Polish forest and in White Russia. After the war, Elena's rescuers decided to move to Sopot, a northern Polish port, until she was "taken away" by her aunt to Lòdz and then to Israel, which was, in her mind, another forced displacement. Only after several years of continuous attempts was Elena's uncle able to bring her to Mexico City.

THE JOURNEY TO LATIN AMERICA: IN TRANSIT TO NEW HOMES

Reconstructing travel routes based on testimonies is a complex task given the lack of precise information in many cases. But testimonies

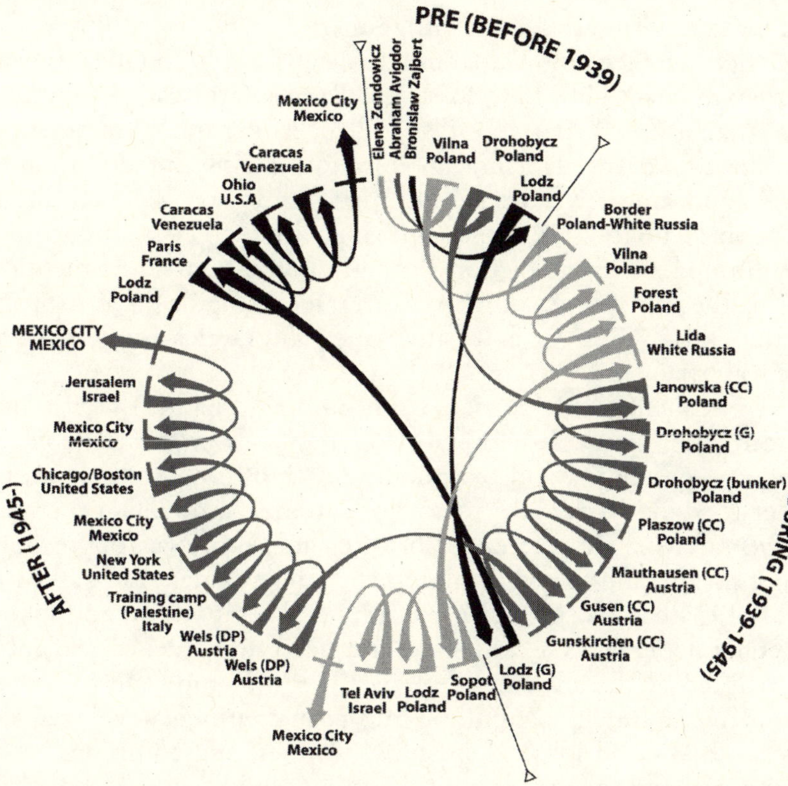

Fig 7.6. Trajectories of Holocaust survivors who immigrated to Mexico. Courtesy of the authors.

shed light on escape and exit points, stops along the way, and final destinations. The existing literature points to Italy, France, and Portugal as countries transited by Jews escaping Nazism as the possibilities for escape began to disappear with the outbreak of war.[28] The journey from Europe to Latin America was, for the most part, in ships, although in the postwar years the means of transportation diversified. This meant that journeys generally lasted between three weeks and one month depending on the final destination. Those who journeyed from Italy, France, or Portugal to Mexico made stops in Casablanca, the Azores, Bermuda, the Dominican Republic, and Havana. Survivors who left European ports for Barranquilla, Cartagena, or Buenaventura in Colombia stopped in the Caribbean islands of Trinidad and Tobago, and Curacao. The service of Latin American passenger ships in the *Italia* fleet left Genoa to Valparaíso, Chile, with stops on the outward journey in Marseilles, Barcelona, Las Palmas, Trinidad, La Guaira, the Panama Canal, Barranquilla, Callao, Arica, and Antofagasta.[29] Recollections of travel include the duration of trips, the conditions of travel, food, and arrival dates. Most survivors do not talk much about the people who traveled in the same ship with them, perhaps because they limited social interaction to their families, but some mention sharing the journey with other Jewish families escaping Nazism, Spanish Republican refugees, and Latin American travelers, diplomats, or political personalities.

Consequently, the journeys from Europe to Latin America may be seen as an interlude between two completely different life experiences, geographies, and temporalities.[30] However, neither can be understood independently from prior patterns of mobility generated by the survivors' desperate search for escape from Nazi oppression, dispossession, and forced displacement. The experience of survivors before 1933 had its singular geography and temporality, and it was generally depicted as a contented and peaceful existence, violently interrupted by the advance of Nazism across Europe and the onset of war. When leaving behind the European continent—villages and cities, schools and jobs, friendships, families, and communities—survivors abandoned biographical and family histories anchored in traditions. But leaving Europe also meant escaping and surviving, thus leaving behind a topography and a time of horror and anxiety. The second experience of survivors implied rebuilding a life project in Latin America. Their journeys may be seen as the continuation of previous mobility, encompassing multiple displacements in Europe—from homes to ghettos, from ghettos to camps, from towns to cities, and from cities to embarkation ports—but they may also be conceived as socio-emotional ruptures with the past, given that survivors affirmed their social agency through the recovery of a human condition that had been threatened.

Not every journey was experienced without threats or dangers related to the context of war and mined oceans, or to the risks of visas obtained by bribing diplomatic authorities. Walter Berchheim and his family emigrated from Germany to Uruguay because his father paid a bribe in English pounds to the vice-consul of Uruguay in France, in exchange for the visas. However, their plans did not work out as expected:

> We embarked there on the *General Artiga* of the German company . . . in the journey we learned that they would not allow us to disembark in Uruguay because the matter exploded, the consul did not provide part of the bribe (*coima*) to the Ministry, but there was a Latin American conference, and the Chilean delegate that I think was Dr. Natalio Berman, the communist member of parliament from Concepción, who knew what was happening contacted don Pedro Aguirre Cerda, God may keep him in his blessed memory and there our visa was authorized . . . We were in Uruguay under police protection in lodgings . . . and my father with another gentleman went to the Argentinean consulate to get the famous transit visa in order to take the Trasandino, and the man opened the passport and the same thing happened, so we headed for Punta Arenas.[31]

On these journeys, survivors might have left behind fears, threats, or repressed traumatic experiences, but traveling was also a time of anxiety and uncertainty on the one hand and entertainment and relaxation on the other, especially for children and adolescents. Indeed, the narratives show differences in the way survivors lived during their journey, depending on their age and their previous experience under Nazism. Marion Mostny remembers: "we had a good time, trip to Chile, we traveled luxury on a ship, because . . . they were the only ship tickets you could get, April of 1939 was already pretty late . . . so he got three tickets for the four of us . . . and I remember the trip was very nice . . . I mean you are a kid, we had all new clothes . . . we enjoyed it, I was ten, eleven years old, my brother was ten."[32]

References to food were expressed as sensory memories of what was eaten on board the ship or upon arriving in the first Latin American countries. In contrast to the scarcity of food in Europe, the food on board was often abundant in the recollections of the survivors. Alberto Bejarano, who emigrated from Bulgaria to Mexico with his family in 1948, remembers that when he boarded the ship in Bordeaux, their first priority was to eat. He tells how they quickly grabbed (*se abalanzaron*) a bread basket, but they had to leave it and wait two more hours until their turn came. The materiality of the ships is also remembered:

sleeping cabins, dining rooms, bathrooms, and what seemed either luxurious or uncomfortable, depending on whether they traveled first, second, or third class.

In contrast to the children's memories of adventure, the testimonies show that parents and other adults expressed worries given that they were traveling with limited economic means, and without knowing the language or having a job in the place of destination. As the ships became more distant from the European continent, the hope of creating a new life rose while pain and fear also became more intense. These feelings were particularly acute for those who had left family members behind in Europe.

The first geographical, social, and cultural encounters by survivors with Latin America occurred in these journeys, which expanded their spatial conceptions of the region.[33] Physical contacts with Latin American ports brought the migrants closer to local otherness. Sensory memories also acquire relevance in encounters with Latin American climates (the warm tropics), landscapes, food, and culture. Meeting local people produced a sense of oddness (*extrañeza*). Lea Kleiner remembers:

> We continued the trip until, well open sea, until . . . Buenaventura, I think we docked in Colombia . . . it was the encounter with the Caribbean, with the black people . . . I remember the comments of adults, let's say, facing . . . these people they had never seen and never, I do not know if they imagined that there existed black people in South America, in Caracas there was yellow fever . . . one could not visit and, well, we continued traveling, slowly, towards the South.[34]

In a humorous way, Alberto Bejarano reflects on the port: houses of palm, hats, and *machetes*: "We thought that if these were the Americas they would eat us alive; they were anthropophagous. But nothing happened [*No pasó a mayores*]. We did not disembark, we could not disembark."[35]

Survivors continued to emigrate to the region in the period from the 1950s to the 1970s, but in smaller numbers. Only a minority in our sample left shortly after arriving, for either study or work reasons, or because they found it difficult to adapt to local community and societal settings. However, years later some survivors emigrated elsewhere, within the region or overseas. Chile's political history and exile had an impact on emigration decisions. Two survivors who immigrated to Chile returned to Germany in times of crisis, but came back when the national politics stabilized. In 1973, following the military coup by Augusto Pinochet which overthrew the socialist government of Salvador Allende, Gunter Seelmann—an active supporter of Allende—was sent as a political prisoner to a concentration camp on the island of Quiriquina, where he stayed for several months until he was exiled to Germany. He stayed there with his wife and children until 1985, when he returned to Chile. In contrast, had it not been for the fear of a socialist political takeover, Marion Mostny and her family would have probably stayed in Chile. However, in the 1964 elections, as it became more likely that the socialist Salvador Allende would be elected president, her family emigrated to San Mateo, California. Her second emigration, like the first, constituted a very significant event in her life. Unlike Gunter, Marion decided to stay in the United States. Three survivors in our sample mention leaving Chile for Argentina, the United States, Australia, and also Germany for reasons that were not political: the country's underdevelopment, poverty, earthquakes, their desire to reunite with family members, or simply to try their luck elsewhere.

A larger number of survivors left Colombia. For Gary Simonsohn, born in Germany, Colombia was a transit destination. Gary remembers that after meeting his father they left together for Bogotá. Although Colombia represented a place of initial hardship for Gary's father, who was an "intellectual" and not a businessman, he adapted and benefited from local opportunities. Gary went to university, got married, and had several occupations but decided to emigrate to the United States, where he finally settled. Due to family affairs, work opportunities, or simply because a random door was opened, Colombia did not remain a long-term possibility. Nevertheless, more research is required to examine if these factors intersected with the sense of insecurity that characterized Colombia during the second half of the twentieth century.[36] Mexico became the residence of a large number of survivors. Some emigrated from Mexico to Israel, the United States, Chile, or Venezuela. Those who left did so for professional and personal reasons, or due to the difficulties they faced in adapting to a country characterized by socio-economic inequality. Some regarded Mexico only an intermediate step towards the United States, their preferred destination from the outset.

ARRIVAL IN LATIN AMERICA

Yi-Fu Tuan argues that "to be always on the move is, of course, to lose place, to be placeless and have, instead, merely scenes and images," adding that journeys "increase awareness, not for exotic places but of home as a place."[37] Survivors talk about their memories of childhood or youth as recovering details of their towns and cities, sites of family homes and shared experiences, celebrations, cultural practices, traditions and religion. They remember with emotion their school, vacations, streets and plazas, synagogues, forests and outdoor activities. In general, these are happy and colorful memories through which survivors appeal to their belonging to towns, cities, and countries of origin. Nevertheless, the threat of Nazism and forced displacements and migratory journeys led to a fracture in their sense of having a home. Their arrival in Latin America allowed survivors to recover this sense in a safe place.

Facing an impossible return—both physical and emotional—nostalgia turned into a search for meaning and the building of a place in the host countries. In a sense, survivors underwent—as Feng and Breitung describe for general migratory experiences—different competing and interacting *factors* at work when a sense of home is built up or transformed, where the idea of "roots" can still be strong.[38] Both roots and memories are nostalgic sources of home construction; the former mostly imagined, the latter mostly experienced.[39] Arrival may be seen as the moment of touching Chilean, Colombian, or Mexican soil, or when they first saw the ports from afar. It was also the encounter with local inhabitants and the recognition of the cities where they settled, meeting families and reuniting with parents and siblings. These were emotional moments for children who had been sent in the *Kindertransport* to England and later emigrated to Chile, but they were also uneasy encounters for orphaned children who came to Mexico. These first experiences were very important but not definitive; some of them changed as survivors interacted with local people and learned about their culture, thus reconciling themselves to their otherness.

Initially some survivors felt uncomfortable and wanted to return home. Ida Benadon, an adult Sephardic survivor of Auschwitz from Greece, remembers: "Well, I arrived in Mexico, my impression . . . was horrible . . . I came from Athens . . . cosmopolitan and Mexico seemed like a town. I was shocked . . . I wanted to take the airplane and go home."[40] Pola Blatman and Ingeborg Grzymisch make similar remarks about Colombia and Chile, as both underdeveloped and primitive countries.[41] In contrast, survivors like Margot Guthman had completely different impressions of Latin America: "I remained with my mouth open when I arrived in Chile, I did not imagine . . . Chile was not known, in books very short articles were published . . . Valparaíso fascinated us, in Santiago we did not need anything, all the trunks arrived, we lived in my uncle's house."[42]

In contrast to Chile and Mexico, where capital cities became the principal settlement centers, survivors lived in diverse locations in Colombia: Bogotá, Cali, Medellin, Armenia, and Manizales.[43] This may be related to the regional presence of Jewish communities and the availability of economic opportunities, given the more regionalized character of the country. Each of these cities were spaces of reception and settlement that became interchangeable over time according to individual and family preferences, and this was probably due to the presence of larger Jewish communities in them.

Most survivors who stayed in Latin America found warm welcomes, opportunities for work and education, Jewish spaces for socialization, and the possibility to live in freedom and safety. In their minds, the region acquired a fixed character.[44] Carrying intense mobility trajectories, Holocaust survivors constructed notions of rootedness, belonging, and self-understanding of what it meant to be part of a mobile community-victim of genocide, in diverse ways: some found mobility associated with their "cosmopolitanism" or "adaptation capacity," while others related it to the difficulty of re-creating a homeland.

New geographies acquired meaning in relation to close interactions with families and organized Jewish communities. Family members became helpers: they provided housing, got them a job, supported them finding a school, and overcome their initial cultural shock.[45] When asked about the type of welcome they had from host families, a large number of survivors represent it in positive terms. But in some cases, survivors mention having been silenced by their close relatives or told not to publicly share their Holocaust stories. Survivors found organized Jewish communities in the three countries,[46] even if still growing. According to census data, the Jewish communities of Chile and Mexico increased significantly from 1930 until 1950. By 1950 the Jewish community of Mexico was the largest with 17,574 people, compared to 11,496 in Chile.[47] It may be inferred, based on later data, that the Jewish community in Colombia was smaller.

The moment of arrival could be extended to the first months when work and educational opportunities were still limited, survivors struggled to learn the local language, and housing met basic needs only. Only in Mexico do survivors remember not being able to work because of visa restrictions, working illegally, and facing the threat of deportation instead. In contrast, in Chile and Colombia, the majority of young adults and adult survivors refer to working immediately after their arrival, without references to having done so illegally. But despite initial challenges, a large number of survivors experienced arrival as the end of displacement. The narratives sometimes refer to a sense of relief resulting from their arrival in a place where they were no longer persecuted, but they also emphasize the difficulties faced in surviving and only gradually developing a new life project. The survivors seldom mention state or social antisemitism as a local problem.

Given the ethnic and demographic character of the three host countries, notions of "foreignness" and the legitimacy of minorities were constructed in singular ways. In Chile, mass European immigration had led to a multiethnic society with a *de facto* tolerance toward minorities, counterbalancing the primordial, territorial, and religiously homogeneous profile that the state aspired to achieve. In contrast, in Mexico and Colombia, immigration was not encouraged, and the original ethnic composition of the population enhanced the content of national identity in its homogenous character. Even when the ruling classes were of Spanish descent, the large majority of the population was Indian or *mestizo*. The fact that Mexico rooted its conception of national identity on an ethnic-religious cultural model—*mestizaje*—based on fusion, assimilation, and the merging of the Spanish Catholic and indigenous populations, this might have impacted the survivors' self-perception as "foreigners."[48] Their testimonies also reveal a sense of inferiority, together with a perceived lack of understanding or empathy on the part of their hosts, even fellow Jews. Alberto Bejarano, a child survivor who emigrated with his family from Bulgaria, noted: "For a certain period of time we were not happy here. Of course, we were foreigners, my parents' Spanish was rusty, it was *ladino*, the children's Spanish was very limited. We felt a little bit, truly, of less value. Our clothes, what we looked like . . . we felt inferior . . . out of place."[49] In Chile, survivors did not feel excluded, marginalized, or inferior, and in relation to the existing Jewish community, their integration was swift, similar to Colombia. Regardless, the survivors in all three countries found spaces for socialization and adaptation in Jewish community venues.

Jewish economic networks helped survivors not only immigrate but also settle in the three countries. When Rosita Kugler went to Armenia, Colombia, with her family, she remembers having become part of the economic realm: "my father had his business there . . . it was a coffee region, the best coffee of Colombia and the world . . . of which we feel very proud."[50] Like Rosita, other survivors settled in the economically vibrant coffee area in Colombia, where Jewish networks were strong.

Arrival was also shaped by national political contexts. Survivors who arrived in Colombia in the first years after the war remembered "the violence" (*La Violencia)*, the period of civil war that began in 1948 and was detonated by the assassination of the left-wing leader Jorge Eliecer Gaitán. This period was characterized by the systematic dispossession of rural communities and forced displacement across the country, which was evidently difficult for survivors who had very recently escaped Nazism. Jaime Bromberg, from Poland, noted that: "On April 29, 1948, I still found ashes in Barranquilla, buildings of the revolution still burning. We had to go the following day to Bogotá . . . it was worse than in Barranquilla, here there was a curfew, they could not go out on the streets because there were so many bad guys."[51] The survivors' memory of the war was still very fresh, and thus it was not surprising to connect the violence in Colombia with their Holocaust experience: "The war is after us."[52]

Natural disasters were also traumatic events for survivors. On January 24, 1939, there was an earthquake in the Chilean city of Chillán. It affected nearby cities, leaving several neighborhoods completely destroyed. Ingeborg Grzymisch remembers that she arrived in the city of Temuco, not far from Chillán, several months later: "I visited . . . that house and the tremor began, the . . . building . . . in the apartment, every lamp moved . . . we hugged each other because . . . you never know . . . I told my mother: I will not stay here."[53] Soon after arriving in Chile, Ingeborg and her mother emigrated to Argentina, where they stayed. Although other survivors were also sent by authorities to cities affected by the earthquake, their testimonies do not make connections between this devastating event and Nazi persecution, in contrast to the violence in Colombia.

Emigration may have been experienced as a radical break from the Holocaust, but the Holocaust remained an interpretative reference point for national events in the region. Marion Mostny, originally from Germany, remembers how their later migration from Chile to the United States in the mid-1960s was in response to political conditions there, but it was also profoundly framed by their experience in Nazi Germany:

> When the communists were coming to Chile or it looked as if they were, we decided . . . paranoia or threat or whatever that was, we said we are not going to wait until 1939 . . . this is 1933, it's coming, we can sell our business, we can sell our house, we can take our children wherever we want to . . . that was part of this feeling of . . . we said we are not going to repeat the mistake they made.[54]

In her view, her parents' mistake was not to take the rise of Hitler in 1933 seriously, thinking that it would be a temporary event or that the Nazis' antisemism did not refer to them, German Jews.

Some survivors experienced emigration as closure to their process of mourning. However, most survivors refer to how the memory of Holocaust remained present in their lives: nightmares, spontaneous reminders of traumatic experiences, fear and pain. Nevertheless, the majority of survivors rebuilt their lives in a region that they valued highly. Their testimonies were given many years after the end of World War II. In Chile, survivors gave testimony in larger numbers when there was a memory boom regarding the civil-military dictatorship in the 1990s. Until then, they spoke very little with others about their Holocaust experiences, including their relatives, and tried to lead a normal life in spite of their trauma. While testimonies show different layers of mourning, it is possible to distinguish the return from the Holocaust and profound trauma from a later peaceful life of achievement. To some extent it seems a closed cycle, one with a happy starting point in prewar Europe and a peaceful point of closure in Latin America. The Holocaust defined the life of the survivors, but migration to Latin America enabled them to build histories and places, giving new meanings to their past and present.

CONCLUSIONS

The emigration of Jewish survivors to Colombia, Chile, and Mexico had two principal meanings: it was the means by which they survived

Nazi persecution; and migration offered the possibility of a new beginning in completely different and distant settings. Although the narratives show that survivors never lost their historic agency, the migratory journey enabled them to reclaim aspects of it. Emigration to Latin America was in many cases preceded by intense mobility before and during the war, which generated a rupture in the survivors' biographies.

Although none of the three countries were destinations sought or desired by these emigrants, the vast majority found rootedness in them, building new spaces both socially and culturally, endowing them with meanings and appreciating them more with the passage of time. Colombia, however, is different from Chile and Mexico. It was not always the final destination for survivors. This transmigration or route interruption requires further research, given that the survivors' narratives provide only vague references to their reasons to emigrate once again. The rootedness of the majority, however, restored a sense of permanence and fixity. Despite this, however, political events such as *La Violencia* in Colombia and Allende's presidency and the Pinochet dictatorship in Chile still shaped the personal trajectories of a minority of the survivors, leading to new voluntary migrations and political exile in the Chilean case.

Emigration to Latin America needs to be conceived as a phenomenon at a continental scale in which political-national contexts and events in Europe and Latin America overlapped with personal and family biographies, and especially with the decisions and possibilities of action by survivors. How temporalities—national and personal—interacted in the diverse scenarios of Europe and Latin America is a problematic that requires further study and the analysis of a wider sample of testimonial and archival sources.

NOTES

1. Latin America attracted little attention as a place of refuge until 1935 and 1938, following James G. McDonald's visit to the region, *Kristallnacht,* and the Evian Conference.

2. Not every government had the same immigration policy, and different numbers of Jewish refugees arrived in each country: Chile received the third largest number of Jewish refugees (13,000), after Argentina (between 32,000 and 39,000) and Brazil (23,500). In contrast, Mexico received only 1,800–2,000 Jewish refugees, while Colombia received about 4,000. For its part, Bolivia became a recipient of Jewish refugees escaping Nazism when

Argentina, Brazil, Chile, and Mexico denied them access. Haim Avni, "The Role of Latin America in Immigration and Rescue during the Nazi Era (1933–1945)," in *A General Approach and Mexico Case Study* (Washington, D.C.: Woodrow Wilson International Center for Scholars, 1986); Avraham Milgram, *Entre la aceptación y el rechazo: América Latina y los refugiados judíos del nazismo* (Israel: Yad Vashem, 2003).

3. Migration studies of Holocaust survivors to Latin America were initially developed in the 1980s. See Haim Avni, "Latin America and the Jewish Refugees: Two Encounters, 1935 and 1938," in *The Jewish Presence in Latin America*, ed. Judith Laikin Elkin and Gilbert W. Merks (Boston: Allen and Unwin, 1987), 45–68.

4. Avni, "Latin America and the Jewish Refugees," 68; Haim Avni, "The War and the Possibilities of Rescue," in *The Shoah and the War*, ed. Asher Cohen, Yehoyakim Cohen, and Yoav Gelber (New York: Peter Lang, 1992), 373–92; Haim Avni, *Argentina and the Jews: A History of Jewish Immigration,* 2nd ed. (Tuscaloosa: University of Alabama Press, 2002); Leonardo Senkman, *Argentina, la Segunda Guerra Mundial y los refugiados indeseables, 1933–1945* (Buenos Aires: Grupo Editor Latinoamericano, 1991); Leo Spitzer, *Hotel Bolivia: The Culture of Memory in a Refuge from Nazism* (New York: Hill and Wang, 1999); Jeffrey Lesser, *Welcoming the Undesirables: Brazil and the Jewish Question* (Berkeley: University of California Press, 1995); Allen Wells, *Tropical Zion: General Trujillo, FDR, and the Jews of Sosúa* (Durham, N.C.: Duke University Press, 2009); Marion Kaplan, *A Dominican Haven: The Jewish Refugee Settlement in Sosúa, 1940–1945* (New York: Museum of Jewish Heritage, 2008); Milgram, *Entre la aceptación y el rechazo*, 10; Judit Bokser Liwerant, "Cárdenas y los Judíos: Entre el exilio y la inmigración," *Canadian Journal of Latin American and Caribbbean Studies* 20 (1996): 39–40; Irmtrud Wojak, *Exil in Chile: Die deutsch-jüdische und politische Emigration während des Nationalsozialismus 1933-1945 (Berlin: Metropol Verlag,* 2007); Daniela Gleizer, *Unwelcome Exiles: Mexico and the Jewish Refugees from Nazism, 1933–1945* (Leiden: Brill, 2014).

5. Some works mention aspects of Jewish immigration to Colombia, but there are no in-depth case studies. Colombia's immigration policy changed from being more open under President Alfonso López Pumarejo to placing conditions on the reception of Jewish refugees and turning into a highly restrictive policy by 1939. See Avni, "Latin America and the Jewish Refugees," 53–57; Avni, "War and the Possibilities of Rescue," 379; Sonia Galvis and Alberto Donadio, *Colombia Nazi* (Bogotá: Siglo del Hombre, 2002). We found one study of German immigration to Colombia: Lina Leal, "Colombia frente al antisemitismo y la inmigración de judíos polacos y alemanes 1933–1948" (unpublished master's thesis, Universidad Nacional de Colombia, 2011).

6. A new study of Jewish immigration to Ecuador has as its main focus the period from 1933 to 1945. Daniel Kersffeld, *La migración judía en Ecuador: Ciencia, cultura y exilio 1933–1945* (Quito: Academia Nacional de Historia, 2018).

7. Milgram's *Entre la aceptación y el rechazo* uses a case-study approach and a comparative perspective to examine the relation between the type of government and the immigration policy towards Jewish refugees.

8. Some exceptions are the works of Leo Spitzer, Marion Kaplan, Jeffrey Lesser, and Allen Wells which address not only the arrival of survivors in Bolivia, the Dominican Republic, or Brazil, but also their acculturation and integration processes.

9. On transnational experiences of survival in the former Soviet Union, see *Shelter from the Holocaust: Rethinking Jewish Survival in the Soviet Union*, ed. Edele Mar, Sheila Fitzpatrick, and Atina Grossman (Detroit, Mich.: Wayne State University Press, 2017).

10. Simone Gigliotti, *The Train Journey: Transit, Captivity, and Witnessing in the Holocaust* (New York: Berghahn Books, 2009). Although Gigliotti refers to the train deportations of Jews in the Holocaust, thus considering a different context and situation, we consider that the three moments of departure, journey, and arrival help frame the migration experience of survivors to Latin America.

11. Alessandro Portelli, "Sobre la diferencia de la historia oral," in *Historias orales: Narración, imaginación y diálogo,* ed. Alessandro Portelli (Rosario: Prohistoria, 2016), 23. On the two possibilities offered by oral history, see Lynn Abrams, *Oral History Theory* (London: Routledge, 2010), 22.

12. Research on Holocaust survivors' immigration and social integration is less common. The studies analyze processes of migration, acculturation, and integration after the Holocaust, but do not include Latin America in their geographical scope. See Francoise S. Ouzan and Manfred Gerstenfeld, *Postwar Jewish Displacement and Rebirth 1945–1967* (Leiden: Brill, 2016). More is known on Argentina than Chile, Colombia, or Mexico. From 1945 to 1949, an estimated maximum of 1,500 Jews entered Argentina legally. Haim Avni's *Argentina and the Jews*, as cited in Natasha Zaretsky, "Child Survivors of the Shoah: Testimony, Citizenship and Survival in Buenos Aires," in *The New Jewish Argentina: Facets of Jewish Experiences in the Southern Cone*, ed. Adriana Brodsky and Rein Raanan (Leiden: Brill, 2013), 315–40. Based on published works and testimonies of Holocaust survivors, a new study sheds light on the reasons why survivors migrated to Argentina, their integration into the national society, and the ways in which the local environment influenced them. Yossi Goldstein, "Between Memory and History: Holocaust Survivors in Argentina: A Case Study," *Moreshet: Journal for the Study of the Holocaust and Antisemitism* 15 (2018): 219–52.

13. According to Noah Shenker, testimonies emerge not only from individual experiences, but also from institutionally embedded practices with particular aims. Noah Shenker, *Reframing Holocaust Testimony* (Bloomington: Indiana University Press, 2015). *Voces de la Shoá Memoria Viva* can be accessed in the U.S. Holocaust Memorial Musuem's virtual archive.

14. We thank the USC Shoah Foundation for providing access to its Visual History Archive (VHA) during the Interdisciplinary Research Week (08/17). The Fortunoff collection was accessed from the U.S. Holocaust Memorial Museum (Silberman follow-up grant, 07/17).

15. We follow the flexible and inclusive conception of Dwork and Van Pelt, as well as Grossman's definition of "survivor." Debórah Dwork and Robert Jan Van Pelt, *Flight from the Reich: Refugee Jews, 1933–1946* (London: W. W. Norton, 2009); Atina Grossman, *"Remapping Survival: Jewish Refugees and Lost Memories of Displacement, Trauma, and Rescue in the Soviet Union, Iran, and India," USC Shoah Foundation,* https://sfi.usc.edu/news/2016/05/11429-atina-grossmann-lecture-summary.

16. The projection of these data through circular migration plots has implied the use of open-source software packages; in this case, we used Circos to customize migration plots in R. Later on, in order to make it suitable for this publication's format, some of these plots were made graphically adequate with Adobe Publisher.

17. Nikola Sander, Abel Guy, et al., "Visualizing Migration Flow Data with Circular Plots," *VID Working Papers* 2 (2014): 8–9.

18. In migration studies, circular visualizations in plots depict large sets of information reflecting locations of origin and destination, volume, direction of flows, and main corridors of movement. See Sander, Guy, et al., *"Visualizing Migration Flow Data,"* 8–9; and Nikola Sander, Abel Guy, and Fernando Riosmena, "The Future of International Migration: Developing Expert-Based Assumptions for Global Population Projections," *VID Working Papers* 7 (2013): 25. We used open-source software packages for the projection of these data into circular migration plots. Circos was used to customize migration plots in R, and Adobe Publisher to represent them graphically.

19. Anne Kelly Knowles, Tim Cole, and Alberto Giordano, eds., *Geographies of the Holocaust* (Bloomington: Indiana University Press, 2014). On global refugee movements in the twentieth century, see Tony Kushner and Katharine Knox, *Refugees in an Age of Genocide* (London: Routledge, 2001). See also Tony Kushner, *Journeys from the Abyss: The Holocaust and Forced Migration from the 1880s to the Present* (Liverpool, Eng.: Liverpool University Press, 2017).

20. Simone Gigliotti, "A Mobile Holocaust? Rethinking Testimony with Cultural Geography," in *Hitler's Geographies: The Spatialities of the*

Third Reich, ed. Paolo Giaccaria and Claudio Minca (Chicago: University of Chicago Press, 2016), 329–47.

21. Klara Sternbach remembers that she knew Chile "like you or me, you know, of the darkest Africa." Klara Sternbach, interviewed by Voces de la Shoá Memoria Viva, Santiago, Chile, 2010.

22. Recent studies of migration include a comparative lens to understand push-and-pull factors as a convergence between groups, places, time periods, and institutions that either facilitate or complicate journeys. Irene Bloemraad, "The Promise and Pitfalls of Comparative Research Design in the Study of Migration," *Migration Studies* 1 (2013): 27–43.

23. Enrique Brahm and Jorge Montes, "Obstáculos jurídicos y consulares a la inmigración judía durante el gobierno de Arturo Alessandri 1932–1938," *Revista de Estudios Histórico-Jurídicos* 35 (2013): 523–45. On Chile, see Wojak, *Exile in Chile*, 34. On Mexico's immigration policy, see Liwerant, "Cárdenas y los judíos," 248–50, in Milgram, *Entre la aceptación y el rechazo*, 248–76; and Gleizer, *Unwelcome Exiles*, 33–35. On Colombia, see Leal, "*Colombia frente al antisemitismo*," 24–27.

24. USC Shoah Foundation VHA, Interview with Eva Gutmann (Mexico City, Mexico, 1998).

25. The World Jewish Congress (WJC) was founded in 1936. During the Holocaust, it tried to persuade neutral countries and the International Red Cross to rescue Jews. On the WJC's activities during the Holocaust, see Gregory J. Wallance, "The World Jewish Congress during World War II," in *The World Jewish Congress: 1936–2016*, ed. Menachem Rosensaft (New York: World Jewish Congress, 2017), 25–45; and Zohar Segev, "The World Jewish Congress during the Holocaust: Between Activism and Restraint," in *New Perspectives on Modern Jewish History* (Berlin: de Gruyter Oldenbourg, 2017).

26. HICEM was founded in 1927 to concentrate emigration efforts, with the exception of emigration to Palestine. It was formed by HIAS, ICA, and EMIGDIRECT.

27. Joint promoted Jewish emigration to Latin America from the end of the nineteenth century. In the Southern Cone, it became a key element of the project of the Jewish Colonization Association. Yehuda Bauer, *American Jewry and the Holocaust: The American Jewish Joint Distribution Committee* (Detroit, Mich.: Wayne State University Press, 1989), 146.

28. Vicki Caron, *Uneasy Asylum: France and the Jewish Refugee Crisis* (Stanford, Calif.: Stanford University Press, 1999); Greg Burgess, *Refuge in the Land of Liberty: France and Its Refugees, from the Revolution to the End of Asylum, 1787–1939* (New York: Palgrave Macmillan, 2008); Susan Zuccotti, *The Italians and the Holocaust: Persecution, Rescue, and Survival* (Lincoln: University of Nebraska Press, 1996); Liliana Picciotto Fargion,

"The Shoah in Italy: History and Characteristics," in *Jews in Italy under Fascist and Nazi Rule, 1922–1945*, ed. Joshua D. Zimmerman (Cambridge: Cambridge University Press), 209–23; Irene Flunser Pimentel and Claudia Ninhos, "Portugal, Jewish Refugees, and the Holocaust," *Dapim: Studies on the Holocaust* 29, no. 2 (2015): 101–13.

29. Spitzer, *Hotel Bolivia*, 61.

30. Leo Spitzer writes about the "in-between" passage between continents and existences, which sparked a complex constellation of emotions and responses. Spitzer, *Hotel Bolivia*, 58.

31. Walter Borchheim, interviewed by Voces de la Shoá Memoria Viva, Santiago, Chile, 2010.

32. USC Shoah Foundation VHA, Interview with Marion Mostny (San Mateo, California, 1998).

33. Place and space are understood in the terms used by geographer Yi-Fu Tuan, for whom space is a "container of human activity" while place is described as a "center of felt value." Cited in Knowles, Cole, and Giordano, *Geographies of the Holocaust*, 4.

34. Voces de la Shoá Memoria Viva, Interview with Lea Kleiner (Santiago, Chile, 2011).

35. USC Shoah Foundation VHA, Interview with Alberto Bejarano (Mexico City, Mexico, 1997).

36. Haim Avni, *Pertenencia y alteridad: Judíos en/de América Latina, Cuarenta años de cambio* (Madrid: Iberoamericana; Frankfurt: Vervuert, 2011).

37. Yi-Fu Tuan, *Space and Place: The Perspective of Experience* (Minneapolis: University of Minnesota Press, 2011), 411.

38. Dan Feng and Werner Breitung, "What Makes You Feel at Home? Constructing Senses of Home in Two Border Cities," *Population, Space, and Place* 24, no. 3 (2018).

39. Blunt finds the term "nostalgic" negatively connoted when directed at an unattainable past. Alison Blunt, "Collective memory and productive nostalgia: Anglo-Indian homemaking at McCluskieganj," *Environment and Planning D*, 21(6), (2003): 717–38. Cited in Feng and Breitung, "What Makes You Feel at Home?"

40. USC Shoah Foundation VHA, Interview with Ida Benadon (Caracas, Venezuela, 1997).

41. USC Shoah Foundation VHA, Interview with Pola Blatman (North Miami Beach, Florida, 1996); Interview with Ingeborg Grzymisch (Buenos Aires, Argentina, 1997).

42. Voces de la Shoá Memoria Viva, Interview with Margot Guthman (Santiago, Chile, 2009). See also USC Shoah Foundation VHA, Interview with Rosita Kugler (Miami Beach, Florida, 1997).

43. Bogotá is the capital city, but other cities or regions are economi-

cally relevant: Barranquilla, Manizales, Armenia, Medellin, Buenaventura, and Cali.

44. For the notion of fixity and movement, see Gigliotti, "*A Mobile Holocaust?*" 335. In our study we refer not only to objective fixity (i.e., being confined in a ghetto or a camp), but to the re-creation of a sense of permanence or stability in a Latin American destination following migration from Europe.

45. Voces de la Shoá Memoria Viva, Interview with Ursula Michels (Santiago, Chile, 2009).

46. There had been a Jewish presence in the region since the colonial period and the arrival of Sephardic and crypto-Jews. But the immigration that set the demographic foundations and the shape of contemporary Jewish life there began in the late nineteenth century and continued until the mid-twentieth century. See Avni, "Latin America and the Jewish Refugees," 49.

47. Sergio Della Pergola, "Demographic Trends of Latin American Jewry," in *The Jewish Presence in Latin America,* ed. Elkin Leikin and Gilbert Merks (Boston: Allen and Unwin, 1987), 85–134.

48. See Avni, "Latin America and the Jewish Refugees," 52–53; Judit Bokser Liwerant, "Latin American Jewish Identities: Past and Present Challenges: The Mexican Case in a Comparative Perspective," in *Identities in an Era of Globalization and Multiculturalism: Latin America in the Jewish World,* ed. Judit Bokser Liwerant et al. (Leiden: Brill, 2008), 81–105.

49. USC Shoah Foundation VHA, Interview with Alberto Bejarano (Mexico City, Mexico, 1997).

50. USC Shoah Foundation VHA, Interview with Rosita Kugler (Miami Beach, Florida, 1997).

51. USC Shoah Foundation VHA, Interview with Jaime Bromberg (Manizales, Colombia, 1998).

52. USC Shoah Foundation VHA, Interview with Karolina Teicher (Cali, Colombia, 1998).

53. USC Shoah Foundation VHA, Interview with Ingeborg Grzymisch (Buenos Aires, Argentina, 1997).

54. USC Shoah Foundation VHA, Interview with Marion Mostny (San Mateo, California, 1998).

III. D·I·G·I·T·A·L M·E·T·H·O·D·S, D·I·G·I·T·A·L M·E·M·O·R·Y

Adrien Dallaire

A Different Approach to Microhistory: The Arrests of the Jews of the Vaucluse as Seen through Quantitative Prosopography

HOW THREE-QUARTERS OF THE JEWS OF FRANCE SURVIVED THE Holocaust has long been a subject of debate between historians. Perhaps this has something to do with the fact that the first answers were provided in the immediate aftermath of the war. After the Liberation, top Vichy officials—such as Pierre Laval and Xavier Vallat—sought to frame their participation in the persecution of the Jews during the war in the best light possible. Consequently, they were among the first to articulate what came to be known as the "shield thesis." The Vichy regime, so the argument went, had served as a shield against the worst of the German demands regarding the Jews. This, they argued, had the happy result of saving thousands of Jews—and in particular, those of French origin—from destruction. Some former bureaucrats were willing to admit that *l'État français* had occasionally done some distasteful things, but only half-heartedly and only with the best intentions. The conclusion to be drawn was clear: the death toll would have been significantly higher had it not been for the actions (or deliberate inaction) of some high-ranking Vichy officials.[1]

This interpretation of events was later rehashed by some of the most prominent scholars in the field. "In France, the process by which the Jews were destroyed was the result of the Franco-German armistice," argued Raul Hilberg in his seminal work *The Destruction of the European Jews*:

> From 1940 to 1944, the unequal relationship between victor and vanquished translated itself into an unending flow of German demands, which would have been difficult to oppose. Among these

> demands was the destruction of the Jews. In its reaction to German pressure, the Vichy government attempted to maintain the destruction process within certain limits. These limits were essentially intended to slow the evolution of this process in its entirety. The French authorities sought to avoid all radical action. They recoiled before the adoption of measures without historical precedent. When German pressure intensified in 1942, the Vichy government withdrew behind a second line of defence. The foreign Jews and the immigrants were abandoned to their fate, while an attempt was made to protect Jewish nationals. To a certain extent, this strategy worked. By forsaking a fraction, a large part of the totality was saved. If the Vichy Regime was able to negotiate the fate of the Jews with the victors, this was because of one very simple reality: the Germans needed the help of the French.[2]

According to Hilberg's interpretation, then, the Vichy authorities were, at best, reluctant participants in the destruction process; at worst, they were pragmatists willing to sacrifice one group—the foreign-born Jews—in order to save another—the French *Israélites*.

The "shield thesis" in its various forms has not gone unopposed. Indeed, since its formulation, certain elements of it have largely been refuted. In their groundbreaking *Vichy France and the Jews*, Michael R. Marrus and Robert O. Paxton challenged the idea that, in France, the destruction of the Jews had simply been the product of a German diktat, made possible by the power disparity between France and the Third Reich. Rather, they saw the impetus for the anti-Jewish measures that ultimately facilitated this destruction as having come primarily from the Vichy regime itself with, at least initially, little or no prodding from the Germans. Thus, far from having been reluctant participants in the destruction of the Jews, Vichy officials had, in the eyes of these authors, actively contributed to their persecution.[3]

To a certain extent, Marrus and Paxton also took issue with the idea that certain Jews—in particular, those of foreign extraction—were deliberately sacrificed in order to protect those of French origin. Such a theory, they argued, presupposes that the Vichy government had a clearer understanding of the intentions and long-term goals of the Germans than the contemporaneous evidence seems to suggest. Their main objection, however, was that even if Vichy had, to the detriment of the foreign-born, shown a clear preference for sparing their Jewish compatriots from deportation, nothing suggests that this objective had ever been part of a concrete, well thought-out plan or that it was ever given priority over other, more immediate goals.[4]

In truth, the second pillar of the "shield thesis" (what could be dubbed the "French-foreign dichotomy") has been considerably more resilient to criticism than the first (the idea that the Germans forcibly coerced the Vichy regime to participate in the destruction process), with many authors continuing to insist that, in France, the foreign Jews were sacrificed so that their French coreligionists could be saved. Looking at the victim ratio between these two "categories" of Jews, it is not very difficult to see why. Of the 80,000 Jewish victims of the Holocaust in France, approximately 25,000 of them were French and 55,000 of them were foreign.[5] Since French and foreign Jews numbered, respectively, 195,000 and 135,000 in 1940, it is clear that, both numerically and proportionally, one group suffered significantly higher losses than the other.[6] Indeed, although the numbers vary slightly from one source to another, it is estimated that 39–42 percent of the foreign-born Jews living in France during the Second World War were murdered, while this was the case for "only" 12–13 percent of those of French origin.[7] In many instances, this discrepancy has been viewed through the lens of the "shield thesis." "The proportion of Jews of French origin which were victims of the Final Solution is greatly inferior to that of the foreign and stateless Jews," wrote Serge Klarsfeld. "Vichy, in its concessions to the Germans, placed the French Jews at the back of the line."[8]

This chapter challenges what has become *the* framework for understanding the Holocaust in France, by analyzing the arrests of the Jews of the department of Vaucluse in southeast France[9] through the prism of quantitative prosopography. Ultimately, it argues that, through its repeated appeals to the French-foreign dichotomy, the historiography has placed far too much emphasis on one factor for explaining the fate of the Jews in France during the war. Part of this stems from the fact that this dichotomy brings together very different individuals into two artificially homogeneous groups and, in so doing, obscures other, more important differences between them.

QUANTITATIVE PROSOPOGRAPHY

Prosopography—in Lawrence Stone's influential definition, "the investigation of the common background characteristics of a group of actors in history by means of a collective study of their lives"—has, in recent years, continued to gain in popularity and is being applied by historians of all periods to answer an ever-increasing number of questions on a wide range of topics.[10] Historians of the Holocaust have not been absent from adopting this approach. Christopher Browning's classic *Ordinary Men* can be seen as a qualitative collective biography of one group of German perpetrators.[11] More recently, Nicolas Mariot and Claire Zalc have mixed quantitative and qualitative approaches in their study of 991 Jewish victims from Lens.[12]

Some authors believe that it is a mistake to try and define prosopography as either a quantitative or a qualitative approach since, in their view, it is both.[13] They would, therefore, almost certainly object to the use of the adjective "quantitative" to describe the particular form of prosopography used here. In many ways, their objection would be warranted because prosopography is, in fact, a hybrid of sorts: a *qualitative* approach is used to extract the information contained in the sources, while a *quantitative* one is at the heart of the statistical analyses performed on the collected data. In this case, however, the qualifier is appropriate because of the preponderant role played by quantification in the current study.

By collecting and analyzing vast quantities of data on the individuals belonging to the group being investigated, the particular traits and characteristics of that population as a whole become visible. This reduces the risk of giving undue weight to exceptional and, consequently, unrepresentative individual cases.[14] Prosopography also has the added advantage of enabling researchers to detect previously hidden links between variables. In this regard, there is an obvious affinity between microhistory and prosopography. Indeed, just as the microhistorical approach has enabled historians, by narrowing the scale of observation, to uncover things that would have remained difficult—if not impossible—to perceive at a larger, or macro, scale, the use of quantitative methods and statistical analyses allows for the identification of patterns that would not be discernible otherwise, that is, not even at a traditional micro scale. Nevertheless, one should not overestimate the potential of the prosopographical method or view it as some kind of panacea for the standard difficulties involved with historical research. In fact, as one author has noted, prosopography sometimes reveals only "partial linkages" between variables and often allows for only "statistically modest generalizations." "The statistical modesty of those conclusions," the same author nonetheless asserted, "does not deny their historical value."[15]

There has been some hesitation over whether prosopography is best described as a "method," a "technique," an "approach," or an "analytical tool." The reluctance to attribute the label of "method" to prosopography stems from the fact that prosopography is not uniformly applied in all circumstances. Indeed, one's approach to it varies depending on the sources at one's disposal, the questions needing to be answered, and the data analysis tools available. Thus, there is not one single and unique way to conduct prosopography, but many. As Katharine S. B. Keats-Rohan remarked, "Prosopography is . . . a plural rather than a singular beast, so attempts at definition are necessarily more descriptive than prescriptive."[16]

Even if the intermediary steps vary from historian to historian and from subject to subject, prosopographical research is largely conducted in two stages. First, there is the collection and the compiling of the data pertaining to each individual in the identified group. Second, there is the analysis and the interpretation of that data. Regardless of the chosen topic or the time period considered, the creation of a database is often necessary to both of these tasks. This database, moreover, will generally be quite elaborate, given that the goal is to systematically collect a vast array of information on the individuals concerned. For this study, the database contains the following information—and, indeed, much more—on the Vauclusian Jews: age, gender, nationality, place of origin, marital status, education, military service, profession over time, and movements throughout the war. In total, the database is comprised of over three million cells, including 1,125 variables for 2,826 Jews.[17]

SOURCES

The database that underlies the current research is the product of a systematic gathering and compiling of a large number of different sources from several archives:[18] files on individual Jews, police and arrest reports, deportation lists, concentration camp records, and, most importantly, lists and censuses of the Jews of the department. There are a total of 177 lists recording the names of Jews in the Vaucluse, or 183 when the postwar commemorative plaques (which are scattered throughout the department) are factored in. The lists—which contain anywhere from one or two names to several hundred, and, in certain cases, in excess of 1,500—provide the names of, and a wide range of socio-demographic information on, 9,445 individuals, many of whom can be found on multiple lists.[19] Typically, they provide the following information on the individuals concerned: surname and given name, date and place of birth, nationality, profession, marital status, and address. There are, in general, four different types of lists: first, censuses conducted with the deliberate intent of tracking the Jews, including the two department-wide censuses of July 1, 1941, and May 13, 1944, as well as the local ones (the *États des Israélites*) conducted in fall 1943; second, lists recording the names of the foreign Jews targeted for—or evading—arrest (1942); third, lists concerning the Jews who were part of a *Groupe de travailleurs étrangers* (foreign labor battalion) (1942); and finally, lists of those having received the "Jewish stamp" on their identification papers and ration cards (1943).

Lists are also the basis for identifying the Jews who were apprehended by the authorities. Much like those discussed above, these too are not entirely uniform, and vary in content depending on the year in question. In the summer of 1942, the prefecture of Vaucluse prepared a list of the foreign Jews who had been singled out for arrest during the large-scale roundup operation that was planned for, and executed on, August 26. In the wake of the operation, the prefecture produced a second list. This one provided the names of those who had been successfully apprehended and taken to the camp des Milles in Aix-en-Provence, in order to await their transfer to the Occupied Zone and subsequent deportation to the East.[20] Although these lists enable one to determine the identities of those who were targeted and apprehended during the operation, they do not provide any context behind the event itself. Fortunately, they are complemented by detailed police reports, which offer insight into most—though not all—of the arrests carried out on that fateful day in August 1942.

While similar to those discussed above, the lists concerning the years 1943 and 1944 are, nevertheless, quite different. There are, in fact, two sets of lists that help track the arrests that took place in the department of Vaucluse during those years, though neither of them exclusively concerns the Jews. The first is something of a master list. Dated November 24, 1944, the document is titled "List of persons arrested for political motives by the German police forces."[21] Among other things, this list provides the date of, and the motive for, the arrest of the 565 persons apprehended in 1943 and 1944, of whom 106 were Jews. It also indicates the name of the authority that conducted the arrest. The second set of lists—individually titled "Monthly statement of the arrests of French nationals operated by the German authorities" (or, occasionally, "by the Italian authorities")—present a month-by-month breakdown of the arrests that took place in the Vaucluse from April 1943 to July 1944. In general, these "monthly statements" provide much of the same information as that contained in the "master list." Both sets of lists are needed to identify arrested Jews, however, as some names appear on only one of them.

All of these sources are, both in terms of quality and quantity, well suited for a study privileging a quantitative approach. They are, however, for lack of a better word, dry. Indeed, with the impersonal nature of the various lists used, it would be easy to lose sight of the human element of the story. But that, precisely, is the most important part. An attempt was therefore made to give a voice to the victims themselves using the testimonies of thirty-one Jewish survivors of the department of Vaucluse, found in the USC Shoah Foundation's Visual History Archive, to complement the otherwise dispassionate documents.

ARRESTS OF THE VAUCLUSIAN JEWS, 1942–1944

On the afternoon of March 13, 1944, Ginette Cherkasky and three of her relatives were arrested at her family's residence at 72 Rue Joseph Vernet in Avignon. Recalling the event many years later, Ginette believed that the operation had been a targeted one, but not in the conventional sense of the word. The Gestapo, it seemed to her, had not set out to arrest specific Jews, but rather specific "types" of Jews.

> I returned home [after lunch]. When I entered, the Gestapo was in the hallway. And they were asking my father, "Are you a Jew?" So, I said to them, "They are not Jews. Leave them alone!" . . . My father, my brother, and my nephew were made to take off their pants in the kitchen. They were not even given the opportunity to show their [fake] Orthodox or Protestant baptismal certificates. Perhaps if I had not said anything . . . Because my mother was home, a cousin was home . . . and her daughter [was as well] . . . , and they were not arrested. . . . *They* [the Germans] *had come to take the men*. I was there, and I opened my mouth, so they [prob-

> ably] told themselves, "Well, it's only one more [person]. That's not a problem." If I had not said anything, maybe [I would not have been arrested] . . . But, in the end, . . . who knows.[22]

Out of at least seven Jews present, only four were taken into custody. All of them were French citizens and all of them—with the exception of Ginette—were "men," although not of military age.[23] All four were taken to the local prison in Avignon and transferred to Les Baumettes in Marseille two days later. From there, they were sent to Drancy.[24] Exactly one month after their arrest, they were deported to Auschwitz, aboard convoy 71.[25] Only Ginette returned.

Raids of this nature were more commonplace than one might believe, as the following example shows. Having been separated from their children for several months, Joseph (Szloma) Waysenson and his wife, Yenta, managed to reunite their family in the winter of 1943 in a small village named Goudargues, located about fifty kilometers northwest of Avignon.[26] "In [this] village of [the department of] Gard," recalled their second eldest son, Adolphe, "we had the impression that the war would end and that we will have survived."[27] Sadly, however, this was not to be the case for all of them. Joseph was arrested on March 9, 1944, and was deported to Kaunas/Reval a few weeks later.[28] Neither his wife nor his children "ever saw him again. Never again."[29]

The context surrounding Joseph's arrest is known through the testimonies of two of his sons, Adolphe and Léon, who were eleven and fifteen years old respectively when their father was apprehended. Although they had both been eyewitnesses to the event, the two men do not describe it in exactly the same way. In one account, Joseph was home when a single German officer arrived to arrest him. Given a few minutes to pack a small piece of luggage, he was forced onto a truck and was taken away.[30] According to the second account, one or two German officers, accompanied by several soldiers, presented themselves at the Waysenson residence. Informed by Yenta that Joseph was not home but at work, the Germans proceeded to arrest him there instead.[31] Although the two accounts differ in a number of ways (proving, if proof were needed, that memory is a fickle thing), they come together in their observation that only one category of Jews had been targeted by the operation: adult males. "Other men had been rounded up in the village," remembered Adolphe. "He [the German officer] said . . . , 'Today, we come for the men. . . . Later, we will come for you. So do not leave.' . . . They never did come back to get us."[32] Thus, like the roundup of the Cherkasky family four days later, the arrest of Joseph Waysenson was another instance in which a male Jew of a certain age was singled out by the authorities and apprehended, while their younger or female relatives were not.

But was there really a link between a Jew's age and gender and whether or not they were arrested, as these examples suggest? In order to answer this question, one turns to quantitative analysis of the database. Two Chi-square (χ^2) tests of independence[33] were performed to assess the relationship between the fact of—or of not—having been arrested and one's gender and date of birth. In both cases, the analyses revealed that the relationship was statistically significant. For each of these variables, moreover, there was only a 0.1 percent (or a 1 in 1,000) chance that the results that were obtained could be attributable to chance.[34] Consequently, being arrested was not independent of one's age and gender. This is not to suggest, however, that the association between the independent variables ("date of birth" and "gender") and the dependent variable ("arrest") was strong. Indeed, when the Cramer's V measure (which is similar to a correlation coefficient) was taken into account, it was observed that both had only a very weak effect on the variable "arrest."[35] A weak—and even a very weak—effect is an effect, nonetheless.

When one takes a closer look at the numbers, it appears that male Jews between the ages of 35 and 65 were—if ever so slightly—more vulnerable to arrest than others (see tables 8.1 and 8.2). Of the 527 Vauclusian Jews arrested, 332—or 63 percent—were male, and 192—or 36.4 percent—were female.[36] From these figures, one might be tempted to conclude that men were much more likely than women to be apprehended. It is, however, important to consider the number of males and females arrested in relation to the total number of those of each gender. Numbering 1,475 and 1,311, respectively, male and female Jews were—in terms of their gender—arrested in the following ratios: 22.5 percent and 14.6 percent. Thus, Jewish men were not only arrested in greater numbers than their female counterparts, but were also apprehended in larger proportions to their share of the total Jewish population than women.

Interpreting the statistics concerning the Jews' age is considerably more difficult, because the contingency (or cross-tabulation) table pertaining to this variable is, unlike the one for the variable "gender,"

Table 8.1. Arrests of the Vauclusian Jews according to Gender

Gender (χ^{2***})	Arrested	Not Arrested	Total
Male	332 (22.5%)	1,143 (77.5%)	1,475 (100.0%)
Female	192 (14.6%)	1,119 (85.4%)	1,311 (100.0%)
Total	524 (18.8%)	2,262 (81.2%)	2,786 (100.0%)

If the information pertaining to the variable under discussion was not known, it was not included in the analyses.
Legend: *** indicates that the relationship between the variables was significant and that the "*p*-value" (or probability value) was smaller than 0.001 ($p < .001$), meaning that there was a 0.1 percent (or a 1 in 1,000) chance that the results that were obtained could be attributable to chance; ** indicates that the relationship was significant and that $p < .01$, meaning that there was a 1 percent chance that the results that were obtained could be attributable to chance; * indicates that the relationship was significant and that $p < .05$, meaning that there was a 5 percent chance that the results that were obtained could be attributable to chance.

not a simple binary. Although the Jews were either male or female, they could be of a multitude of different ages. From a statistical point of view, it was thus necessary to group these into several smaller categories or age groups. This, however, made interpreting the data much more difficult and also increased the risk of error when doing so. The numbers nevertheless point to a few general trends, even if, once again, the association between the two variables ("date of birth" and "arrest") was very weak. When looking at table 8.2, one notices that—both in terms of hard numbers and in terms of ratios—the Jews born between 1880 and 1909 were slightly more vulnerable to arrest than those from other age groups, while those born before 1880 or between 1940 and 1944 appear to have been the least vulnerable.[37]

But could this truly have been the case? Were middle-aged Jews—that is, individuals who were between 35 and 65 years old at the time the arrests took place—more vulnerable than younger and, likely, more physically capable Jews, especially those of military age, who represented a greater danger to the German occupation authorities? As counterintuitive as it may seem, it must be remembered that Léon Cherkasky and Joseph Waysenson were both within this age group at the time of their arrest, at 60 and 48 years old, respectively. The two men shared common features in addition to their age, however. Both

Table 8.2. Arrests of the Vauclusian Jews according to Date of Birth

Date of Birth (χ^{2***})	Arrested	Not Arrested	Total
1940 to 1944	5 (9.4%)	48 (90.6%)	53 (100.0%)
1930 to 1939	32 (13.7%)	202 (86.3%)	234 (100.0%)
1920 to 1929	71 (17.7%)	330 (82.3%)	401 (100.0%)
1910 to 1919	76 (18.7%)	330 (81.3%)	406 (100.0%)
1900 to 1909	135 (23.8%)	432 (76.2%)	567 (100.0%)
1890 to 1899	107 (24.0%)	339 (76.0%)	446 (100.0%)
1880 to 1889	66 (21.4%)	243 (78.6%)	309 (100.0%)
Before 1880	33 (9.6%)	310 (90.4%)	343 (100.0%)
Total	525 (19.0%)	2,234 (81.0%)	2,759 (100.0%)

of them were married and were arrested while in the presence of their wife and children, who, for the most part, were not apprehended alongside them.

One wonders, therefore, if factors such as marital status and familial situation hold the key to explaining the greater vulnerability of the Jews within this particular age group. It certainly seems to be part of the explanation. When Chi-square tests were performed to assess the relationship between the variables "marital status" and "number of children" and the variable "arrest," the analyses revealed that the relationship was once again statistically significant.[38] Married Jews were, for instance, arrested nearly one-and-a-half times more frequently than their single counterparts. In addition, parents with a greater number of children appear to have been more vulnerable than those with fewer of them in their care.[39] Is it possible that the sheer size of certain families hindered their mobility and thus their ability to hide (as Nicolas Mariot and Claire Zalc suggest in their study of Lens),[40] thereby making certain members of these households—and in particular, the patriarchs—even more vulnerable to arrest measures? It is a distinct possibility.

Missing from the discussion thus far is an analysis of the relationship between the Jews' arrest and their "status"—that is, whether they were viewed as French or foreign by the German and Vichy authorities.[41] As has previously been pointed out, the French-foreign dichotomy—a central pillar of the "shield thesis"—has held and, indeed, continues to hold a rather predominant position in the historiography. But is this justified? Indeed, is the French-foreign distinction really as important in explaining the fate of the Jews in France during the war as it has generally been made out to be? Or does it bring together very different individuals into two artificially homogeneous groups, thereby obscuring other, possibly more important differences between them?

These questions are not intended to suggest that French and foreign Jews were equally vulnerable to arrest. They were not. Even to the naked eye, the numbers would seem to indicate that one group—foreign Jews—found themselves in the authorities' crosshairs (see figure 8.3). But what do the statistics say? The analyses once again revealed that there was a statistically significant relationship between the two variables ("status" and "arrest"). This time, however, the association between them was considerably stronger than it had been for the variables "gender" and "date of birth." Rather than being very weak, the strength of the association was, in this instance, moderate. And since the contingency table is a relatively small one (three-by-two), it is not very difficult to see why (see table 8.4). The rates of arrest between the two categories of Jews are particularly instructive: 262 (of 949) foreign Jews—or 27.6 percent—were arrested, while that was the case for only 165 (of 1,492) French Jews—or 11.1 percent. Thus, foreign Jews were apprehended nearly two-and-a-half times more frequently than their French counterparts.

But was "status" truly the decisive factor when it came to arrests? In other words, did one's fate hinge on a couple of labels—"French" and "foreign"—more than anything else? Or was there more at play? In addition to the analyses performed on the variable "status," others were conducted on the variables "nationality" and "country of origin"—variables that, at first glance, appear to be quite similar. They are not the same, however, nor do they provide identical results. Both point to the same conclusion, nonetheless: that the French-foreign dichotomy is rather simplistic and is thus of dubious explanatory value when attempting to understand why certain Jews were arrested, while others were not.

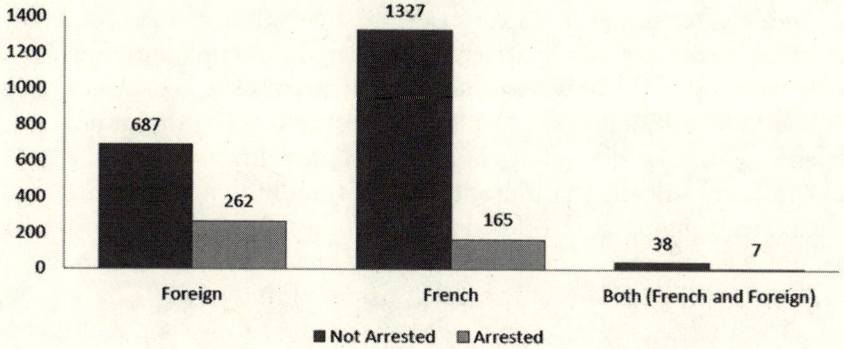

Fig. 8.3. Arrests of the Vauclusian Jews according to Status. Courtesy of the author.

Table 8.4. Arrests of the Vauclusian Jews according to Status

Status (χ^{2***})	Arrested	Not Arrested	Total
French	165 (11.1%)	1,327 (88.9%)	1,492 (100.0%)
Foreign	262 (27.6%)	687 (72.4%)	949 (100.0%)
Both	7 (15.6%)	38 (84.4%)	45 (100.0%)
Total	434 (17.5%)	2,052 (82.5%)	2,486 (100.0%)

Much as it had been for the Jews' date of birth, it was necessary to group the variables "nationality" and "country of origin" into fewer categories.[42] These variables were, moreover, coded in a couple of different ways, in order to allow for a multilayered analysis of the data. The first method was to group the countries of origin into three categories based on their geopolitical situation during the war: first, France or Country of French North Africa; second, German-Occupied or German-Allied Country; and third, Enemy or Neutral Country. Thus, if a Jew had been born in Switzerland, their "country of origin" was coded as "Enemy or Neutral Country." If, on the other hand, they had been born in Tunisia, they were included in the category "France or Country of French North Africa." The same logic applied to the Jews' nationality. If, for example, one was a Belgian national, they were counted as a "Citizen of a German-Occupied or German-Allied Country." If, however, they were British, they were considered a "Citizen of an Enemy or a Neutral Country." Coding the variables in such a way allowed for the grouping of nationalities and countries of origin that—although different—were, for all intents and purposes, the same. This approach offered the possibility of observing trends that would have remained imperceptible had the numerous nationalities and countries of origin only been considered in isolation.

The analyses revealed that there was a statistically significant relationship between the variables "country of origin" and "arrest," even if the strength of the association between them was weak. In many ways, the numbers seem to confirm what was found with the analyses concerning the variable "status," namely, that Jews born in France or in French North Africa were less vulnerable to arrest than others. There is, however, a distinction to be made between those who were born in countries that were occupied by, or allied to, Germany and those who were not, with the former being more vulnerable to arrest than the latter (see table 8.5). There was thus, quite visibly, a hierarchy within the group commonly referred to in the historiography by the generic term "foreign Jews," a fact that, in and of itself, suggests that the traditional framework (i.e., the French-foreign dichotomy) for understanding the fate of the Jews in France during the Holocaust should perhaps be reassessed. This is all the more evident when the Jews' nationalities are taken into account.

With another Chi-square test, it was observed that a statistically significant relationship existed between the variables "arrest" and "nationality," when the latter was coded along the same lines as the variable "country of origin." The difference, in this instance, was that the association between them was moderate rather than weak. Initially, the results did not appear all that different from those that had been obtained from the previous analyses. In terms of their vulnerability to arrest, French Jews (and those who were citizens of a country of French North Africa) seem to have had the upper hand over those of foreign nationalities. Upon closer examination, however, it was discovered that the category "Citizen of an Enemy or a Neutral Country" contained an unrepresentative subgroup with the numerical strength to distort the conclusions drawn. Indeed, of the 35 Jews of this category to have been apprehended, 30 of them—or 86 percent—were Turks. In the

Table 8.5. Arrests of the Vauclusian Jews according to Country of Origin

Country of Origin (χ^{2***})	Arrested	Not Arrested	Total
France or Country of French North Africa	192 (12.9%)	1,293 (87.1%)	1,485 (100.0%)
German-Occupied or German-Allied Country	272 (29.2%)	660 (70.8%)	932 (100.0%)
Enemy or Neutral Country	57 (21.6%)	207 (78.4%)	264 (100.0%)
Total	521 (19.4%)	2,160 (80.6%)	2,681 (100.0%)

presence of such a subgroup, it was decided to rerun the analyses while excluding the Turkish Jews. The results were fascinating.

Looking at table 8.6, one can see that the Jewish citizens of an enemy or a neutral country were *less* vulnerable to arrest than those of France or of a country of French North Africa—with both groups being considerably less vulnerable than those with the citizenship of a German-occupied or German-allied country. Thus, contrary to what is generally believed, in the case of the department of Vaucluse, it was preferable to be a *foreign* Jew during the Second World War, *provided* that one was of the "correct" nationality. Indeed, it was best to be a citizen of a country that was at war with the Third Reich or had chosen to remain neutral (with one exception: Turkey). The Jews in the greatest danger were those of a nationality of a country that was occupied by, or allied to, Germany. Even here, however, there were certain gradations.

As has been mentioned, the variable "nationality" was grouped and coded in a number of different ways. Although it had been useful to group the different nationalities based on the corresponding nations' geopolitical situation during the war, it was also deemed necessary to consider them individually. This was not initially possible, however, because the number of nationalities represented by only a handful of Jews prevented any attempts at statistical analysis. Thus, the choice was made to include only the nationalities that, numerically, were above a certain threshold. The threshold was set at twenty-seven Jews—or (when rounded) one percent of the total Jewish population of Vaucluse.

Table 8.6. Arrests of the Vauclusian Jews according to Nationality

Nationality (χ^{2***})	Arrested	Not Arrested	Total
Citizen of France or of a Country of French North Africa	197 (11.7%)	1,492 (88.3%)	1,689 (100.0%)
Citizen of a German-Occupied or German-Allied Country	238 (30.4%)	545 (69.6%)	783 (100.0%)
Citizen of an Enemy or a Neutral Country (Including Turkey)	35 (19.0%)	149 (81.0%)	184 (100.0%)
Citizen of an Enemy or a Neutral Country (Excluding Turkey)	*5 (6.2%)*	*75 (93.8%)*	*80 (100.0%)*
Total (Including Turkey)	470 (17.7%)	2,186 (82.3%)	2,656 (100.0%)
Total (Excluding Turkey)	*440 (17.2%)*	*2,112 (82.8%)*	*2,552 (100.0%)*

Statistically significant, the relationship between the individual nationalities and the variable "arrest" was the strongest one yet, at moderately strong.[43] Although many observations could be made from these analyses, only the most important ones will be discussed here. Of the nine nationalities having met the established threshold, two had been significantly more vulnerable to arrest than the others—German and Austrian Jews (see table 8.7). In fact, more than half of the Vauclusian Jews of these nationalities were ultimately arrested. It was, thus, an arrest ratio far exceeding that of the seven other nationalities. Indeed, the runners-up on the vulnerability ladder were the Romanians, at an arrest rate just below 30 percent—with three more (Turks, Greeks, and Poles) not far behind.

But what could account for such a large disparity? Part of the explanation seems to lie in the various policies that the countries occupied by—and more importantly, allied to—Germany had toward their Jewish nationals living abroad: policies that, in many instances, changed on account of the evolving military and geopolitical situation. Take Romania, for example. Although the country's Jews were eligible for arrest and deportation through the year 1942, they were declared off limits as of April 1943, a fact that spared a certain number of them living in France.[44] Other governments were also occasionally successful in protecting—if only for a certain period of time—their Jewish citizens from arrest and deportation. In the case of the German and Austrian Jews, however, there was no one to mitigate their

Table 8.7. Arrests of the Vauclusian Jews according to Nationality (2)

Nationality (χ^{2***})	Arrested	Not Arrested	Total
French	197 (11.7%)	1,491 (88.3%)	1,688 (100.0%)
Belgian	4 (14.8%)	23 (85.2%)	27 (100.0%)
German	65 (52.4%)	59 (47.6%)	124 (100.0%)
Austrian	25 (52.1%)	23 (47.9%)	48 (100.0%)
Polish	99 (25.0%)	297 (75.0%)	396 (100.0%)
Russian	2 (3.9%)	49 (96.1%)	51 (100.0%)
Romanian	12 (29.3%)	29 (70.7%)	41 (100.0%)
Turkish	30 (28.8%)	74 (71.2%)	104 (100.0%)
Greek	12 (25.5%)	35 (74.5%)	47 (100.0%)
Total	446 (17.7%)	2,080 (82.3%)	2,526 (100.0%)

destruction. Thus, although it is difficult to say for certain, it seems likely that this fact helps explain the rather lopsided arrest ratios of the Jews of these two nationalities in particular.

The variable "nationality" was not the only one to have had a moderately strong (and, indeed, borderline strong) effect on the variable "arrest," however. One's date of arrival in France also appears to have been important. As can be seen from table 8.8, Jews who arrived in the country in the post-1933 period were considerably more vulnerable to arrest than those who had immigrated prior to that time. The numbers relating to Austrian and German Jews are emblematic of this fact. Of the forty-three of them who were arrested and whose date of arrival in the country is known, only one had immigrated to France prior to 1933. Five had entered the country between 1933 and 1935, while the remaining thirty-seven had done so after 1936.

To a certain extent, this can be explained by the massive roundup that had taken place throughout the Unoccupied Zone in August 1942: a roundup that had initially targeted the foreign Jews having entered

Table 8.8. Arrests of the Vauclusian Jews according to Date of Arrival in France

Date of Arrival in France (χ^{2***})	Arrested	Not Arrested	Total
Prior to 1933	19 (33.3%)	38 (66.7%)	57 (100.0%)
Between 1933 and 1935	8 (80.0%)	2 (20.0%)	10 (100.0%)
1936 or Later	116 (66.3%)	59 (33.7%)	175 (100.0%)
Total	143 (59.1%)	99 (40.9%)	242 (100.0%)

France after January 1, 1936, but which was subsequently extended to include certain categories of those who had done so between 1933 and 1935.[45] Since this operation alone netted over 15 percent of all the Vauclusian Jews arrested during the war, it is perhaps not that surprising that the criteria which had underpinned it would have had a certain influence on the variable "arrest." What all of this suggests is that, for the Jews of Germany at least, there really had not been a "right time" to flee the country following Hitler's rise to power. Whether one had left for France in the wake of the "anti-Jewish demonstrations of 1933" (like the Franck family) or whether one had only been prompted to do so following *Kristallnacht* in November 1938 (like the Eichbergs and the Kempowskis) mattered very little.[46] Both groups were at a greater risk of arrest than those who had made the journey westward prior to the advent of the Nazis: Jews who, in the words of Susan Zuccotti, "had had more time and opportunity to put down roots, learn the language and customs, and make the local contacts indispensable for survival."[47]

In the final analysis, it would appear that the French-foreign dichotomy, which continues to pervade the historiography, is too narrow a framework for understanding the fate of the Jews in France during the war. When it came to arrests, other factors (including one's age, gender, nationality, and date of arrival in France) were equally as important as—if not more important than—one's "status." The analyses performed do not, however, enable one to determine precisely which of these had the greatest influence on the variable "arrest." Indeed, even if the present statistics provide a means for determining the strength of the association between different variables, they do not allow one to compare the degrees of association between themselves. Nor do they indicate which factor prevailed at any one given moment, as the case of the De Ciavès family illustrates.

Although none of them were born in the Netherlands, Moïse and Rachel De Ciavès, and their son, Elie Lucien, were considered foreign Jews of Dutch nationality by the German and Vichy authorities.[48] Of the three, only one—Moïse—was arrested and deported.[49] Was he singled out because of his age and gender, much like Joseph Waysenson had been? And why were Rachel and Elie Lucien allowed to walk free? Was it because the former was a woman and the latter was a young child? Or did it have more to do with their countries of origin? After all, Moïse was born in Turkey, while his wife and son were, respectively, born in the United Kingdom and France, making them, in theory, less vulnerable to arrest.[50] Was one of these factors primarily responsible for the differences in their fate? Or did each of them play a role? It is, in truth, anybody's guess.

NOTES

1. Michaël R. Marrus and Robert O. Paxton, *Vichy et les Juifs* (Paris: Calmann-Lévy, 1981), 475.

2. Raul Hilberg, *La Destruction des Juifs d'Europe, Volume II* (1985; Paris: Gallimard, 2006), 1122–23.

3. Marrus and Paxton, *Vichy et les Juifs*, especially chapter 1 ("*Les Premières Mesures*"), 17–43.

4. Marrus and Paxton, *Vichy et les Juifs*, 477.

5. The breakdown of these 80,000 Jewish victims is as follows: 76,000 deported to the "east"; 3,000 deceased in French concentration camps; and 1,000 executed in France. See Serge Klarsfeld, *Mémorial de la déportation des Juifs de France* (Paris: Fils et filles des déportés juifs de France, 2012), 17.

6. Serge Klarsfeld, *Vichy-Auschwitz: Le Rôle de Vichy dans la Solution finale de la question juive en France, 1943–1944* (Paris: Fayard, 1985), 179–81.

7. These estimates are based on the numbers provided by Klarsfeld. See Klarsfeld, *Vichy-Auschwitz*, 179–81; and Klarsfeld, *Mémorial*, 17. See also Susan Zuccotti, *The Holocaust, the French, and the Jews* (New York: Basic Books, 1993), 283–84.

8. Klarsfeld, *Vichy-Auschwitz*, 190.

9. The Vaucluse is a French administrative division comprised of 151 communes (cities, towns, and villages) with its capital in Avignon.

10. Lawrence Stone, "Prosopography," *Daedalus* 100, no. 1 (Winter 1971): 46. See also Koenraad Verboven, Myriam Carlier, and Jan Dumolyn,

"A Short Manual to the Art of Prosopography," in *Prosopography: Approaches and Applications: A Handbook*, ed. Katharine S. B. Keats-Rohan (Oxford: University of Oxford Press, 2007), 69.

11. Christopher R. Browning, *Ordinary Men: Reserve Police Battalion 101 and the Final Solution in Poland* (New York: Harper Perennial, 1993).

12. Nicolas Mariot and Claire Zalc, *Face à la persécution: 991 Juifs dans la guerre* (Paris: Odile Jacob, 2010). See also Alberto Giordano and Anna Holian, "Retracing the 'Hunt for Jews': A Spatio-Temporal Analysis of Arrests during the Holocaust in Italy," in *Geographies of the Holocaust*, ed. Anne Kelly Knowles, Tim Cole, and Alberto Giordano (Bloomington: Indiana University Press, 2014), 53–88.

13. Katharine S. B. Keats-Rohan, "Introduction: Chameleon or Chimera? Understanding Prosopography," in *Prosopography: Approaches and Applications*, ed. Keats-Rohan, 12.

14. Verboven, Carlier, and Dumolyn, "A Short Manual," 36.

15. William Bruneau, "Toward a New Collective Biography: The University of British Columbia Professoriate, 1915–1945," *Canadian Journal of Education* 19, no. 1 (1994): 67.

16. Keats-Rohan, "Introduction: Chameleon or Chimera?" 20.

17. 2,826 Jews represents nearly 1 percent of the total Jewish population in France at the outset of the war. See Hilberg, *La Destruction des Juifs d'Europe*, 2,1131.

18. The research for this chapter was conducted using sources from the following archives: Archives Départementales de Vaucluse (Avignon, France); Archives Nationales de France (Pierrefitte-sur-Seine, France); Centre de Documentation Juive Contemporaine (Paris, France); Archives of the International Tracing Service (U.S. Holocaust Memorial Museum, Washington, D.C.); USC Shoah Foundation's Visual History Archive (accessed via the University of Ottawa); and Yad Vashem's "Central Database of Shoah Victims' Names" (available online).

19. The majority of these lists are found in two boxes at the *Archives Départementales de Vaucluse* in Avignon (hereafter ADV)—7W15 and 7W16. The others are located in boxes 20W10 and 3W265.

20. See Prefecture of Vaucluse, "Liste des Israélites étrangers entrés en France depuis le 1er janvier 1936 qui doivent faire l'objet des mesures prévues par les instructions de M. le Ministre Secrétaire d'État à l'Intérieur en date des 5 et 15 Août 1942," and "Liste des Juifs étrangers ayant fait l'objet des mesures de regroupement prévues par les instructions de M. le Ministre Secrétaire d'État à l'Intérieur en date des 5 et 15 août 1942 et ayant rejoint effectivement le camp des Milles (B.D.R.) du 23 au 26 août 1942," undated documents (probably August 1942), ADV, 7W16.

21. Division Commissioner and District Chief of Police in Avignon,

"Liste des personnes arrêtées pour des raisons politiques par les services de police allemands," November 24, 1944, ADV, 6W37.

22. USC Shoah Foundation Visual History Archive (hereafter VHA) 25852, Interview with Ginette Kolinka (1997) (emphasis added).

23. Ginette's father, Léon, was sixty years old at the time. Her younger brother, Gilbert, was twelve, and her cousin, Georges Marcou, was "fifteen years old . . . fourteen and a half, but he looked eighteen." USC Shoah Foundation VHA 25852, Interview with Ginette Kolinka (1997).

24. USC Shoah Foundation VHA 25852, Interview with Ginette Kolinka (1997).

25. Deportation list of convoy 71, Centre de Documentation Juive Contemporaine (hereafter CDJC), C71_10 and C71_36.

26. USC Shoah Foundation VHA 32680, Interview with Adolphe Waysenson (1997).

27. USC Shoah Foundation VHA 32680, Interview with Adolphe Waysenson (1997).

28. Deportation list of convoy 73, CDJC, C73_34.

29. USC Shoah Foundation VHA 32680, Interview with Adolphe Waysenson (1997).

30. USC Shoah Foundation VHA 32680, Interview with Adolphe Waysenson (1997).

31. USC Shoah Foundation VHA 32673, Interview with Léon Waysenson (1997).

32. USC Shoah Foundation VHA 32680, Interview with Adolphe Waysenson (1997). Léon, for his part, remembered overhearing one of the German officers telling the mayor of Goudargues that "'We no longer have room on the trucks. You are responsible for the [Waysenson] family. We will come back soon to pick up the rest of the family.'" USC Shoah Foundation VHA 32673, Interview with Léon Waysenson (1997).

33. The Chi-square (χ^2) test is used to examine the relationship between two variables. Specifically, it allows one to determine whether there is a statistically significant association between them, with the null hypothesis being that they are independent of one another. Once the Chi-square test has been performed, a significance level is calculated to determine the probability of finding the observed results. A statistically significant result is one where the "p-value" (or probability value) is smaller than 0.05 ($p < .05$), meaning that there is a 5 percent chance that the result that was obtained could be attributable to chance (for other p-values, see the legend below table 8.1). Neither the Chi-square nor the p-value provides an indication as to the strength of the association between the two variables, however. In order to measure the strength of this association, one must use either the Phi or Cramer's V measures, depending on the size of the contingency (or cross-tabulation) table.

34. This was determined by way of the *p*-value (or probability value), which, in both cases, was smaller than 0.001.

35. The Phi measure was only used in the few instances in which the contingency (or cross-tabulation) table was a simple binary, such as it was for the variable "gender." In every other instance, the Cramer's V measure was used instead.

36. The gender of three arrestees—or 0.6 percent of the total—could not be determined.

37. The eldest and youngest Jews may have been the least vulnerable to arrest because they were often the least mobile of all of them. Reduced mobility could at times be a sufficient motive to exempt a particular individual from arrest measures. See the Report by the Prefect of Vaucluse to the Minister of the Interior (also communicated to the Regional Prefect of Marseille) concerning the roundup of August 26, 1942, September 12, 1942, ADV, 7W16.

38. The *p*-value of the analyses performed for the variable "marital status" was smaller than 0.001. Based on the Phi measure obtained, the strength of the association between the variables "marital status" and "arrest" was very weak. With regard to the variable "number of children," the *p*-value was smaller than 0.01. The Cramer's V measure indicated that the strength of the association between the variables "number of children" and "arrest" was weak.

39. Parents having five or more children were the most vulnerable to arrest, while those having just one or two were the least vulnerable. Those having three or four children in their care were, for their part, in the middle of the vulnerability spectrum.

40. In their study of the Jews of Lens, Nicolas Mariot and Claire Zalc found that the most important factor determining whether Jews remained at their place of residence or fled was not their age, their nationality, or their perception of danger, but the size of their family. The individuals who had children were more likely to stay, while those who were single or married but without children left in greater numbers. Moreover, the more children one had, the more likely they were to remain. "The increase in the number of persons in a family considerably reduced the mobility of each of its members." Mariot and Zalc, *Face à la persécution*, 126–28.

41. The category to which a particular person belonged can be gleaned from the various lists that differentiate between these two "types" of Jews. The department-wide censuses of July 1941 and May 1944, for instance, are both comprised of two parts: one concerning the French Jews; the other, foreign Jews. One's "status," it must be stressed, appears to have been only tenuously linked with one's nationality and place of origin. Indeed, one sometimes gets the impression that the labels "foreign" and "French" were somewhat

inconsistently applied. For example, Salomon Chazine, a Russian Jew born in Berdychiv in 1895, and who obtained French citizenship through naturalization, was invariably considered a French Jew. On the other hand, Joseph and Victor Léon—two French Jews born in Paris—were identified on separate occasions as belonging to each of the categories. A possible explanation is that their parents, Abraham and Sultana Léon (née Behau), had both been born in Turkey and were themselves considered foreign Jews. For information concerning Chazine, see Police Commissariat in Apt, "État des Juifs s'étant présentés dans nos services pour l'apposition de la mention 'Juif,'" February 9, 1943, and "État des Israélites—Ville d'Apt," September 1, 1943, ADV, 7W15; Prefecture of Vaucluse, "Liste nominative des Juifs français (13 mai 1944)," May 13, 1944, ADV, 7W15. For information concerning the Léon family, see Prefecture of Vaucluse, "État nominatif des Juifs français résidant en Vaucluse au 1er juillet 1941," July 1, 1941, ADV, 7W15; "Liste des étrangers qui désireraient retourner dans leur pays d'origine," undated document (after March 1943), ADV, 7W16.

42. This was necessary because the Vauclusian Jews were a group comprised of individuals of thirty nationalities, having been born in thirty-seven different countries (based on a map of 1939). Further complicating the situation was the fact that, in many instances, there were only a handful of Jews (often three or fewer) belonging to a certain nationality or having been born in a particular country. In order not to violate the assumptions of the Chi-square test, however, no more than 20 percent of the cells of the contingency table can have a count less than five.

43. In fact, the Cramer's V measure indicated that the strength of the association between the variables was just shy of being outrightly strong, rather than only moderately so.

44. Georges Wellers, *L'Étoile jaune à l'heure de Vichy: De Drancy à Auschwitz* (Paris: Fayard, 1973), 75–76.

45. See Director General of the National Police to the Regional Prefect of Marseille, August 5, 1942, and Regional Prefect of Marseille to the Prefects of the Region of Marseille, August 24, 1942, ADV, 7W16.

46. See Letter from Friedel Franck to the Prefect of Vaucluse, August 26, 1940, ADV, 3W265; USC Shoah Foundation VHA 42083, Interview with Irene Osborne (1998); USC Shoah Foundation VHA 48360, Interview with Marcel Kempowski (1998).

47. Zuccotti, *The Holocaust, the French, and the Jews*, 284.

48. Prefecture of Vaucluse, "État nominatif des Juifs de nationalité étrangère résidant en Vaucluse au 1er juillet 1941," July 1, 1941, ADV, 7W15.

49. Deportation list of convoy 76, CDJC, C76_18_19.

50. Prefecture of Vaucluse, "État nominatif des Juifs de nationalité étrangère résidant en Vaucluse au 1er juillet 1941," July 1, 1941, ADV, 7W15.

Anne Kelly Knowles, Paul B. Jaskot, Tim Cole, and Alberto Giordano

Mind the Gap: Reading across the Holocaust Testimonial Archive

INTERVIEWS WITH HOLOCAUST SURVIVORS HAVE BECOME INDISPENSABLE sources in Holocaust studies over the past fifteen years, particularly as a portion of the video interviews recorded by the USC Shoah Foundation has been made available online through its Visual History Archive (VHA). The VHA, like any collection of survivor interviews, privileges each testimony as a vital act of individual memory. The interviews are rich with personal experiences, observations, and particular places and events which are unique for each person. Yet, while the VHA interviews have been used in hundreds of classes and have stimulated numerous scholarly studies, the video archive poses significant problems for research that seeks to go beyond the scale of the individual. This methodological challenge stems in part from the framework that shaped the interviews and in turn shapes the archive. As Noah Shenker and Todd Presner have suggested, in some ways the VHA can be seen as telling one story 54,000 times, because the basic structure and focal points outlined in the interview guidelines so strongly influenced the narrative arc of most accounts.[1] In this sense, the structure of the interviewing process and its digital interface can unintentionally flatten out certain crucial aspects of individual experience, which can work against a critical investigation of multiple testimonies across the archive. Is there a way, however, to find undetected patterns across the testimonial archive that may be just as rich and telling as the individual narrative accounts? What interests us is the untapped potential of survivor interviews to reveal significant commonalities and differences that the technologies of video recording and digital streaming make difficult, if not impossible, to discover.

One of the less appreciated aspects of the VHA project holds partial answers to this dilemma, namely, its extremely detailed index. Trained volunteers and staff tag names, places, organizations, actions, and events in every minute of audio, drawing on a specially made, carefully structured thesaurus of terms related to the Holocaust.[2] Being able to search on any one, or any combination, of terms enables scholars to identify and study subsets of interviews with important traits in common, such as place of birth, language, a particular concentration camp or ghetto, or kinds of experience, such as forced labor. Christopher Browning, for example, worked with 123 VHA interviews with survivors of the slave-labor camp in Starachowice, Poland.[3] Tim Cole pulled 236 testimonies from the VHA using the search term "postwar visits to sites of persecution" and "Auschwitz Birkenau."[4] Better than most traditional archival finding aids, the index makes it possible to identify from the immense archive which are the "right" testimonies—and moreover the "right" segments from the "right" testimonies—to use in a case study focused on certain people, places, or events. The VHA index may have no equal as a search tool for a single archival collection.

Marvelously useful as it is, the VHA index has some drawbacks. Its approximately 62,882 terms[5] offer a wealth of avenues into the interviews' content, but without full transcripts of all of the interviews, one cannot search systematically for words and concepts that are not included in the index. Researchers then face the daunting task of listening to possibly useful interviews in hopes of finding the key words and phrases that are relevant to their interests. We encountered this problem when we realized that almost all places included in the index are proper nouns (i.e., place names). A few of the unnamed places we hoped to study are indexed, such as "barracks," but many, such as "home," are not. Others are somewhat bound by the hierarchical relationships of preset associations, such as "attic" being listed under the larger category of "hiding places." The structural hierarchy reflects the dominant categories of analysis that shaped scholarly understanding of the Holocaust in the 1990s, when the index was created. New research fields and ideas suggest new categories and terms. And although many people mentioned in interviews are listed in the index, not all are.[6] Despite these drawbacks, the VHA index represents a very large and scarcely explored collection of data in its own right.[7] By tagging millions of words and phrases in testimony, the index facilitates a radical disaggregation of historical memory, and a means of reaggregating disparate interviews for study, without disturbing the original form of each interview.

Moving beyond the given categories and terms of the VHA index, however, requires opening the entire corpus to reexamination. If researchers were able to interrogate the entire archive according to the words, phrases, concepts, and linkages relevant to their research, whatever their field or line of inquiry, the possibilities for Holocaust studies and related fields would be very exciting. In addition, enabling the analysis of any number of interviews (instead of a few, tens, or hundreds, potentially thousands and even tens of thousands) could bring a sea change in the scale and scope of studies based on survivor testimony. In anticipation of the intended eventual transcription of all of the VHA's Holocaust interviews, how should we think about approaching a corpus of perhaps as many as 300 million words, which will be one of the largest digital corpora of speech in the world?[8] What methods may be useful for analyzing this large body of information while preserving individual voices? And what methodological strategies could be developed to bridge the persistent gap in Holocaust studies between the microhistory of the individual, the mezzohistory of social groups, and the macrohistory of the systemic, political-economic project of the Nazi regime and its perpetration of genocide?

One approach to these questions draws on the geographic concept of scale.[9] The spatial patterns of the Holocaust can be found at many different scales, from the details revealed in highly localized studies of events to the broader, more general patterns apparent in the continental-scale planning by National Socialist Germany. We examined a number of the scales at which the Nazi genocide was implemented in our first set of studies based on the use of geographic information systems (GIS) and other geographic methods.[10] Holocaust scholars are very familiar with the different views and values of each scale of analysis, even if they speak of them in non-geographical terms. For instance, comparing a young woman's experience of forced movement, imprisonment, separation from family, and periods of hiding to the patterns of all women from her home region can help one gauge how representative or exceptional her experiences may have been. Conversely, establishing the sequence of major events, such as the German conquest of foreign territory or the building of death camps, provides context for understanding what was happening to whom, and when, in the course of the war and the genocide. The inherently scalar practices of providing background for context, and personal stories to illuminate larger events, structure many historical narratives and interpretations.

Yet a more sensitive geographical awareness of the nature of scale—and particularly the fact that analysis at one scale is usually inadequate to describe or explain a phenomenon viewed at a different scale—reveals that the gaps between scales of historical analysis of the Holocaust reinforce the bifurcation between perpetrator studies and victim studies that Saul Friedländer identified, and tried to overcome, years ago.[11] Ramification of the divide comes from the fact that most victim studies operate at the up-close, detailed scale of the individual and her or his immediate surroundings and experience, while perpetrator studies span a much wider range of scales, up to the most distant, abstract, regional, or global view of Hitler's inner circle and the bureaucrats and planners who translated their ideas and ideology into imperial master plans.[12] If the full texts to which the VHA index refers were available for digital analysis, however, we could visualize the narratives of many thousands of cases of forced movement during the Holocaust that the interviews contain, using scale to generalize within and between regions and nations. Developing a method to approach survivor interviews as a whole would give us at least some large-scale social perspective of Holocaust victims.[13] This method could open up valuable new fields of inquiry, given that, at the scale of the entire system, this history has been told time and again (by necessity, given the sources) from the Nazi leaders' continental perspective of the planning and implementation of genocide. With more comprehensive analysis of survivors' accounts, we could potentially see the establishment of thousands of camps and ghettos eastward across Europe and into German-occupied Soviet territory in relation to how thousands of people experienced these developing policies. Such views would not just be background, for they would still contain the strands of the individuals whose interviews collectively provide skeins of information. Our methodological goal is to find ways to combine multi-scale visualization and analysis with attention to the individual experience, memory, and narration that lie at the heart of testimony. Sensitivity to the scale of research questions as well as one's methodological approach provide new possibilities for analyzing the relationship between Nazi and Jewish histories of the Holocaust.[14]

In what follows, we will explore these issues through two related sections. First, we will discuss the development of our own spatial thinking and spatial questions over the last decade, attending to the possibilities for and problems raised by our experimental uses of GIS. The second section will explain how the problems we encountered inspired a turn to testimony, adopting methods of textual analysis that are unusual in Holocaust studies.[15] We decided to test the potential of analytical methods from corpus linguistics and natural language processing to seek, and interpret, narratives and specific expressions in oral interview transcripts. We particularly wanted to learn whether these methods could identify spatial stories and the expression of spatial experiences in testimony better than the preset terms and search methodology provided by the VHA index. After laying out the basic methodological strategies of this analysis, we will describe how we applied them to a small subset of interviews with Polish and Hungarian Jews who were involved in certain kinds of forced labor during the Holocaust. As with GIS, this digital approach has its limitations and inherent difficulties, which we will discuss toward the end of the chapter. We will argue, however, that corpus methods may provide important new means of mediating the historiographic and geographic gaps between individuals and the system, as well as bridging local, regional, and continental events.

FROM GIS TO INDUCTIVE VISUALIZATION

The concept of scale was a structuring device that guided our initial engagement with GIS. Each chapter in our edited volume, *Geographies of the Holocaust*, examined the implementation of genocidal policies at different scales, organized according to a spatial hierarchy from the continent (SS camps) to the nation (Italy), the city (Budapest), the camp (Auschwitz), and the body (evacuations). We used a wide range of methods of data exploration and spatiotemporal argument in these projects. For example, the studies of SS camps and the Budapest ghetto were based on spatiotemporal databases built in GIS, which were then visualized cartographically after subjecting the data to various GIS analytical techniques. The Italian study employed more spatial analytical methods whose visual products included maps, as well as other kinds of data visualizations. The Auschwitz project, which focused on the design and construction of the camp's built landscape, used computer-assisted design (CAD) and three-dimensional digital modeling software to create estimates of visibility within the landscape, in addition to more conventional mapping with GIS and digitally augmented historical maps.

We learned that mapping with GIS and searching for spatiotemporal patterns with quantitative methods have specific limitations for the study of the Holocaust, ones that our approach shares with broader structural analyses of the period.[16] Our most mappable data—the data with the most certain location, time, and specific attributes—was derived primarily from perpetrator documents. The absence of individuals from the majority of our maps and analyses thus stemmed from our sources as well as our methods. The challenge of representing individual victims and their experiences became most obvious in a study of evacuations from Auschwitz in January 1945. Authored by Simone Gigliotti, Marc Masurovsky, and Erik Steiner, this chapter drew on the only substantial record of the traumatic events, namely, oral interviews with survivors. The initial topographical mapping of evacuation routes showed where the victims were marched but not the nature of their experiences, as recorded in their interviews decades later. As a result, the project team decided not only to work with conventional mapping, but to also develop more experimental visualizations of a subset of six interviews with women who endured one of the evacuation marches. The team developed a series of maps that decomposed and distributed the words of the six interviews along the death march route. What emerged was a shared spatiality, with clusters of commentary about certain places interspersed with blank spots along the route.[17]

These visualizations inspired us to think afresh about how we might approach testimony as something that can be mapped and visualized in ways that are quite different from GIS-driven cartography. In another close study, this time of three survivor interviews, Knowles and team members Levi Westerveld and Laura Strom set aside GIS in favor of very low-tech exploratory methods. After listening to an interview many times, taking notes and sketching spatial ideas, they drew visual summaries of, for example, where along the course of Leon Wells's narrative major stories emerged, then colored the route/narrative according to the degree of agency or constraint he expressed in relation to events. Slow listening,[18] drawing, and diagramming revealed temporal structures within video interviews as well, structures whose patterns could help researchers more quickly search for the segments in testimony that contain survivors' spatial experiences. Although the team also used digital visualization software to test and represent their discoveries, using manual methods in the first phase of source exploration—the method Knowles dubbed "inductive visualization"—helped them remain open to what the material might suggest about victims' spatial experiences.[19]

As the evacuation routes' graphics and Knowles's work with inductive visualization indicate, we were beginning to look for ways to approach testimony that could counterbalance the foregrounding of perpetrators' sources in our GIS analyses. While we were already thinking in scalar terms with GIS, we needed a different way to bring out the scale of the individual, the particular, and the micro-analysis of spatial experience in the places where the Holocaust registered in an individual's life. However, we still had to make the leap from the particular investigation of individual interviews to the systemic level of the genocide as a whole. The challenge was clear: how to analyze spatial experience not just in a few testimonies, but in dozens, hundreds, thousands—that is, how to *scale up* the analysis in a numerical rather than geographic sense, with the goal of preserving the granularity and particularity of individual experiences within the systematic analysis of the Holocaust afforded by GIS. The answer appeared to lie in using multiple approaches to testimony and digital visualization to scale up the analysis of oral interviews without reducing victims' experience to the abstraction of perpetrator documents or the binary constraints of the database. Multiple methods would be necessary, including traditional close reading and listening, but also methods new to Holocaust studies, such as corpus linguistics and natural language processing.

CORPUS METHODS

Corpus linguistics (CL) is a set of computational methods for analyzing large bodies of text (corpora). It was originally developed in the 1960s as an empirical methodology using real language samples to study a variety of linguistic research questions and features such as grammatical structure, the frequency of words, and the emergence of neologisms. One of the earliest applications of CL, the approximately one million-word Brown Corpus of Standard American English, was drawn from samples of text found in books, government documents, periodicals, and other miscellaneous texts published in a single year (1961). Soon, much larger corpora were developed, such as the 100-million-word British National Corpus. Corpus linguistic methods were adopted to create and update dictionaries and to study the changing meaning and spelling of words over time. Examples of the latter are the many literary studies of early modern English literature and correspondence.[20] Natural language processing (NLP), a related branch of computer science, focuses on developing computational methods to analyze the semantics of words and phrases across corpora. These methodological approaches are central to what is called *text mining*, an umbrella term for using computerized searching and analysis to discover, extract, and make sense of patterns within large bodies of text. Franco Moretti's *Graphs, Maps, Trees* (2007) was a breakthrough book that introduced many humanities scholars to what CL and NLP, paired with basic visualization, could reveal about the structure of literary texts, their content, and the historical emergence and decline of authors and genres. Literary scholars soon became the dominant users of text mining techniques, although the approach has also been adopted by historians.[21] Todd Presner was among the first scholars to apply text mining to Holocaust material, specifically the content of the VHA index.[22]

Corpus methods and geographic information science, including GIS, are similar in two ways. They are both big data techniques with visualization capabilities and they are both used to discover and visualize patterns—spatial in the case of GIS and textual in the case of CL and NLP. Given their potential to visualize patterns, we wanted to see what CL and NLP methods might reveal about the structure and content of the VHA interviews. We were particularly interested in whether it would be possible to discern the spatial aspects of victims' experiences, building on our close reading of individual testimonies by survivors from Hungary and Poland. We hoped that such a proof of concept would help us develop methods that could be scaled up much further than any previous study.[23] This methodological move was initially inspired by the omission of many terms from the VHA index that are crucial for geographical research and spatial analysis. For example, the index tags the names of firms that employed forced labor, but not key terms associated with the kinds of work many captives were forced to do, such as "dig" and "carry," "build" and "we made." We therefore needed a way to create new search terms that we could then apply systematically across a large number of testimonies. This would be an iterative process, like so much digital research,[24] since we would use our initial terms to interrogate the corpus of testimony, refine the terms, apply them again, and so on, to develop a dictionary of empirically derived terms for spatial, phenomenological Holocaust analysis. Our long-term goal is to use corpus methods to explore patterns of experience and expression in hundreds and eventually thousands of interview transcripts.

The first step was to test the feasibility of these methods with a small set of sample testimonies. We chose ten VHA interviews with five Jewish women and five Jewish men who were either part of the Hungarian deportations in 1944 or were Poles who went through a number of labor camps where there was forced-labor construction activity.[25] In addition to undertaking a traditional close listening, we also analyzed them—individually, collectively, and comparatively—with five basic CL and NLP methods:

1. *Concordance*—displays a select word or phrase in the sentences in which it occurs.
2. *Frequency*—how many times a word or phrase occurs in a given corpus.
3. *Relative frequency*—compares frequency in the target corpus to frequency in a larger reference corpus. For example, comparing women's use of a term to all people's use.
4. *Collocation*—returns the instances where two or more words occur within a preset distance from one another. For example, "train" and "Auschwitz."
5. *Annotation*—also known as "tagging," annotation attaches information to words and phrases to enable semantic analysis. For example, annotation can identify parts of speech and place names. Semantic tags identify words and phrases as belonging to any of a number of preset conceptual categories, such as "movement" or "family" or "religion."

Jaskot and Knowles explored the potential of these methods to discover the spatial experiences of forced labor in Polish interviews. Cole and Giordano used them to analyze gendered differences in Hungarian interviews related to movement through the system.

WORK AND LABOR

In addition to identifying where a word occurs in a given text or set of texts, CL methods can visualize its occurrence in the temporal sequence of the interview. In the testimony of Ben Zion Gutman, for example, different words show up in different segments of his narrative, as can be seen using the concordance plot feature in AntConc (figure 9.1).[26]

This tool generates a horizontal bar chart of the text, or the corpus as a whole, and marks each incidence of a specified term's usage in the text. When Gutman referred to "work" (he never uses the term "labor") he was usually not talking about his experiences in Majdanek or Auschwitz. Nor does "work" correspond closely to his time in the "ghetto," despite the fact that he and his brother set up a rickshaw transportation business during their time in the Warsaw ghetto. Gutman talked about construction but used "job" and "work" relatively infrequently. He referred most to "work" in relation to the year and a half he spent at Monowitz and the Buna factory complex. He described Monowitz as a relative paradise compared to Majdanek and the main camp at Auschwitz because he got somewhat better food there. The work itself (bridge construction, then electrical jobs) also seemed to be of more interest to him, and he highlighted doing a good job in order to survive. Finally, this space and time were also associated with severe danger, as he injured himself at the construction work site and begged his kapo to send him to another job in the electrical unit. There, a civilian Dutch foreman gave him extra bread or left him alone to do his work and recover. The visualization in figure 9.1 points to this moment as a section of the interview with particularly frequent mentions of work and a particular place. It raises the question of whether labor connected to survival may leave distinctive temporal and spatial traces in testimonies, traces that may point to the importance of places outside the well-known environs of major concentration camps and ghettos. The term "work" had a particular meaning to this survivor. Do similar patterns exist across thousands of interviews? To answer this question, we need a thesaurus of work-related terms to parse specific kinds of forced-labor spaces, experiences, and chronologies.

In moving from labor to socially significant relationships, Gutman spoke of his brother Leiby many times while relating their early years growing up in Błędów, Poland, during ghettoization when they

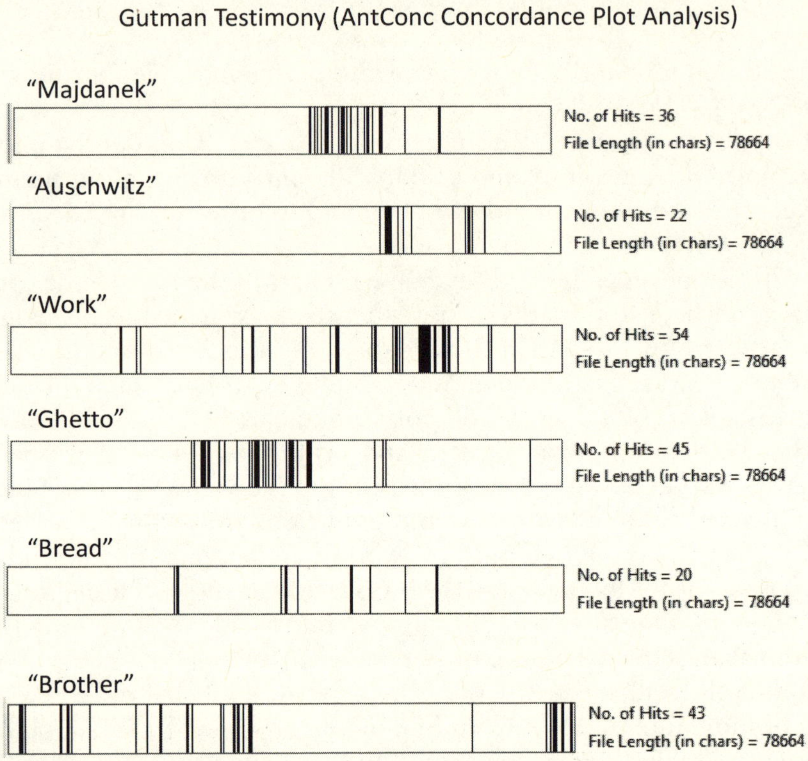

Fig 9.1. Words in the temporal sequence of Ben Zion Gutman's Holocaust video interview. This concordance plot shows when in the sequence of the interview Gutman used each of the six words noted on the left. He referred to work at many points, sometimes but not always in close relation to his narrative of experiences in Majdanek and Auschwitz. The silence about his brother marks their sudden parting and Gutman's sad reflections on his death while reflecting on family mementos at the end of the interview. Image by the authors.

worked together, and when talking about his life after the Holocaust. His brother's death, and the loss of many others in his family, were marked in the long gap—a visualization of absence—during the periods when Ben was transported out of the Warsaw ghetto (1943), his lonely struggle to survive starvation ("bread" often correlates with getting "only a little" or nothing to eat), the last violent phase of the war, and his intensive labor. These points of analysis could be drawn out by listening closely to the interview. What the CL method suggests is that it may be possible to find—and then analyze—similar periods of social connection and isolation, deprivation and labor, looking across many more interviews.

Other methods allowed us to look at the spatialization of labor during the genocide in different ways. Wmatrix, a set of CL and NLP tools developed at Lancaster University, includes a word cloud function that visualizes unusually common words in a select text in comparison to a reference corpus.[27] We used this tool to explore terms for the places and experiences that individuals emphasized, comparing each interviewee's word usage to that in the other transcripts in our test corpus.

The first word cloud visualizations we generated showed more or less what we expected to see (figures 9.2 and 9.3). Compared to the other victims in the sample, Gutman (figure 9.2) and Paul Schneiderman (figure 9.3), both of whom experienced many kinds of forced labor, more often mentioned places where they were sent to work (Buchenwald, Buna). Other uncommonly frequent words in their interviews were names of family members (for Gutman, Leiby and Naphtali) and spatial terms related to other places and experiences that they discussed in greater detail or length than other interviewees, such as "ghetto," "Warsaw ghetto," "march" (meaning forced movement), and "trains." The categorical semantic analysis available in Wmatrix's NLP toolbox attaches semantic tags to words and phrases, in essence assigning them to categories of meaning. Applying this method to Gutman and Schneiderman's texts, again in comparison to the other sample interviews, revealed some interesting differences between the two men's narratives (figures 9.4 and 9.5). Although both of them worked in a variety of manual trades in forced-labor camps, for example, Gutman's interview appeared to be more dominated by the theme of work and employment (figure 9.4).

Because there is, theoretically, no limit to the number of texts one could include in a corpus for linguistic analysis, the ability to compare individuals and subgroups to the larger population of Holocaust survivors might lead to new insights into labor within, and movement between, ghettos and camps. Comparing the language in our sample of ten to the enormous reference corpus of British spoken English[28] highlights a number of terms that we might expect would be disproportionately common in survivor interviews. For example, "camp," "ghetto," "Germans," "Jewish" and "Jews," and "Auschwitz" were

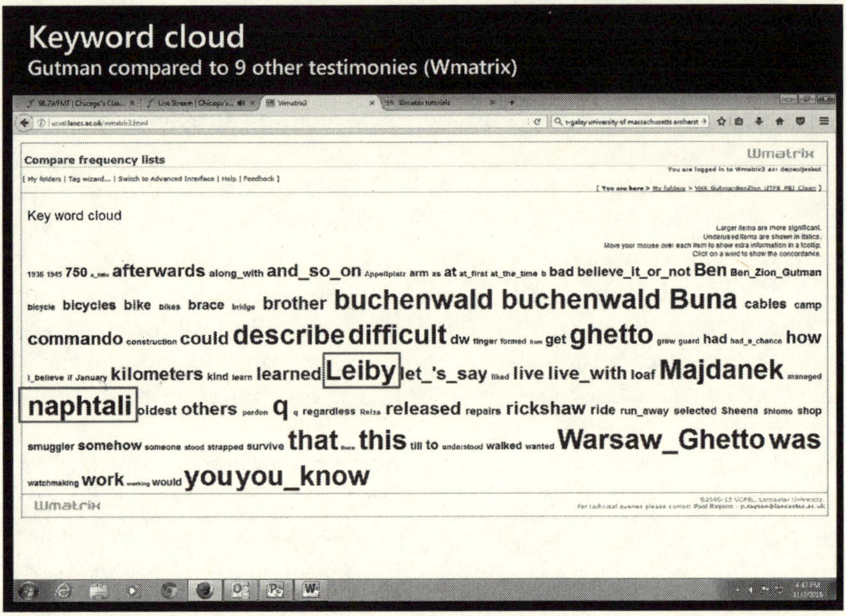

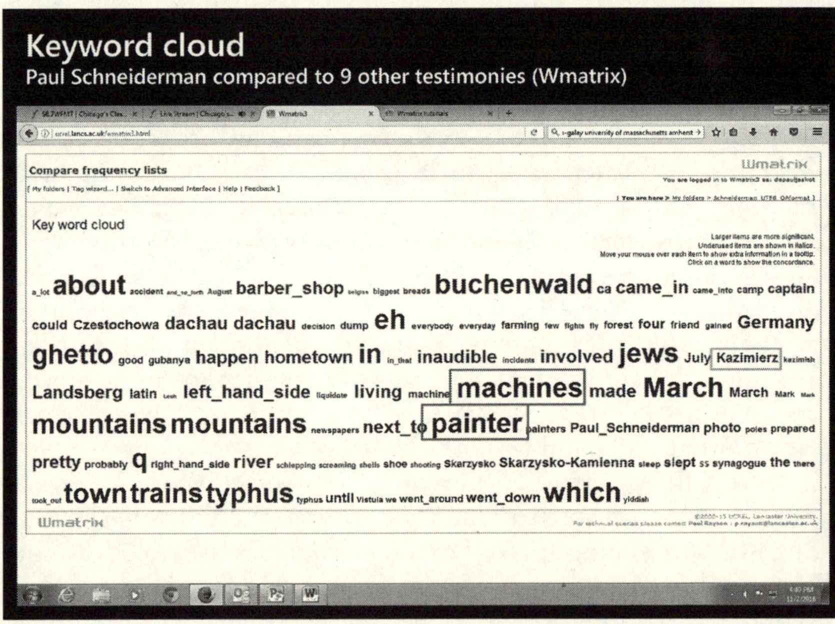

Figs. 9.2 and 9.3. Keyword cloud visualizations use the relative size of words to indicate the degree to which they are overrepresented in the source relative to a reference corpus; in this case, all other testimonies in our test set of ten testimonies. Gutman's unusually frequent words (top) include Buchenwald and names of family members. Paul Schneiderman (bottom) spoke less about family and more about the kinds of work he did at labor camps. Images by the authors.

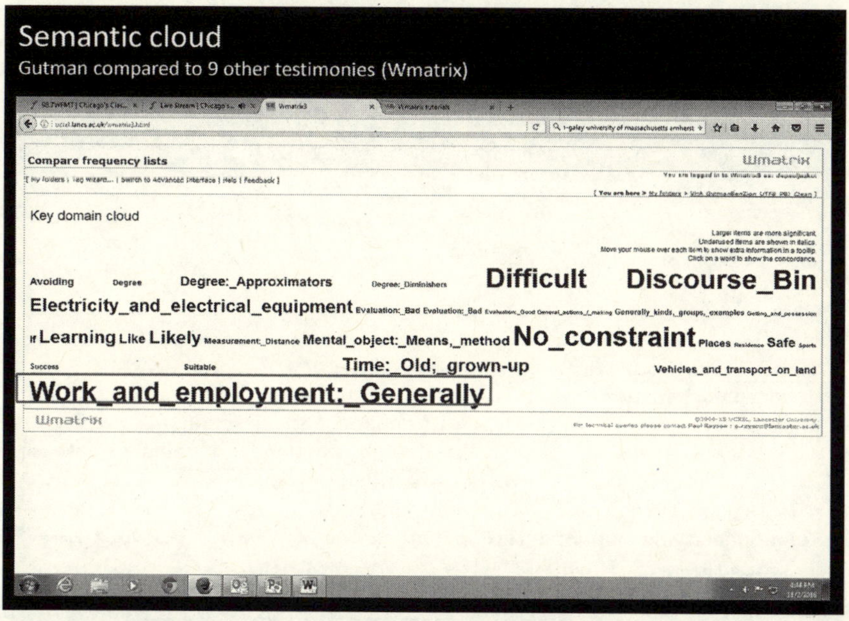

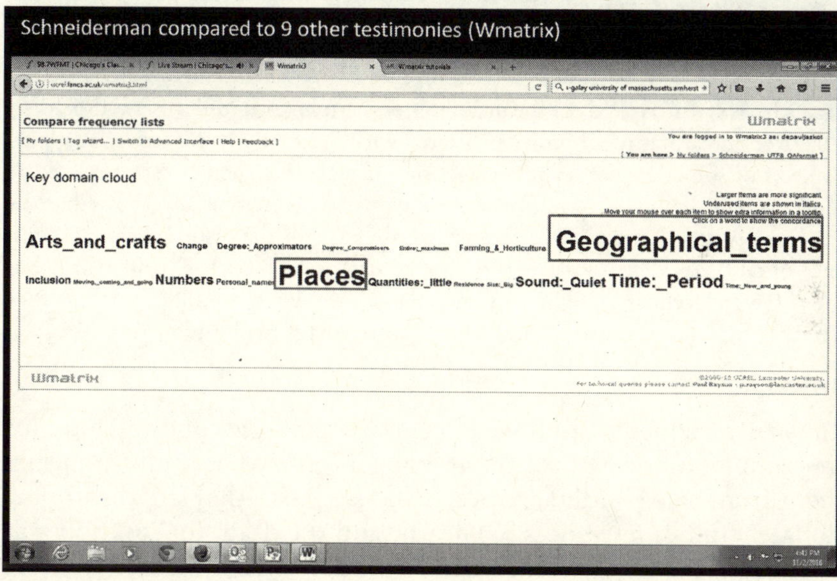

Figs. 9.4 and 9.5. Applying the word cloud method of visualization to semantically tagged testimonies reveals the relative prominence of particular themes in Gutman's testimony (top), including his focus on labor, and Schneiderman's unusual awareness of places (bottom). The category "Discourse bin" is attached to terms the semantic tagger does not recognize. In Gutman's testimony, some foreign place names landed in this bin, along with other foreign terms, pointing to the need for Holocaust-specific semantic categories, dictionaries of terms, a multilingual gazetteer, and manual checking of terms. Images by the authors.

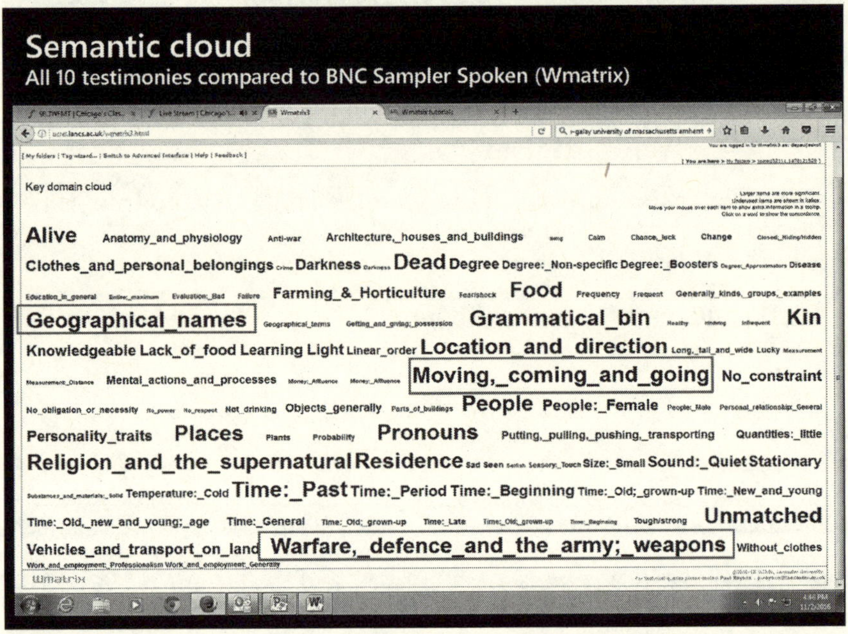

Fig. 9.6. Keyword clouds of the group of ten sample testimonies showed predictable overrepresentation of terms associated with the Holocaust. Semantic tagging picked out some less predictable categories of meaning, such as terms related to movement and unusual numbers of place names. This analysis also showed us the need to develop a specialized reference vocabulary, for the disproportionate presence of terms related to warfare were not actually references to World War II but the survivors' frequent mention of "barracks," meaning the buildings where they were housed in concentration and labor camps. Image by the authors.

unusually frequent. But if we look at the semantic concept cloud for the sample interviews, we get a stronger sense of what distinguishes them from more ordinary speech (figure 9.6). They are disproportionately full of references to "death" and the dead, to "location and direction," "moving, coming and going," specific places (some of which have an almost totemic resonance), and war. The Holocaust narratives also contain many unrecognized terms ("unmatched" and "Grammatical bin" are catchalls for words that the semantic tagger does not have in its dictionary of speech terms). This is not surprising given that the interviewees were not native English speakers, that they referred to many foreign places, and that their accented speech may have been difficult to transcribe accurately. These are not trivial problems.

Our preliminary efforts to map the movements of survivors from their testimony confirm our earlier sense that this evidence may, in some cases, reveal less about the places an individual inhabited or moved through during the Holocaust than about how individuals sought to make sense of profound dislocation and the threats to existence that can affect people's ability to orient themselves and to establish lasting memories of place.[29] "Positive" spaces of survival associated with important turning points in the speaker's experience also come to the fore. Through painstakingly plotting the many places that Leon Wells mentions in his VHA interview, Levi Westerveld found that the narrative jumbled together the places where Wells was at given moments with references to places from the past and places far away.[30] Such mixing of place references may not be unusual in spoken language, but as yet we do not know for certain. Scholars have only recently begun to apply automated, or semi-automated, methods to extract place sequences (or topologies of place) from a given corpus,[31] and the meaning of places in relation to time in oral interviews is, as far as we know, uncharted territory in linguistic analysis. As a first step for geographical analysis, place references in texts can be located for mapping through a process called geoparsing, which tags each place with its geographic coordinates, provided the place in the text matches a place in a prepared list that includes coordinate locations.[32] Geoparsing places in our test sample of ten survivor interviews proved difficult in the first round of analysis, primarily because many of the places mentioned are relatively obscure or because of variant spellings and mistranslations in the transcription. These difficulties could be significantly redressed by building a comprehensive historical, multilingual gazetteer of the Holocaust.[33] Referencing transcribed interviews to such a gazetteer would lessen the number of omitted or misidentified places in geoparsing.

GENDER: THE SPATIAL IS SOCIAL, THE SOCIAL IS SPATIAL

Another potential area for working with linguistic textual analysis is the set of questions central to work on gender and the Holocaust. In an important intervention in debates over whether Jewish women activated social networks more fully than did Jewish men, Pascale Rachel

Bos questioned whether the gendered differences identified by scholars such as Joan Ringelheim simply reflected gendered narratives—that is, that women tell different stories than men, and they tell Holocaust stories differently.[34] This was one of the questions that we sought to examine by including an equal number of men and women's interviews in our test sample. Corpus methods enable one to search through an individual text or to compare one text, or group of texts, to others. Thus as an analytical approach, CL and NLP methods do not differentiate between one interview and 54,000 interviews; the methods can be applied to any size corpus, although generally, the larger the corpus, the more meaningful its results are likely to be. While our sample was small and statistically unreliable for generalization, we were testing a proof of concept which, in this case, needed to see whether any pattern in a computational analysis of a particular interview transcript could be confirmed through close watching of the video interview. The small sample size served this purpose. We could easily toggle between computational and analog methods to think about what a larger and more rigorous study should focus on.

Working with two sample sub-corpora (transcripts of five interviews by women, five by men) was suggestive. Running a simple word list frequency count between the women and men pointed to differences in their usage of the pronouns "I" and "we." We expected the oral histories to shift between these social referents as survivors spoke of themselves and their own, individual story, then the story of wider collectives, such as family, friendship groups, spatial units such as their home town, the camp barracks where they slept and ate, their work group, and so on. However, what became clear was that these ten women and men differed in their retelling of the Holocaust as "my" story or "our" story. The women in the sample more frequently used "we" than "I," while the men did the opposite. In addition to the gender-neutral plural, "we," women were more prone to speak of other women and girls ("she," "her," "woman/women"), and were more likely to mention family relationships ("father," "mother," "sister," "aunt," etc.).

To probe this difference further, we visualized the use of these terms across a number of individual interviews using the concordance plot feature in AntConc (as discussed above). Taking the testimony of Helen Farkas and Morris Farkas, two survivors sent to Auschwitz during the Hungarian deportations in 1944, we visualized the usage

Figs. 9.7 and 9.8. AntConc concordance plots of the occurrence of "I" (top) and "we" (bottom) in the testimonies of Helen Farkas and Morris Farkas. Images by the authors.

of the terms "I" and "we" in each interview. The two plottings are almost mirror images of one another. Morris almost constantly used the pronoun "I" (figure 9.7), while "we" recurred over and over in Helen's interview (figure 9.8). This test suggests that deploying CL tools could be valuable for comparative analysis of oral history interviews along the lines of gender and other kinds of social relationships.

We see CL methods as one tool among many, including archival work, close reading of texts, and the distant reading methods of the digital humanities, within an iterative research process.[35] As an example, consider the spatiality of the collective pronoun "we" in the testimony of Helen Farkas and the other women in our sample. One of the striking moments in Helen's interview comes in a self-reflective aside to the interviewer about her use of "we," as she retells the story of the group of women with whom she struggled to survive during an evacuation (a death march for some) in early 1945. She explained: "And we looked, we, there, I'm talking in the plural because my five in a row and my sisters and my niece, and we looked there and we saw a woman standing and blood on the snow . . ."[36] Here, Helen not only signaled her awareness that she retold her story as that of a wider collective; she also described who was included in the collective, and how they were literally shaped by the spatial ordering of the prisoners into "a row" of five. This spatial, human form originated in the camp system for ease of counting and food distribution—a conceptual and physical technology of discipline and order.[37] It continued into the evacuations as a form that helped make the moving column of marchers fit the roads while keeping prisoners visible and manageable for the guards.

Having discovered a possible connection between "we" and "five," we ran a concordance for the word "five" in all of the women's interviews. We found that "five" was also a significant term for another survivor of the Hungarian deportations, Anna Patipa.[38] For both women, the row of five became a critical social unit. The row of five was a means of place-making for them as well, one that they used consciously, when they could, to keep loyal friends and relatives close and to maintain bonds of trust and understanding in an otherwise alien and hostile environment. To give just two examples:

> We were my aunt, my cousin, my sister, my niece and I, we were five . . . we were five so my aunt would save—the five, we would get a bread about the size of a brick and we would eat the thin slice of bread in the evening and we would leave some for the morning . . . (Anna Patipa)[39]
>
> . . . We had to line up in five rows and usually it was the same people. We chose each other. So we chose a Slovakian girl to us when we were in Block 10 from the second day on. And she was in our line—our fifth to the line for as long as we were in Auschwitz. We had to have someone that you knew and you got used to because we had to share a bread . . . And we had to divide it in five equal pieces . . . So we were responsible for each other, all five of us. Now that we were all together, all four of us and this Slovakian girl . . . (Helen Farkas)[40]

The connection of place to specific social relationships in the camps is not unknown in Holocaust studies. Indeed, our investigation brought us back to a canonical but often forgotten 1978 text, Falk

Pingel's *Häftlinge unter SS-Herrschaft: Widerstand, Selbstbehauptung und Vernichtung im Konzentrationslager* (Inmates under SS Control: Resistance, Survival, and Destruction in the Concentration Camp). Pingel took a sociological approach to concentration camp inmates as a group, rather than looking at individuals or the camps from a perpetrator perspective. He argued that key factors (such as political affiliation) which inmates valued before they were caught up in the SS camp system preconditioned the potential for survival. He also combined archival perpetrator documents on conditions in the camp with analysis of first-person interviews, memoirs, and other accessible testimony.[41] In many ways, Pingel's text was an attempt to do an "integrated history" *avant le lettre*. His sociological approach never really took hold, due to the rising dominance of the intentionalist and functionalist debate and, most importantly, the difficulty of gathering and analyzing the voluminous first-person accounts required for studies of social groups. But Pingel's forays into trying to analyze victim experiences at a larger scale resonate with our investigations, especially in terms of the social patterns of experience just described. Far from rejecting key interests in Holocaust studies, computational methods extend them in new ways that make some analyses possible across the system for the first time. However, as we came to realize, these methods—like any methodology—are not without problems.

CONCLUSIONS

Most of the authors of this chapter, and all of the researchers involved in the *Geographies of the Holocaust* project, were new to CL and NLP when we embarked on exploring VHA interviews computationally. In retrospect, we approached the methods a bit naively and perhaps with too many expectations. We discovered that corpus methods would indeed enable certain kinds of scaling up, potentially to move from analyzing one interview transcript to studying many thousands. The methods readily answered questions about the relative frequency of single words, such as the gendered patterns of personal pronouns. Even in this simple case, however, interpretation can be problematic because of the importance of the context and the non-sequentiality of human speech. To understand the meaning of the five women's more frequent use of "we" and "she," we had to study the context of each reference to determine, for example, whether the pronouns were used in relation to events during the Holocaust or some other period of their lives. The CL methods of concordance and collocation can help sort this out for a handful of interviews, but analyzing context is much more difficult to do at scale. Tagging, or "annotation" in CL parlance, has the potential to tackle some of these issues, but this process has significant costs in terms of time and effort.

The many languages of Holocaust survivors' testimony pose additional problems. One is that semantic tagging tools, first developed for studying English corpora, have only in the last five to ten years been adapted to analyze other languages. Semantic tagging software is now available, or in development, for many other languages.[42] While linguistic differences present some interesting research opportunities, they could also make direct comparison quite difficult. For example, in Italian the pronouns "I" and "we" are not needed in front of a verb as they are in English, because the conjugation of the verb tells the listener or reader whether it refers to the first-person singular or plural. Thus, an analysis of the gendered use of the pronouns *io* ("I") and *noi* ("us") would be essentially meaningless in Italian, and in some other languages as well. As with context, this would become a problem were we to engage in comparative analysis of not only the approximately 35,000 English-language VHA interviews but all 54,000 of them.

Despite these limitations, thinking spatially with a variety of digital and nondigital approaches to testimony helped us to identify patterns that link survivors' narratives to the broader, systemic level of the genocide. At this early stage, CL and NLP appear useful as tools for searching for patterns in large textual archives and for developing customized indexes. We also see potential for these methods to support temporal analysis, such as comparing narratives from different periods of the Holocaust or the war, and for studying how the content of testimony changes over the arc of interviews.[43] Geoparsing also shows promise for enabling at least the preliminary mapping of places, and perhaps some kinds of movement, based on words and phrases in testimony. Another very interesting possibility is using corpus methods to compare testimonies according to the period they were recorded and the organization that conducted the interviews.

These methods reminded us of the need to retain the particularity of experience and space for the Holocaust, its millions of victims, and the policies and practices of the perpetrators. We hope that the spatial and textual methods we explored in this chapter may be of use to a range of interpretative problems in Holocaust studies. For us, they demonstrate the value of thinking at different scales, as well as with varied sources and methods. The possibilities of computational tools like CL and NLP also point to the need for more collaborative scholarship in Holocaust studies, given the complexity and size of the textual source collections and the need for multiple modes of analysis. Collaborative work is the only way that we will be able to approach a truly "integrated history" of the Holocaust. It will require the preparation of large datasets, more training of Holocaust scholars in digital methods, bringing computational specialists into Holocaust projects, and, of course, rigorous attention to the historical sources that have always been part of Holocaust scholarship. We should seek not only to integrate history, but our scholarly practice.

NOTES

The authors acknowledge assistance from Maël Le Noc, Paul Rayson, and Ian Gregory in preparing this chapter.

1. Noah Shenker, *Reframing Holocaust Testimony* (Bloomington: Indiana University Press, 2015); Todd Presner, "The Ethics of the Algorithm: Close and Distant Listening to the Shoah Foundation Visual History Archive," in *History Unlimited: Probing the Ethics of Holocaust Culture*, ed. Claudio Fogu, Wulf Kansteiner, and Todd Presner (Cambridge, Mass.: Harvard University Press, 2016), 175–77.

2. Presner, "The Ethics of the Algorithm."

3. Christopher R. Browning, *Remembering Survival: Inside a Nazi Slave-Labor Camp* (New York: W.W. Norton, 2010).

4. Tim Cole, "'Crematoria, Barracks, Gateway: Survivors' Return Visits to the Memory Landscapes of Auschwitz," *History and Memory* 25, no. 2 (2013): 102–31.

5. The number of index terms in 2017.

6. In his testimony, for example, Gilberto Salmoni—USC Shoah Foundation VHA, 40749–35, Interview with Gilberto Salmoni (February 18, 1998)—mentions his daughter, son-in-law, and grandchildren, but only the grandchildren are indexed.

7. To our knowledge, the only published analysis of the VHA index as data is Presner, "The Ethics of the Algorithm."

8. On the Shoah Foundation/ProQuest venture to transcribe all oral interviews in the VHA Holocaust collection, see http://www.proquest.com/products-services/USC-Shoah-Foundation-Visual-History-Archive.html.

Word estimate by Anne Knowles, based on a very approximate average of 200 words per page × 30 pages × 54,000 interviews.

9. Andrew Herod, *Scale* (London: Routledge, 2011).

10. Anne Kelly Knowles, Tim Cole, and Alberto Giordano, eds., *Geographies of the Holocaust* (Bloomington: Indiana University Press, 2014).

11. Saul Friedländer, *Nazi Germany and the Jews*, vol. 1, *The Years of Persecution 1933–39* (New York: HarperCollins, 1997), and vol. 2, *The Years of Extermination 1939–45* (New York: HarperCollins, 2007).

12. Paolo Giaccaria and Claudio Minca, eds., *Hitler's Geographies: The Spatialities of the Third Reich* (Chicago: University of Chicago Press, 2016).

13. Attempts at seeing the victims at scale have been few. One exception, which we elaborate further on, is Falk Pingel, *Häftlinge unter SS-Herrschaft: Widerstand, Selbstbehauptung und Vernichtung im Konzentrationslager* (Hamburg: Hoffmann und Campe, 1978).

14. These overlapping experiences have come together profoundly most recently in the work of microhistories of killing sites and events. See the now-canonical Jan T. Gross, *Neighbors: The Destruction of the Jewish Community in Jedwabne, Poland* (Princeton, N.J.: Princeton University Press, 2001); the essays in Claire Zalc and Tal Bruttmann, eds., *Microhistories of the Holocaust* (Oxford: Berghahn, 2016); as well as the contributions (especially that of Jan Grabowski) in Alexandra Garbarini and Paul B. Jaskot, eds., *Lessons and Legacies XIII: New Approaches to an Integrated History of the Holocaust: Social History, Representation, Theory* (Evanston, Ill.: Northwestern University Press, 2018). The persisting gap between microhistorical analysis and an integration with the system of genocide is what we are trying to address here.

15. See, for example, the many works by Henry Greenspan and Lawrence Langer, among others. See also the diverse approaches gathered in the volume edited by Jürgen Matthäus, *Approaching an Auschwitz Survivor: Holocaust Testimony and Its Transformations* (Oxford: Oxford University Press, 2009).

16. One might point to the excellent analysis of the developing political economy of the Nazi state and its genocidal ambitions in Adam Tooze, *Wages of Destruction: The Making and Breaking of the Nazi Economy* (New York: Penguin Books, 2008), though Tooze includes no perspective of the victims in his broad approach.

17. Simone Gigliotti, Marc J. Masurovsky, and Erik Steiner, "From the Camp to the Road: Representing the Evacuations from Auschwitz, January 1945," in *Geographies of the Holocaust*, ed. Anne Kelly Knowles, Tim Cole, and Alberto Giordano (Bloomington: Indiana University Press, 2014), 192–225. See also the debate about this essay's visual interventions in Claudio Fogu and Todd Presner, "Interview with Anne K. Knowles, Tim Cole, Alberto Giordano, and Paul B. Jaskot, Contributing Authors of *Geographies of*

the Holocaust," in *History Unlimited: Probing the Ethics of Holocaust Culture*, ed. Claudio Fogu, Wulf Kansteiner, and Todd Presner (Cambridge, Mass.: Harvard University Press, 2016), 240–56.

18. The notion of slow listening—listening repeatedly, replaying parts of an audiovisual testimony—is adapted from Daniel Kahneman, *Thinking, Fast and Slow* (New York: Farrar, Straus and Giroux, 2013).

19. Anne Kelly Knowles, Levi Westerveld, and Laura Strom, "Inductive Visualization: A Humanistic Alternative to GIS," *GeoHumanities* 1, no. 2 (2016): 233–65.

20. Hans Lindquist, *Corpus Linguistics and the Description of English* (Edinburgh: University of Edinburgh Press, 2009); Tony McEnery and Andrew Hardie, *Corpus Linguistics: Method, Theory, and Practice* (Cambridge: Cambridge University Press, 2012); Tony McEnery and Andrew Hardie, "The History of Corpus Linguistics," in *The Oxford Handbook of the History of Linguistics*, ed. Keith Allan (Oxford: Oxford University Press, 2013), 727–46.

21. For an important recent corrective to Moretti that grapples with the relationship between textual analysis and social history, see Carolyn Lesjak, "All or Nothing: Reading Franco Moretti Reading: A Review of *Distant Reading* and *The Bourgeois: Between History and Literature* by Franco Moretti," *Historical Materialism* 24, no. 3 (2016): 185–205.

22. Presner, "The Ethics of the Algorithm."

23. For a compelling example of how space and genocide can come together through an analysis of a focused sample of the testimony of survivors and bystanders, see Jan Grabowski, "A Study in the Microhistory of the Holocaust: The *Liquidierungsaktion* in Węgrów Ghetto," in *Lessons and Legacies XIII: New Approaches to an Integrated History of the Holocaust*, ed. Alexandra Garbarini and Paul B. Jaskot (Evanston, Ill.: Northwestern University Press, 2018), 141–66.

24. See Anne Kelly Knowles, "GIS and History," in *Placing History: How Maps, Spatial Data, and GIS Are Changing Historical Scholarship*, digital supplement edited by Amy Hillier (Redlands, Calif.: ESRI, 2008), 1–25.

25. The Hungarian deportations included Jews living in borderland regions that were included in the expanded wartime boundaries of Hungary. Our sample video interviews from the USC Shoah Foundation's Visual History Archive were Anna Patipa (VHA no. 52616), Helen Farkas (53123), Morris Farkas (52328), Anna Hollander (53400), Miriam Samuel (53047), Ben Zion Gutman (02132), Philip Riteman (21342), Tania Rozmaryn (03411), Paul Schneiderman (00991), and Henry Tiger (22576). The first five interviews (Patipa, the Farkases, Hollander, and Samuel) were recorded by the Jewish Family and Children's Services San Francisco Holocaust Center; the others by the USC Shoah Foundation. We had the videos

transcribed by a commercial service, then proofed the transcripts against the videos before analysis.

26. The concordance plot is a visualization tool developed within the AntConc suite of tools. AntConc was developed by Laurence Anthony. See http://www.laurenceanthony.net/software.html.

27. In addition to the corpus of our ten testimonies, the large reference corpus we used was British National Corpus (BNC Sampler). For an introduction to WMatrix, see http://ucrel.lancs.ac.uk/wmatrix/.

28. Reference corpora also exist for American spoken English. In future analyses, it may be more appropriate to use an American corpus because of many interviewees' long residence in the United States.

29. On the spatiality of retelling difficult stories, see Tim Cole, "(Re) Placing the Past: Spatial Strategies of Retelling Difficult Stories," *Oral History Review* 42, no. 1 (2015): 30–49.

30. See Knowles et al., "Inductive Visualization," figure 10.

31. David Cooper and Ian N. Gregory, "Mapping the English Lake District: A Literary GIS," *Transactions of the Institute of British Geographers* 36, no. 2 (2011): 89–108.

32. Claire Grover, Richard Tobin, Kate Byrne, Matthew Wollard, James Reid, Stuart Dunn, and Julian Ball, "Use of the Edinburgh Geoparser for Georeferencing Digitized Historical Collections," *Philosophical Transactions of the Royal Society A*, 368 (2010): 3875–89; and C. J. Rupp, Paul Rayson, Ian Gregory, Andrew Hardie, A. Joulain, and D. Hartmann, "Dealing with Heterogeneous Big Data When Geoparsing Historical Corpora," *Proceedings of the 2014 IEEE Conference on Big Data* (2014): 80–83.

33. An excellent introduction to the structure, content, and uses of historical gazetteers is *Placing Names: Enriching and Integrating Gazetteers*, ed. Merrick Lex Berman, Ruth Mostern, and Humphrey Southall (Bloomington: Indiana University Press, 2016).

34. Pascael Rachel Bos, "Women and the Holocaust: Analyzing Gender Difference," in *Experience and Expression: Women, the Nazis and the Holocaust*, ed. Elizabeth Baer and Myrna Goldenberg (Detroit, Mich.: Wayne State University Press, 2002), 23–50.

35. Franco Moretti, *Distant Reading* (London: Verso, 2013); Anne Kelly Knowles, "A More Humane Approach to Digital Scholarship," *Parameters: Knowledge under Digital Conditions*, Social Science Research Council, August 3, 2016, http://parameters.ssrc.org/2016/08/a-more-humane-approach-to-digital-scholarship/.

36. USC Shoah Foundation VHA, 53123, Interview with Helen Farkas (September 13, 1990). This interview was originally undertaken by the JFCS Holocaust Center.

37. Tim Cole, *Holocaust Landscapes* (London: Bloomsbury, 2016).

While Foucault's analysis of physical spaces was abstract at best, his epistemological connection between spatial formations, discipline, and order seems useful as a broader context for understanding this and other testimony. See Michel Foucault, *Discipline and Punish: The Birth of the Prison* (New York: Vintage Books, 1995).

38. USC Shoah Foundation VHA, 52616, Interview with Anna Patipa (February 13, 1989). This interview was originally undertaken by the JFCS Holocaust Center.

39. USC Shoah Foundation VHA, Interview with Anna Patipa (February 23, 1989).

40. USC Shoah Foundation VHA, Interview with Helen Farkas (September 13, 1990).

41. Pingel, *Häftlinge unter SS-Herrschaft.*

42. Scott Piao et al., "Lexical Coverage Evaluation of Large-Scale Multilingual Semantic Lexicons for Twelve Languages," in *Proceedings of the 10th Edition of the Language Resources and Evaluation Conference (LREC2016)* (Portoroz, Slovenia, 2016): 2614–19.

43. On the structures of institutional Holocaust interview corpora, see Shenker, *Reframing Holocaust Testimony.*

Hannah Pollin-Galay

When the Index Is Wrong: Exploring Black Holes in Victim Memory

ON THE WEBSITE "REVILNA," USERS ARE INVITED TO "EXPLORE THE Ghetto on their own."[1] Taking up this invitation, I find a gray-toned digital map of contemporary Vilnius, punctuated with colored markers and a yellow border, demarcating the area of the former Vilna ghetto. (See figure 10.1.) I click on a green circle on the northwest corner of the ghetto. I learn that this is where the ghetto prison was located, on Straszun 6, now Zemaitijos 4. I walk (with my mouse) down from this circle on Straszun 6 to a blue one on Straszun 2. Here, I learn, is where the Zionist soup kitchen was located, a place where the "Haluts Youth organization would gather, and where the Zionists would often hold their meetings." If I needed to get from the soup kitchen to the children's sledding hill, on Szawelska (Šiauliu) 8, or to the place where the Jewish partisans built a barricade, Oszmianska (Ašmenos) 3, or even way out to the HKP 562 work camp on the outskirts of the city, the map could surely guide me with great precision—so much precision that I feel as though I am there. Especially since the website offers a GPS option, designed for mobile phone use while on the site, I feel my body invited into this landscape. If I am at a distance of several thousand miles from Vilnius while looking at my computer, that is just a technicality, a temporary setback. At any moment, the map seems to tell me, I could board a plane to Vilnius and "explore" these streets, feeling the history beneath my feet. The digital, satellite image is a placeholder, touching the landscape for me until my arrival.

This invitation toward the physical, offered by the "reVilna" map, calls to mind the reflections of the literary critic Hans Ulrich Gumbrecht in his book *The Production of Presence*.[2] In it, Gumbrecht nar-

Fig. 10.1. Digital map of the Vilna ghetto from the website reVilna. Printed with permission from Menachem Kipnis.

rates a personal and intellectual journey over the course of which he found himself, in the twenty-first century, tired of words. According to Gumbrecht's observation, he and his colleagues had learned to privilege labyrinthine interpretations and interpretations of interpretations at the expense of any recognition of the physical, spatial aspects of being human. In response, Gumbrecht "seeks to make a pledge against the tendency in contemporary culture to abandon and even forget the possibility of a presence-based relationship to the world."[3] What he means by presence is "a spatial relationship to the world and its objects. Something that is 'present' is supposed to be tangible for human hands, which implies that, conversely, it can have an immediate impact on human bodies."[4]

Who in the field of Holocaust studies cannot relate to the fatigue that Gumbrecht describes? The perennial debates on terminology alone seem overwhelming: some scholars object to the term "Holocaust," advocating instead for the less Jewishly particular term "genocide" or, alternatively, for the *more* Jewishly particular terms "Shoah" or "Churban/Khurbn."[5] Objections have similarly been sounded regarding the term "survivor,"[6] since it overemphasizes the positive, heroic aspects of victimhood. Referring to perpetrators as "Nazis" has also come under fire, since it limits the burden of guilt to those individuals with direct political ties to the National Socialist Party.[7] As for those who helped the Nazis (or Germans), scholars have debated whether to term their participation in violence "collaboration" or "cooperation."[8] While each of these discussions has produced fruitful insight on its own, the cumulative effect could result in a verbal fatigue similar to that which Gumbrecht describes.

Indeed, a yearning for presence seems apparent in a number of arenas connected to Holocaust scholarship and education. At the site where the Sobibor death camp was located, archaeologists Yoram Haimi and Wojciech Mazurek have been working on a historical excavation since 2007. Haimi explained the importance of the project as follows: "When we find items like the medallion of Carolina Cohen [a young Jewish victim], we are able to touch the Shoah, not just to talk about it."[9] Haimi's public rationale for this challenging archaeological dig relates less to the novelty of the information it has revealed than to the pathways of physical, embodied perception that it enables. Similarly, regarding the exhibits at the United States Holocaust Memorial Museum, Noah Shenker points out an increasing emphasis on material objects over verbal testimony.[10]

It is within this presence-hungry atmosphere that the field of Holocaust studies has also witnessed a spatial turn of sorts,[11] with digital maps as one important component. The "reVilna" website is part of a growing effort to create digital maps of Holocaust history. Others include Waitman Wade Beorn's "visualization/digital map" of one camp inmate at the Janowska camp,[12] Tim Cole and Alberto Giordano's digital project "Mapping Mobility in the Budapest Ghetto,"[13] and the proposed plan to create an "orthophotomap, or geo-referenced aerial photo," of the Auschwitz grounds in their current state.[14] While diverse in their stated goals and methods, these digital-geographic ventures all promise a reprieve from the problems that Holocaust-words create and allow people to encounter knowledge of the Holocaust as a visual presence. Scholars involved in this Holocaust map-work often labor to specify, in terms of historical reconstruction or new propositions of causality, which insights these maps can produce.[15] But perhaps the power of these maps does not rest primarily on new historical explanations or new analysis, but rather on their capacity to translate verbal stories into visual presence.[16]

Since other scholars have undertaken the project of translating low-technology, verbal (aural or paper) sources on the Holocaust into digital ones, my aim here is to do the reverse, to translate digitally presented Holocaust sources—maps specifically—into the language of human perception, narration, and cultural ethos. At a moment of great enthusiasm for the digital humanities, I propose this reversal as a means of humanizing the digital. It is an acknowledgment that digital-visual resources for the Holocaust are not merely pragmatic tools, but projects that respond to very specific contemporary pressures and desires, among them the yearning to touch or see a physical presence. Rather than simply making research or education more expedient, digital maps engender new situations of memory, ones that make values-laden claims about the Holocaust and human agency. I hope to make these visual claims more explicit through this process of "reverse-translation." This reversal also illuminates certain complexities specific to the mapping of Holocaust experience, reminding us that this is not a typical or easy case of word-to-map correspondence. One such complexity relates to the damage that Holocaust violence did to its victims' capacities to orient and understand space, and to the limitations of conventional cartography in depicting that damage. Another complexity relates to the influence of post-Holocaust migration and to the diverse contemporary places in which witnesses testify. The events of World War II not only rattled the landscapes on which they took place, but also engendered mass postwar migration, for surviving European Jews especially. Now scattered across the globe, the sites in which survivors eventually settled have offered them highly varied ideological and cultural resources for remembering their wartime experiences. Depending on where they currently live and speak, Holocaust witnesses participate in different political and cultural conversations in the very fabric of their geo-narratives. These divergent memory ecologies significantly shape the witnesses' cartographic lens.

As a case study, I will examine the way that digital maps inform the presentation of witness testimony on the USC Shoah Foundation Visual History Archive's viewing platform. In this current apparatus, a human face appears beside a digital map, each narrating different versions of the same story. I argue that the maps awaken a type of geo-curiosity in the listeners/viewers, encouraging us to seek out spatial coordinates as we receive the witness's words. In creating this heightened awareness, these maps reveal their own drawbacks. There are moments when witnesses violate the narrative told by the map, in which all moments of history unfold with uniformly measurable, orientable physical clarity. This occurs most acutely when witnesses share memories of radical physical disorientation, contradicting the way that the maps depict them as oriented beings on an intelligible European landscape. The survivors' loss of physical, indexical orientation is one severe consequence of Nazi persecution and is thus a meaningful, historical truth about the Holocaust. From the perspective of Holocaust victims, these "black holes" were a real element of the violence they endured.

This observation should lead to critical consideration of how digital maps testify, but not to derision or cynicism toward the mapping project in general. In awakening a desire to emplace testimony,[17] these digital maps raise questions about how witnesses consider geography throughout their testimonies—as well as the ways that contemporary geography shapes the memory process. All of these layers of meaning are not necessarily legible in the visual language of digital maps alone. However, these maps can inspire us to return to the spoken record with a new geographic sensitivity. In sum, this chapter argues for a type of dialogue between the verbal and the spatial, in which we allow testimonial speech to challenge the terms of the digital map, and vice versa. In the conflict and encounter between maps and words, there is new insight to be gained.

INDEXICAL MAPS AND USC SHOAH FOUNDATION TESTIMONY

The USC Shoah Foundation introduced the map feature in 2013, allowing the viewer to follow the longitude and latitude of the story at every moment of the testimony.[18] On the next page, for example, is how the map appears on the USC Shoah Foundation viewing platform in the middle of the testimony of Hana Golani.[19] (See figure 10.2.) Golani was born in the Lithuanian town of Tavrig (Tauragė) in the year 1930. During World War II, she was imprisoned in the Shavl (Šiauliai) ghetto and the Stutthof concentration camp. She testified in 1998 in Haifa, Israel, in Hebrew. As Golani speaks to the viewer on the left, the map speaks to the viewer on the right, providing a simultaneous translation of her story in cartographic terms. As her narrative moves from Tavrig, to Shavl to Stutthof, then after the war from Warsaw, to Krakow to Feldafing and then to Haifa, the red and green pins move across the map. This digital activity provides a new framework through which we are invited to receive her voice and her face.

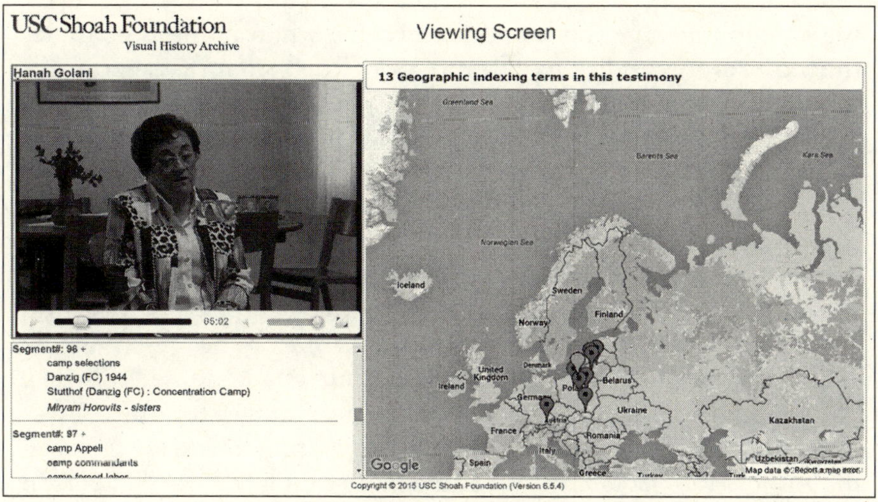

Fig. 10.2. Testimony of Hana Golani, her face appearing beside the map. Printed with permission from USC Shoah Foundation Visual History Archive.

Thinking in semiotic terms, what the map proposes is a new indexical relationship between the speaking witness, the events remembered, and the landscape on which they occurred. An index, according to Charles Sanders Peirce, is a sign that "stands for its object by virtue of a real [i.e. physical] connection with it."[20] A weathervane is an index of wind, since it signifies that object by touching it. A footprint is an index of the human being that stepped on that bit of sand. A photograph is an index of the landscape it captures, since light rays have created a contiguous physical relationship between the photo film and the object. And a satellite-produced map, like the Google maps used by the USC Shoah Foundation, has an indexical connection to the landscape it captures through its satellite signals. Indexical knowledge is of the highest evidential order. Indexes give us the greatest level of assurance that we can know, understand, and act on and within our physical environments by way of our own agency and rational faculties.

Thus, when positioned beside the face of a speaking Holocaust witness, the map makes an ethical proposition: Hana Golani's testimony can and should be understood through a series of indexical relationships to her surroundings, as depicted on the map, as an indexically lived story. The map defines Golani as a finite, corporeal being who was able to orient her body and perceive her whereabouts even under the most severe conditions of oppression. The map infuses her words with a sense of physical clarity: she knew who she was and where she was, and we should too. She was an agent within her body.

This is a message that has great appeal on a number of levels. It depicts the witness in a positive light, as an intelligent, agentive person. It almost creates a sense of parity between her and those who perpetrated violence against her: if the Nazis drew maps in order to rearrange Europe,[21] Golani was able to follow their plan from a bird's-eye view. The map gives Golani the crucial ability to be present, in the way that Gumbrecht uses the word, to sense and be sensed in space. For twenty-first-century viewers like me, also hungry for this sense of presence, the map creates a common geographic language between the witness and her audience. I could retrace Golani's steps, in person or with the satellite intermediary, and come closer to understanding her experience.

Unfortunately, however, these encouraging messages, all of which begin from the indexical quality of the map, stand in stark contradiction to one of the key points that Hana Golani fights to convey as part of her testimony. At the moment that this image was taken, Hana is narrating her deportation to the Stutthof camp from the Shavl ghetto, where she had been imprisoned up until then. For her, moving from the ghetto to Stutthof does not merely entail moving from one point to another on the map, crossing a certain distance in kilometers or elevation. According to Golani's retelling, her relationship to the indexical world eroded at this point in her experience. Stepping off the train, Golani describes a scene of shouting and chaos. She then reveals the name of her destination, but only through a tentative comparison: "If there is a hell on the face of the earth [*gehenom 'al pnei ha'adamot*], that is Stutthof." Golani repeats this metaphor with full certainty several minutes later, this time asserting: "That was hell on the face of the earth." Her literary overtones—inserting phrases like "the unknown" and "hell on the face of the earth"—mark a distinct shift in her own cartographic terms, which have been very physical and precise up until now.

Golani's loss of geographic coordinates does not escape her diligent interviewer. Directing her back toward a knowable cartography, the interviewer asks:

Int: Where is Stutthof located?
Golani: On the Danzig corridor.
Int: What is the nearest city?
Golani: It would seem to be *the city of Danzig* [sarcastically]!

At earlier points in her testimony, Golani cooperated with the interviewer's request to perform geographic knowledge for its own sake. Now, however, Hana mocks such ritualized geographic inquiries, using sarcasm to unveil the rules of the game: the interviewer persistently requests to know location specifics, but does nothing with this knowledge. Moreover, Golani insists that the physical environment of Danzig (now Gdańsk), the place we can locate on a map or visit today, does not relate to her experience of Stutthof, the camp: "The place is pastoral and beautiful on the coast. There is a lake. You can see a lake. There's clean, golden sand. But we were inside the camp." She protests equating the knowable place—what "you can see," what can be perceived indexically—with her memory of the location as a camp prisoner.

Golani becomes only more adamant about this distinction as her narrative progresses. Transported to a satellite work camp of Stutthof, she describes the site simply as "darkness." When the interviewer requests to know the name of this satellite camp, Golani becomes abrasive: "I don't know the name. It was a field in no place [*sham haya sade beshum makom*]." Though Golani demonstrated high geographic precision earlier in the testimony, she has now become forceful in her claim of not knowing. The interviewer urges Hana to cast herself as having remained an agentive, oriented being at the time of slave labor in a Stutthof satellite; Golani insists that such a depiction would be inaccurate. The very capacity to orient herself physically, to read and understand the physical world she touches, to make her way through it of her own accord, is something that the Nazis violently seized from her. The witness talks back to her interviewer at this point when the screenshot was taken, and, in parallel, talks back to the map. If Gumbrecht argues that physical presence is a prerequisite for full human subjectivity, Golani's testimony affirms that suggestion. She asserts that multiple forced transports, extended physical deprivation, and emotional and cultural loss cumulatively destroyed her capacity to self-orient, to know where she was, in all senses of the phrase. The

Nazis suppressed her right to physical presence—and that is a truth important enough to record for posterity.

Hana Golani is far from alone in sharing such a memory of "no-place." To a surprising degree, witnesses from a range of cultural and linguistic settings, whose testimonies differ in a great number of other respects, share similar memories of radical physical disorientation.[22] Meri Gotler, a Yiddish-speaking witness who testified in Lithuania in 1996, and whose testimony couldn't be more different from Hana Golani's in most respects, recalls her arrival at Stutthof in similar terms: "We arrived there by ship. On the occasion of the 50th year anniversary of Stutthof, I noticed that there is actually a sea right there. It was just awful. There was nothing to describe there and nothing to tell."[23] She declares that Stutthof, as recalled through the eyes of a prisoner, was a kind of non-landscape. *Not describing* is the best way to describe the way she saw it then. It is only in retrospect that Gotler is able to grasp the proximity of Stutthof to the sea.[24] That is, even though she had touched both the Baltic Sea and the Stutthof camp physically, she had been unable to compile these indexical connections into a coherent mental map. Another Yiddish-speaking witness, Rivka Geler, echoes a similar spatial disconnection between the Estonian Goldfields camp and its environs: "It was a beautiful place. All around and around it was very beautiful. Because Germans lived there in their houses all around. [Makes circling gestures with her hand.] And we were on the inside. They shoved us in and it was just a fine misfortune [*a guter umglik*]."[25] Geler enlists body and voice to dramatize the perceptual gap between the surrounding topography, which is normal, pleasant, residential, and the camp itself. She did not experience the camp as physically contiguous with its environs.

From an American, English-language setting, the witness Gita Taitz also depicts herself moving *within* Stutthof in similar terms of extreme disorientation:

> I didn't know what was happening to me. In a *blitz* I saw Hungarian women coming to me in white dresses, coming at me. Their heads were shaven and I started to run, like a ghost between people. I didn't know if they were going to kill me or not. I didn't care about anything. I just ran to look for my mother. I didn't know where she was taken. I was just running and I saw barracks. I went in I saw people that also went in for our *apell's* and selections.

> Young and old. I didn't know where I am. And I found my mother in one of these places.[26]

A similar memory emerges from a dialogue between the witness Boris A. and his interviewer in an American, English-language Fortunoff interview, regarding his limited mobility in Dachau:

> **Int**: What do you remember from Dachau?
> **Boris**: I was just at the end. You cannot see too much. You have to stay in the place where you are.

Their conversation circles around this point about lacking vision in Dachau. Interestingly, this witness also reflects on specific violent tactics that caused him to lose his capacity to orient: "When I was there I couldn't see this. You go an inch away, they can shoot you." He attributes his disorientation to the specific violent tactics of SS guards and, more broadly, to the Nazi regime's attempt to create a pure monopoly on spatial agency—similar to what Simone Gigliotti describes as the "political immobilisation of personal mobility."[27]

In some sense, to assert the reality of black holes in victim experiences may seem retrograde, reiterating an argument that scholars made in a previous intellectual moment. After all, notions of the Holocaust as having occurred on a hazy, unmeasurable landscape have been put forth at least since the 1990s, when Holocaust scholars were heavily focused on trauma theory.[28] For example, the central motif of Claude Lanzmann's well-known film *Shoah* is of vast, ghostly, unlocatable fields that seem wholly disconnected to the violent memories shared in words.[29] While this motif may have been stretched and overemphasized to the point of cliché in popular culture, it does fit the experience of radical physical disorientation that many victims remember. Thus, the claim that the Holocaust created "a lost spatial center"[30] is not mere theoretical cant. To lose personal navigation capacities was a real part of what it meant to be a victim of Nazi violence for many people.

While recognizing the deep validity of claims of spatial disruption in the Holocaust, we need not treat these claims as a sufficient stopping point: the scholarly choice is not between praising these maps as one of "the marvels of the digital world"[31] or, alternatively, insisting on pious strictures of Holocaust unrepresentability. Rather, one can utilize the spatial interest that the maps awaken in order to expand the study of *emic* (indigenous, subject-based) notions of place that arise from witness testimony. That is, we can return and reexamine verbal testimony with the "baggage" of visual cartography. In doing so, we should chart not only where the witness stood on the empirical map of the world, but also what kind of map key each witness creates in language.[32]

To better understand each witness's verbal map key, I suggest expanding the analysis of these testimonies on two planes: one is to look at the entire story that the witness tells about space, rather than focusing only on momentary, explicit geographic references; or, on the contrary, to look only at single, climactic episodes of disorientation. After all, these narrators are engaged in verbal map-work throughout the recordings. Their conversations begin with different versions of prewar geography, pictures of their family home and Jewish communal life in eastern Europe. The wartime segments contain a variety of spatial settings, some more disorienting than others. As segments of a larger story, witness memories of "no-place" take on different meaning. The second way that I seek to broaden the spatial analysis of these testimonies is to consider *the location in which the interview takes place*, that is, the witness's current space of memory as it informs her testimony. More than just a physical set of coordinates, the place of testimony provides the witness with a specific ecology of ideas. In describing places of the Holocaust, witnesses participate in broader conversations about politics, ethics, and the body. Interviewers act as mediators between the witness and her contemporary community, helping to connect the testimonial narrative to these larger political questions.

For example, we can reexamine Hana Golani's testimony, locating her declarations of disorientation within her larger cartographic narrative. Looking at her place narrative as a whole reveals a subtle Israeli map key, shaping the way that she recalls each station. At the start of the testimony, the interviewer asks where Golani was born. She gives an informative answer: "I was born in Lithuania. Lithuania is one of the three Baltic states. I was born in Tavrig, which is on the border of Germany." She portrays her birthplace as an objective place on the modern map. She seems to value including geographic data for its own sake. It is as if she anticipates a geographic archive, a scientific map of some sort, that will be created from this interview. At the request of the interviewer, Golani adds even more coordinates to her story. She specifies the distance in kilometers between her birth town, Tavrig (Taurigas), and the town in which she grew up, Riteve (Ritavas). She locates her childhood home "on the corner of Shilel and Kirdakas." None of these geographic coordinates will enter Hana's narrative, or become a reference point for later discussion with her interviewer: Yet, both participants are happy to have this information sounded out loud. Some of these spatial inquiries are briefly recommended in the Shoah Foundation questionnaire.[33] However, the conversations that they elicit in Golani's Hebrew-speaking, Israeli context seem to take on a culturally specific shape. Her ritual demonstration of geographic knowledge, uttering coordinates for their own sake, accords with the value placed on *yediat ha-aretz* (knowledge of the land) within the Zionist ethos.[34]

Golani's treatment of geography begins to change when the war breaks out. Her family attempts to flee from Lithuania once the German invasion began on June 22, 1941. Having left home, Hana describes motion rather than place, mentioning a series of distances between sites and vague descriptions of running "on the main road" and "on the side ride." Upon return from their unsuccessful flight, her family moves to the nearby city of Shavl, where all Jews were forced into the ghetto. "On the first of September, we moved into the poor area, to Vilnius Street. On one side there was Ghetto Kavkaz and on the other side Traku."[35] Though living in destitution, Hana is still able to chart out the violence on the landscape around her. Updating her narrative map, she announces when Riteve was destroyed and specifies when she was taken to the *ABE (Armee-Bekleidungs-Amt)*, the clothing depot just outside of Shavl. The manner in which she depicts herself maintaining self-orientation, even under such duress, contributes to a sense of *amidah* (literally: standing), a type of spiritual resistance valued in Israeli Holocaust discourse especially.[36]

Thus, when Golani depicts Stutthof as a black hole, insisting, "I was in a field in no-place" in the conversation described above, she drastically violates the very geographic terms to which both she and the interviewer have committed up until now. Note that, from the start of the testimony, both Golani and the interviewer preempt the Shoah Foundation's Google map in their interest in empirical geography. They find value in connecting their conversation to the world map whenever possible. The young interviewer wants Golani to present herself as a well-oriented agent and is frustrated and a little embarrassed when she cannot. The manner in which both participants value indexing the body toward space coheres with local emphases on creating an agentive Jewish self, and the weight placed on physical sovereignty in Israeli cosmology. That is to say, Golani both builds and *defies* her map through a specifically Israeli lens. Even her memory of having been *nowhere* takes on specific cultural significance within the larger context of her testimony.

Deportation to a concentration camp, Golani tells us, denied her of something she deeply cherishes: the right to feel, understand, and control her own physical presence in the world. This is a message that argues against the uniformly measured, indexical map at her side; she shows us what the Google map is missing. At the same time, her statement is also a critique of her own contemporary Israeli culture, and its modes of envisioning Jewish subjectivity. No, she seems to say, as much as one might like, Jewish people did not and cannot remain self-possessed, well-oriented agents under all circumstances. That is, Golani's narrative act, her insistence that her memory of "a field in no-place" be fully registered, is both a testament to the extremity of violence that she endured during the war years as well as, in her current context, a type of cultural rebellion. She spells out the limits of the Hebrew-Israeli ethos of *amidah* and shows us the point where people should not expect to find Jewish spatial agency.

Memories of "black holes" cut across geographic and linguistic borders. But within each local contemporary discourse, such testaments to disorientation arise amid a different conversation about place, about the Holocaust, and about victimhood. Compare, for instance, Hana Golani's geo-narrative to that of Jack Arnel, an American English-speaking witness who positions himself in the landscape in a different manner throughout his testimony.[37] Like Golani, Arnel shares critical moments of spatial estrangement, moments when indexical knowledge breaks down. Also like Golani, Arnel contradicts the digital map that appears beside his face on the Shoah Foundation viewing screen. Yet, these memories perform something different for him, within his terms of memory and within the local English-language American context in which he witnesses. In Arnel's testimony, neither he nor his interviewer seem especially concerned with proving their geographic competence. Instead, spatial themes often inspire conversations of an introspective, family-oriented nature.

Within this dialogue, Arnel's memories of radical disorientation do not create arguments, but welcome opportunities to dissect his suffering out loud.

Arnel was born in Vilna in 1929. He survived the Vilna ghetto, the Kailis work camp, and the Dachau concentration camp network. He was interviewed by the Shoah Foundation in 1996 in Woodmere, New York. Arnel and his interviewer establish a certain geographic perspective from the very start of the testimony:

> **Int**: So, you grew up in Vilna?
> **Arnel**: Yes. I lived with my parents and my sister.
> **Int**: What was your life like in Vilna?
> **Arnel**: Well, from what I can remember it was a wonderful life. My father had his own business as a fur maker. My mother had her own business. She was a dressmaker . . . . It was a very, very congenial, loving family.

Arnel and his interviewer do begin with a conscious effort to place his story on an empirical map of the world. But, very quickly, the discussion becomes personal. Depicting life in Vilna means, for Arnel, depicting the personalities and dynamics within his household. A question about an urban entity, "Vilna," leads to a statement about his loving family life.

It is not that Arnel ignores the larger city around him. As he continues to recall prewar life, he proudly mentions multiple institutions and public spaces in the city, such as the "Jewish teacher's seminaries,"[38] "Perlman's *cheder*" where he studied, "Beitar," and "the Real Gymnasium." Nonetheless, Arnel and his interviewer quickly zoom in on his family home, which he locates on "Subotch Street 7." Working together, the two take the listener on a tour inside: Arnel walks us through the courtyard, up the staircase, and then into the apartment. Eventually he arrives at the heart of the house, the most intimate and personal space of all: "My sister and I shared a bedroom when we were little. The windows in the back of the apartment faced into a garden and a Russian church." In addition to plants and flowers, Arnel recalls his view of a Russian Orthodox church from that same viewpoint. Flowers and people, nature and social relations, all earn their place on the map once they are visible from his bedroom window. Though Arnel tries to move on to other topics, the interviewer asks him to return to this compelling view from the window. "You described the view from your room as being of gardens and an Orthodox church. What was your relationship to the Orthodox church?" "Absolutely wonderful," Arnel answers, and recounts how one priest, Father John, would rest a ladder on his window in order to let him down to play. This depiction of interethnic friendship becomes relevant and truthful when considered from the right vantage point, from the inside looking out. The interviewer hopes to see as much as possible in this very manner: "And what about the other side of the apartment, what could you see out the front?" From that private lookout spot, Arnel describes friends, neighbors, and other relations. Arnel's interest in personal relationships and introspection is fully integrated into his map key.

Arnel's story progresses. He recounts the Soviet and Lithuanian annexation of Vilna in August 1940 and the German invasion on June 24, 1941, after which he and his family were evicted from their apartment and imprisoned in the Vilna ghetto. Describing this early stage of the war, he continues to locate his testimony on the indexical map of the world, though empirical precision remains a low priority for him. "One thousand, five hundred or two thousand men were taken. They took them there. They disappeared. They took them to the town of Ponar. Which is I don't know exactly how many miles away from Vilna. Maybe 50 or 40 miles from Vilna. I'm not sure about the mileage. That became the graveyard for the Vilna Jews." Rather than challenging him, pressing for more detail on the whereabouts of Ponar, the interviewer accepts Arnel's loose coordinates, as well as his basic attitude toward the topic, and their conversation moves on to other topics.

As in Golani's testimony, there comes a point at which Arnel openly and prominently attests to an extreme loss of physical orientation. Even if Arnel has kept geographic names and spatial coordinates in the backdrop of his testimony, he still emphasizes this experience of disorientation as a major event. For Arnel, the moment of acute spatial collapse comes at the very end of the war, around the liberation of Dachau in April 1945. At this time, Arnel and his father are being transported westward in a train evacuation from the camp. Under American missile fire, the German soldiers allowed their group of prisoners to escape into the woods.

> We started walking. We didn't know where or what or where to walk. We found a little village. Out of the village came out a German in uniform. He came up to us and asked us what we were doing there. We told him we lost our way and he says, "Go away from here and make sure you don't come back here." Somehow as we were walking without any direction we came all around and back to the same spot. He caught us a second time.
>
> He started shouting and yelling at us. He took out his pistol and he put his pistol right at my temple, right over here. My father dropped to the floor and he started pleading and begging him. "Please don't shoot him. He is my son. Please we only didn't find our way." Somehow he said, "All right. This is your last chance." Disappear from here I don't want to see you again.
>
> We ran with all our last might and we thought that we were going away from this place. But, *believe it or not*, it happened a third time [witness's vocal emphasis].

In his telling, Arnel depicts himself at the mercy of this unnavigable landscape. The forest acts *upon* him in this moment, controls him, in a manner parallel to the German soldier who holds him at gunpoint. While Arnel comments on the implausible quality of the story, he expresses no shame at this loss of agency in relation to the natural environment. Significantly, the interviewer does not interrupt this six-minute segment but gives time and attention to Arnel's detailed recollection of disorientation. Their conversation builds into a specific stance toward victimhood, one that differs from the tacit embarrassment at getting lost that I pointed out in Hana Golani's testimony. Here, to lose spatial agency, or to remember having lost it, is not so embarrassing for Jack Arnel, whose real and imagined audience members prioritize individual self-revelation over a demonstration of resilience or collective knowledge. In fact, as an authentic and perhaps cathartic expression of their experiences of victimhood, those witnessing and listening in an English-speaking American ecology may admire the fact that he confesses to getting so lost. This testimony is taking place at a time when a "confessional mode" of self-presentation was strongly valued in American discourse.[39] Arnel's narrative of "no-place" thus serves two purposes: he too, like Golani and others cited above, attests that Nazi rule disrupted his capacity to orient himself toward the indexical word. Simultaneously, he attests to his fluency in local discourse, and his communal connection to the interviewer, which is based upon their shared value of introspective memory.

CONCLUSION

The testimonies of both Hana Golani and Jack Arnel contradict the digital, indexical maps that remain at their side throughout the testimony. Both, like other witnesses whose testimonies I have studied, assert that their capacity for bodily orientation was violently revoked by Nazi imprisonment, exile, and physical deprivation. This commonality is important and should give rise to critical conversations about how we curate their testimonies in the presence-oriented culture of the twenty-first century, as well as how we use the sophisticated science of digital mapping when studying these sources. At the same time, this common memory of a black hole should not deter spatially minded research. Contextualizing these memories of disorientation within these witnesses' testimonies as a whole, geography becomes significant once again. The witness's current location of testimony puts specific conceptual pressures on the conversation, giving each memory of geographic rift a different meaning, a different cultural message in each case.

Reflecting upon the value of using geographic science in Holocaust research, Anne Kelly Knowles, Paul B. Jaskot, Benjamin Perry Blackshear, Michael De Groot, and Alexander Yule propose that we "see the spatial patterns that analytical mapping reveals as traces of human decision and activity."[40] Indeed, these scholars are right to point out the connection between decision, activity—agency—and map-work. For this very reason, survivor witnesses insist on having lost a connection to the indexical map of the world, precisely when their own will and decision-making powers were most stifled. While such memories of radical physical disorientation cut across cultural and linguistic lines, there are still culturally shaped ways through which witnesses access and discuss these memories. On contemporary viewing platforms, these memories of black holes reveal their importance not *despite* the inclusion of digital maps, but thanks to them: the maps demand that we constantly investigate the witness's indexical knowledge of the world, which calls attention to moments when this knowledge was forcibly suspended.

NOTES

1. Menachem Kipnis, *reVilna*, http://revilna.org/map.html. Place names in this segment are listed as they appear on the reVilna website.

2. Hans Ulrich Gumbrecht, *The Production of Presence: What Meaning Cannot Convey* (Stanford, Calif.: Stanford University Press, 2004).

3. Gumbrecht, *The Production of Presence*, xiv–xv.

4. Gumbrecht, *The Production of Presence,* xiii.

5. Omer Bartov sketches out the implications of each term in *Murder in Our Midst: The Holocaust, Industrial Killing, and Representation* (New York: Oxford University Press, 1996), 57–60. See also Vivian Patraka, "Situating History and Difference: The Performance of the Term 'Holocaust' in Public Discourse," *Jews and Other Differences: The New Jewish Cultural Studies* (1997): 62–63; and David Roskies, *Against the Apocalypse* (Cambridge, Mass.: Harvard University Press), 41–43. This debate has even reached popular forums, as in Josh Fleet, "History and Meaning of the Term 'Holocaust': Are We Still Comfortable with This Term?" *Huffington Post,* January 27, 2012, https://www.huffingtonpost.com/2012/01/27/the-word-holocaust-history-and-meaning_n_1229043.html.

6. Lawrence Langer, *Holocaust Testimonies: The Ruins of Memory* (New Haven, Conn.: Yale University Press, 1991), 5–6. Arlene Stein historicizes this objection in *Reluctant Witnesses: Survivors, Their Children, and the Rise of Holocaust Consciousness* (New York: Oxford University Press, 2014), 105–6. A parallel debate has also taken place in feminist thought. See, for example, Rahila Gupta, "'Victim' vs 'Survivor': Feminism and Language," *Open Democracy*, June 16, 2014, https://www.opendemocracy.net/5050/rahila-gupta/victim-vs-survivor-feminism-and-language.

7. Michael Mann lists possible terms to describe Holocaust perpetrators and their various implications in "Were the Perpetrators of Genocide 'Ordinary Men' or 'Real Nazis'? Results from Fifteen Hundred Biographics," *Holocaust and Genocide Studies* 14, no. 3 (2000): 331–66.

8. Isaiah Trunk, *Judenrat* (New York: Macmillan, 1973).

9. Ofer Aderet, "The Medallion That Saved a Young Girl from Oblivion," *Haaretz Magazine,* November 23, 2017, [Hebrew], https://www.haaretz.co.il/magazine/.premium-MAGAZINE-1.4625213.

10. Noah Shenker, *Reframing Holocaust Testimony* (Bloomington: Indiana University Press, 2015), 91. Regarding embodied experiences in Holocaust tourism more broadly, see Tim Cole, "Touching Landscapes? Embodied Experiences of Holocaust Tourism and Memory," in *Remembering the Second World War*, ed. P. Finney (London: Routledge, 2018), 234–48.

11. For example, Andrew Charlesworth, "The Topography of Genocide," in *Historiography of the Holocaust*, ed. Dan Stone (New York: Palgrave Macmillan, 2004), 216–53; and Anne Kelly Knowles, Tim Cole, and Alberto Giordano, eds., *Geographies of the Holocaust* (Bloomington: Indiana University Press, 2014).

12. Waitman Wade Beorn, "Spatial Testimony," Shanti Interactive, http://viseyes.org/mapscholar/?1116.

13. Tim Cole, Alberto Giordano, Erik Steiner, and Sophia Paliza-Carre, "Mapping Mobility in the Budapest Ghetto," Stanford University, http://web.stanford.edu/group/spatialhistory/cgi-bin/site/viz.php?id=411&project_id=0.

14. Auschwitz-Birkenau Museum, http://auschwitz.org/en/museum/news/digital-geo-referenced-imaging-of-the-museum-grounds,1.html.

15. Note the tension between discussing research process and research findings in Paul B. Jaskot and Tim Cole, "Afterword," in *Geographies of the Holocaust*, ed. Knowles, Cole, and Giordano, 227–32.

16. This corresponds with what Simone Gigliotti, Marc J. Masurovsky, and Erik B. Steiner write: "Unintentionally, the figures also provoked strong emotional responses in us and in audiences with whom we have shared our work," in "From the Camp to the Road: Representing Evacuations of Auschwitz, January 1945," in *Geographies of the Holocaust*, ed. Knowles, Cole, and Giordano, 208.

17. In considering the tension between oral histories and maps, see also Tim Cole, "(Re) Placing the Past: Spatial Strategies of Retelling Difficult Stories." *Oral History Review* 42, no. 1 (2015): 30–49.

18. USC Shoah Foundation, Visual History Archive Online, "places" search, http://www.vhaonline.usc.edu/geosearch/geoSearch.aspx.

19. USC Shoah Foundation VHA 48686, Interview with Hana Golani (Haifa, Israel, 1998).

20. Charles Sanders Peirce, "Prolegomena to an Apology for Pragmaticism," in *Peirce on Signs: Writings on Semiotic by Charles Sanders Peirce*, ed. James Hoopes (Chapel Hill: University of North Carolina Press, 2014), 251–52.

21. On Nazism as a geopolitical project, see Paolo Giaccaria and Claudio Minca. "Nazi Biopolitics and the Dark Geographies of the Selva," *Journal of Genocide Research* 13, no. 1–2 (2011): 67–84.

22. These observations are based on the narrative analysis of 127 oral and audiovisual testimonies of Lithuanian Jews currently living in Israel, the United States, and contemporary Lithuania, drawn from the USC Shoah Foundation's Visual History Archive, the Fortunoff Video Archive for Holocaust Testimonies, the Yale University Library, and the Yad Vashem Video

Testimony Archive, as well as 46 interviews that I conducted in Lithuania in 2004–05. On other aspects of this study, see Hannah Pollin-Galay, *Ecologies of Witnessing: Language, Place and Holocaust Testimony* (New Haven Conn.: Yale University Press, 2018).

23. USC Shoah Foundation VHA 10250, Interview with Meri Gotler (Kaunas, Lithuania, 1996).

24. Simone Gigliotti cites similar examples of severe disorientation upon arrival at concentration camps in *The Train Journey: Transit, Captivity, and Witnessing in the Holocaust* (New York: Berghahn Books, 2017), 169.

25. USC Shoah Foundation VHA 45805, Interview with Rivka Geler (Haifa, Israel, 1998).

26. USC Shoah Foundation VHA 9483, Interview with Gita Taitz (New York, 1995).

27. Gigliotti, *The Train Journey*, 3.

28. As examples of such an approach, see Shoshana Felman and Dori Laub, *Testimony: Crises of Witnessing in Literature, Psychoanalysis, and History* (New York: Routledge, Chapman and Hall, 1992), 256; Michael Bernard-Donals, "Beyond the Question of Authenticity: Witness and Testimony in the Fragments Controversy," in *Witnessing the Disaster*, ed. Michael Bernard-Donals and Richard Glejzer (Madison: University of Wisconsin Press, 2003), 213; and Sidra DeKoven Ezrahi, *Booking Passage: Exile and Homecoming in the Modern Jewish Imagination* (Berkeley: University of California Press, 2000), 16.

29. Claude Lanzmann, *Shoah* (France: New Yorker Films, 1985).

30. Barbara Mann, *Space and Place in Jewish Studies* (New Brunswick, N.J.: Rutgers University Press, 2012), 69.

31. Erick Felinto, "Mediascape, Antropotechnics, Culture of Presence, and the Flight from God," in *Digital Humanities and Digital Media: Conversations on Politics, Culture, Aesthetics and Literacy*, ed. Roberto Simanowski (London: Open Humanities, 2016), 95.

32. There is common ground between my goals here and those of scholars working on "geo-narratives," as exemplified in David J. Bodenhamer, Trevor M. Harris, and John Corrigan, "Deep Mapping and the Spatial Humanities," *International Journal of Humanities and Arts Computing* 7, no. 1–2 (2013): 170–75. However, rather than seeking to create digital maps that capture more of the nuances present in a verbal narrative, I am essentially doing the reverse: I ask how the increasing presence of maps can train us to listen to verbal narratives differently, attending more closely to a variety of spatial aspects.

33. "Topical Questions," Shoah Foundation institutional archives, document dated April 2004, p. 4, questions 6 and 7.

34. Yoram Bar-Gal and Bruria Bar-Gal, "'To Tie the Cords between the People and Its Land': Geography Education in Israel," *Israel Studies* 13, no. 1 (2008): 44–67.

35. Names used for the two ghettos of Shavl. Shmuel Spector, ed., *The Encyclopedia of Jewish Life Before and After the Holocaust,* vol. 3 (Jerusalem: Yad Vashem, 2001), 1175.

36. Yehuda Bauer, *Rethinking the Holocaust* (New Haven, Conn.: Yale University Press, 2001,(120.

37. USC Shoah Foundation VHA 19111, Interview with Jack Arnel (New York, 1996).

38. Likely referring to the YIVO Jewish Teachers Seminary. See Cecile Kuznitz, *YIVO and the Making of Modern Jewish Culture: Scholarship for the Yiddish Nation* (Cambridge: Cambridge University Press, 2014), 38.

39. Stein, *Reluctant Witnesses*, 125. See also Eva Illouz, *Saving the Modern Soul: Therapy, Emotions and the Culture of Self Help* (Berkeley: University of California Press, 2008), 39.

40. Anne Kelly Knowles, Paul B. Jaskot, Benjamin Perry Blackshear, Michael De Groot, and Alexander Yule, "Mapping the SS Concentration Camps," in *Geographies of the Holocaust*, ed. Knowles, Cole, and Giordano, 44.

Meghan Lundrigan

People, Places, Things: Considering the Role of Visitor Photography at the United States Holocaust Memorial Museum

THIS CHAPTER EXPLORES THE USE OF INSTAGRAM AS A MEDIUM FOR engagement and the interpretation of visitor experience within the United States Holocaust Memorial Museum (USHMM) in Washington, D.C. I identify which aspects of the exhibition space help visitors to connect to the materiality of the people, places, and things, and I consider visitor photography as a visual performance of witnessing and memory-making within the museum space. This chapter places visitor photographs shared on Instagram alongside more traditional forms of visitor feedback from the USHMM. Through the visual analysis of photographs of the museum's architecture, the installation of victims' shoes from Majdanek, and the Tower of Faces alongside visitor comments, this work connects visitor photography and Instagram usage to the historical trajectory of visitor behaviors before the advent of social media. The photographs taken by visitors to the USHMM demonstrate that visitors grapple with interpretative and methodological issues similar to those which dominated debates over Holocaust representation before the construction of the museum itself. Photographs are layered, complex cultural artifacts, and each image is an effort to layer visual narratives, experiences, and emotional responses atop the physical space of the exhibit itself. The sharing of photos on Instagram allows the visitor to contribute to an online visual dialogue about the forms that Holocaust memory can take in the twenty-first century beyond the walls of the U.S. Holocaust Memorial Museum. Understanding visitor photography at Holocaust memorial sites allows Holocaust scholars to engage with public perceptions of the Holocaust in the age of evolving digital media, where smartphone photography at Holocaust museum and memorial sites functions as third-generation acts of witnessing and contemporary Holocaust memory construction.

This chapter is rooted in an exploration of how Instagram images—both as acts and digital objects—function within the scope of the tourist gaze at the U.S. Holocaust Memorial Museum, placing it in conversation with fields of Holocaust visuality, photography, and memory studies.[1] As of April 2018, a search for #USHMM on Instagram produces roughly 6,700 images; the tag #holocaustmuseum produces thousands more. These numbers indicate an immense and substantial archive to explore the intricacies of both the Instagram image and the Holocaust Instagram aesthetic created within the digitized space of social media.[2] The visual culture theorist Lev Manovich's analysis of Instagram corpora has demonstrated that "different elements of photo culture that throughout the 19th and 20th century were separate, now have been combined into a simple platform . . . Camera, photo paper, darkroom, exhibition spaces such as galleries, and publication venues such as magazines exist together in one handheld device."[3] This chapter places the authority of the visitor at the center of an academic discussion about the needs and directions of Holocaust memory in our current digital age, and embeds amateur digital photography within a long discussion of the Holocaust and its representability.

Instagram photography at the USHMM can help Holocaust scholars to discern several things. First, Instagram photography helps us to explore points of historical impact for the visitors from almost an entirely visual standpoint, and on the user's own terms of interpretation and representation. Second, these images contribute to the broadening of a twenty-first-century Holocaust visuality, mobilized and available for engagement in tandem with the physical geographies of the Holocaust. Third, Instagram photography at the USHMM allows for the investigation of the relationship forged between the visitor and the memory of the Holocaust in the age of social media. This relationship—governed by the overarching, hegemonic structure of the USHMM itself—is interrogated by the visitor through the photography of people, places, and things housed within the walls of the museum itself. Instagram photography lays bare the visual aspects of the memory of the Holocaust which remain important to modern viewers.

The U.S. Holocaust Memorial Museum has a very active social media, digital, and online presence; it holds accounts on most major social networking websites, including Twitter, Facebook, Pinterest, Instagram, and YouTube. Apart from using these platforms for educational and activist purposes and to communicate the goals and mandate of the museum, the USHMM encourages visitors to share their photos and thoughts on the museum with it over social media, on a variety of platforms, having lifted its ban on photography inside the permanent exhibit in 2015.[4] The museum urges visitors both physically and digitally to "reflect upon the moral and spiritual questions raised by the events of the Holocaust as well as upon their own responsibilities as global citizens."[5] While the development of social media policies targets youth engagement, the USHMM's early digital presence has expanded into a thriving social and digital network for Holocaust education and human rights activism in the age of digital media.[6]

Understanding the relationship between the visitor, the image, and the space begins with an exploration of the relationship between the photograph and historical method.[7] Visitors take photos because they wish to collect, capture, or remember their experiences, with the act of photography being a mnemonic device that helps people to recall their experiences clearly.[8] This capturing of experience is not unlike the drive which historians and archivists feel in documenting and interpreting the past itself. With their smartphones, the visitors can frame, curate, capture, archive, and share their encounters with the Holocaust, all within a matter of minutes. [9] For many American visitors a trip to the USHMM is the closest they will get, spatially, to the materiality of the Holocaust, and the nearest they will find themselves to the artifacts housed by the museum; the visit remains one of the more effective methods of learning about and attempting to understand the history of the Holocaust. Visitors seek to convey the "authentic evidence of the historicity of the Holocaust" through their images.[10] The visitors also seek to convey an affective authenticity through earnest captioning—a self-conscious reflection on what the captured images mean to them, the photographers, in the moment of their capture. These images, their captions, and their interaction with the museum's physical space indicate an effort to communicate the importance of Holocaust remembrance and a learned Holocaust visuality.

Visitors to the USHMM are exposed to an embedded interpretation of the history of the Holocaust, as well as a physical representation of its memory. The photography of the space, the application of filters, and the selection of a variety of other categorization techniques serve as additional layers of interpretation which operate in tandem with the established canon of Holocaust museological interpretation. While there are thousands of Instagram images captured at the USHMM and then shared on the mobile platform, a close reading of a few of these images will readily present the constraints of the platform and the photographic method within a predetermined exhibition space. How, then, does the interplay between the visitor and the museum's hegemonic organization of space, visuality, movement, and power play out on Instagram, and in the eyes and camera phone of the visitor? Many of these interactions are governed by tension between the visitor and the museum. Wulf Kansteiner notes: "the lack of control over structure and content will pose a problem in the long run since the generations of digital natives move in a different digital culture. They are used to shaping their everyday digital environments in the process of communication and consumption."[11] Though a visit to the USHMM does not fall within the purview of the history of the "everyday," it allows us to consider the ways in which tourism, individuality, and agency blend together to complicate our understanding of the Holocaust museum in public life, perhaps contributing to the integration of (post)postmemory in the age of social media.[12]

"THINK ABOUT WHAT YOU SAW": INSTAGRAM AND THE WITNESS

Before even entering the museum itself, the U.S. Holocaust Memorial Museum sets its visitors up in the role of witnesses—of the past, present, and future. Figure 11.1 captures the image of one of the museum's external posters, urging visitors to "think about what you saw (the next time you hear about genocide.)"[13] The museum intends for visitors to experience the concept of "Holocaust" in a simulation which walks them through the same journey as the victims, yet they remain entirely aware that this is a contrived simulacrum of that experience. Visitors are highly aware of how "accurate and real it all seems."[14] As Tim Cole explains, "we aren't taking the same 'journey'

Fig. 11.1. "Think about what you saw," at the United States Holocaust Memorial Museum. 2017. Printed with permission from Kerri Ann Flaccomio.

that Holocaust victims took, but the 'journey' of tens of thousands of tourists."[15] Has tourist photography become a behavior which has simply been integrated into this tourist journey? If so, these images present an excellent opportunity to consider this journey—which has not been easily recorded, tracked, or engaged with until now.[16] In evaluating these photographs as sources, we can consider them as cultural artifacts produced by the performance of Holocaust memory in the twenty-first century.

Despite the tyranny of the "self" on Instagram, I do not agree with Gary Weissman's assertion that all visitors to sites which engage with Holocaust memory are governed by fantasies to *experience* the Holocaust; rather, the visitor chooses to assume the role of witness in order to comply with the USHMM's instruction—to "think about what you saw."[17] This endeavor to *understand* this act of "seeing" as a performative act of witnessing at the USHMM is intricately connected to the use of photography and the sharing of images on Instagram. Visitors do not expect to *experience* the reality of the Holocaust as it was, as Weissman suggests. They do expect to *see* people, places, and things affected by the Holocaust, and to witness its aftereffects and lasting impact from both moral and academic perspectives. This expectation of witnessing is integral to visitors' motivations at the USHMM, whether they take photos or not, and whether they recognize it overtly or not.

The ubiquitous and individual "self" which has become synonymous with Instagram (and social media, writ large) is frequently placed in conflict with spaces which demand careful thought and introspection, contributing to a hesitancy to share the authority of representation with the museum visitor.[18] This requires those of us who explore the impact of contemporary Holocaust memory to consider the image as the product of a visitor's mobile encounter with the Holocaust. The journey through the exhibit constitutes a journey for the visitors—they entered the exhibit as tourists, but left considering themselves purveyors of the past—as witnesses in their own right, far removed from the *actual* experiences of the Holocaust, but visitors characterized by having witnessed its legacy. One visitor explains:

> Of all that I have seen, both beautiful and unbearable, none shall ever measure up to what I have seen today. To walk into the towers full of pictures, looking at faces of people you know will die; to hold in your hand the unknown outcome of a poor soul's life; to see a room of burnt and tattered shoes; and to walk through halls of memorabilia of a thing that should not have happened is an experience that no one, but everyone should endure.[19]

This visitor has embedded their visit to the USHMM within their own lifetime of experiences, simultaneously drawing our attention to people, places, and things which have governed their visit and have imparted meaning; their description of their journey through the universe of the Holocaust builds on the image, belongings, and spaces of the other while drawing the attention back to the museum visitor's sense of self—and a transformation from visitor to witness.

The hesitancy in considering tourist photographs as cultural artifacts *of* Holocaust memory is not unwarranted; granting unilateral authority over representation seeks to ignore the hierarchy of representation, place, and authority which guides contemporary Holocaust memorialization. Holocaust scholars could choose to view these images as moments of understanding akin to Susan Sontag's first encounters with Holocaust photography:

> They were only photographs—of an event I had scarcely heard of and could do nothing to affect, of suffering I could hardly imagine and could do nothing to relieve. When I looked at those photographs, something broke. Some limit had been reached, and not only that of horror; I felt irrevocably grieved, wounded, but a part of my feelings started to tighten; something went dead; something is still crying.[20]

Sontag's encounter with the Holocaust centers on her personal experiences and emotions—efforts to communicate such an encounter without personal sentiment would be difficult indeed. How should the Instagram witness be characterized? If we consider Sontag's encounter to be one of the affective benchmarks for personal encounters with the Holocaust, its history, its legacy, and its visuality, then it seems unfair to cast the Instagram witness in the categories of the self-obsessed. To be a witness requires an individual to observe an encounter, certainly; but it also requires the witness to remember that encounter, embedding it in the present and future of their own individualized actions. Visitors to the USHMM are made witnesses to history and the legacy of the Holocaust; their taking and sharing of photographs on Instagram visually embeds that encounter within the timeline of their own experiences, serving as an extension of the role of witness long after they leave the museum.

The visitor's response serves as an entryway to the analysis of how tourist photography works in this setting, for the tourist photo functions in this same way: to communicate, in summation, that the visitor is thinking about what they have witnessed at USHMM, and how it factors into their everyday life. Instagram user @wileycoyote8's image reinforces this sentiment, their caption reading: "I am a firm believer, that every individual of the human race, should be forced to witness this piece of history; and hopefully take away the feeling of empowerment to prevent these events from happening again. #thinkaboutwhatyousaw #beawitness."[21] The visuality of the Instagram USHMM visitor experience lies at the intersection of a fascination with the people, places, and things of the Holocaust and a conscientious effort to be seen "witnessing" the Holocaust, always drawing the experience back to the importance of the self and the individual—even though the USHMM is a simulacrum, or a holding container, for the memory of the Holocaust itself.[22]

PLACES: ARCHITECTURE AND PHOTOGRAPHING SIMULACRITY

> "The architecture speaks of the heaviness and hopelessness of this time/these people. the building is a monument to those lost; a vessel of their journey of suffering."
>
> —*Visitor comment from the U.S. Holocaust Memorial Museum, Institutional Fonds, July 6, 2002*

Museumgoers are not passive, nor should their photographic journeys be construed as such. Stephanie Shosh Rotem explains: "walking through a museum, visitors enter on a journey that recreates significant and meaningful events—the museum's structure, circulation route, lighting, and architectural design constitute a theatrical setting, while the visitors are its active actors."[23] Museum spaces are steeped in power, through both their design and the controlled experience of the visitor; the USHMM features a set path through which visitors are intended to move, and a set ordering of architecture, spaces, objects, and narratives with which they are intended to interact. This is not to say that museumgoers are without agency; the act of discovery within the museum space remains particular to each individual.[24] Moving through an exhibit is performative and active—visitors are constantly impressed upon to behave a certain way and govern themselves with a certain particularity.[25] Therefore, visitors can be conceived of as actors in a space, who can express agency in particular environments, albeit under the power of the museum space. Wulf Kansteiner aptly states: "the digital humanities in general and Holocaust digital culture in particular primarily serve the purpose of providing a new environment for the pursuit and display of expert culture."[26] The physicality of the museum space reinforces the production of particular types of images; many of the photos included in this chapter demonstrate the ways in which the physical constraints of the space prescribe the capturing of a moment on camera.

Understandably, the museum's architecture serves as the stage in the theatrical setting—where visitors serve as actors and agents. The USHMM acknowledges the importance of the museum's architectural visuality in building a visual brand on social media platforms.[27] Rotem argues that "we should understand that this 'package' is loaded with social, cultural, and political messages that critically construct the museum's narrative."[28] The USHMM has dedicated portions of its social media outreach to architectural meet-ups within the exhibit space. In April 2017 the USHMM hosted #USHMMRemembers—a social media architecture tour for Holocaust remembrance. The event was intended "to draw attention to the unique and sometimes unnoticed symbolism in the Museum's architecture" and to kick off the Days of Remembrance—the United States' annual commemoration of the Holocaust.[29] James Ingo Freed's design of the museum enhances the visitors' emotional experience, and grapples with the "unrepresentability" of the Holocaust—a large part of the discussion which surrounded the construction and design of the museum space in the late 1980s. The space is intended to create a sense of distortion, imbalance, and rupture which sets the stage of memory for the exhibitions housed by the museum.[30] What is more, it is the open-ended nature of the architecture and design which allows visitors to attempt to express themselves and their experiences through photography—especially as it relates to the museum's content.[31] The museum building itself asks a question; the architecture, space, and texts of the USHMM continue to resonate with visitors, and these visual tropes can be identified in the photography shared on Instagram as visitors continue to share this question with the world. A visitor comments: "the light/dark, the architecture, the art . . . the silence . . . even without words this place tells their story."[32] Rotem argues that the architecture of American Holocaust museums is compelling, "even to the extent of overshadowing the museums' displays and becoming itself the central experience of the museum visit."[33] By understanding the importance of the space as a "resonator for the memories of others," the attempt to engage with the architecture of the museum can be viewed as an independent interpretation on behalf of the visitor.[34]

This independence of interpretation is a smokescreen, though at no fault of the institution or the visitor; because the hegemonic built space does not offer its visitors an explicit chance to shape their own narratives, given that "consumers have generally no power over the conceptual framing, narrative emplotment, and visual display of the violent pasts which they are urged to remember."[35] However, this does not mean that visitors do not grapple with how to perform their role as visitors appropriately within the given space of the museum. Many take photos, many do not, and many worry over attempts to resist the photographic impulse. While the arrangement and interpretation of Holocaust history is still wholly in the hands of the museum, visitors still attempt to curate their own encounters through photography, arrangement, filters, and captioning. In this way, the Instagram photos taken at the USHMM serve as an indicator of tensions—environmental, memorial, and performative. Whether or not these images are framed as part of a collaborative visual conversation with the museum itself, space and availability dictate what photographs are taken, and in which spaces. Ultimately, there are finite ways that visitors photograph the museum's architecture, the Majdanek shoes, or the Tower of Faces.

The museum's architecture empowers visitors to communicate that same sense of grief expressed by Sontag. The architecture of the USHMM serves as a placeholder for memory for those visitors who find themselves at a loss—unsure of how to complete their role as museum visitors when confronted with the content of the museum itself. A visitor notes, "I'm too overwhelmed to comment on the content of the museum. What could one say? I will say, however, the architecture of the building is fantastic."[36] A similar sentiment is expressed by the Instagram user @halijisand, through their photograph. The brightness created by the skylights in the top left-hand corner of the image and the rich filter create additional contrast, emphasizing Freed's experimentation with light and shadow. The framing of the image and the alignment of the horizonal, vertical, and diagonal elements of the architecture demonstrate an attempt to impose regulation and order on an imbalanced space, locking all chaos outside the frame; the hashtag—a textual indicator of the archival functions of Instagram—connects this image to a larger networked visual community, and communicates that connection through its composition. @halijisand's caption, "how could one person depict his grief in such a sadly beautiful means?" could refer to the Elie Wiesel quotation, but equally encompasses Freed's architecture, or even their own photograph.[37] In this way, the visitor can lean on the labor of memory conducted by the museum, using its carefully crafted architectural space to communicate a sense of affect they may have trouble describing or representing on their own.

THINGS: MATERIAL REALITIES AND THE VISUAL CANON OF THE HOLOCAUST

> "The shoes, I will never forget the shoes. They make their former wearers come alive again. This to me is the greatest memorial of all!"
>
> —*Visitor comment from the U.S. Holocaust Memorial Museum, Institutional Fonds, March 7, 2002*

In the tourist photographs of the U.S. Holocaust Memorial Museum, objects are omnipresent. They fill the frame; the visitor's internalized understanding of these heaps of personal objects manifests in the structure of their image. Piles of shoes stretch beyond the frame of the image, overwhelming the frame, the visitor, and the viewer. The faces of the town of Eisiskes, Lithuania, stretch upward, into a column of light (figure 11.2). These photos function as fragments of a larger whole, operating as a visual synecdoche within the context of the entire exhibit. Ulrike Kistner reinforces this notion, noting: "While death renders humans indifferent from and to lifeless things, apparently lifeless things retain a trace of life, past and present."[38] It is this trace of life and the lasting legacy of death—the materiality of the Holocaust is emblematic of both—which inspires photography as a form of remembrance within the exhibit space.[39] In addition, the piles of things and the materiality associated with the Holocaust have contributed to the Holocaust's visual cultural legacy in our contemporary world.

The USHMM's collection of artifacts and material objects is central to the museum's message and its function as both a placeholder for memory and as building blocks of evidence.[40] The most photographed objects or "things" within the museum space are these very items which contribute to the evidentiary nature of the Holocaust Museum—wooden barracks from Auschwitz-II, piles of shoes from Majdanek, and sometimes the *Karlsruhe* freight car on rails from Treblinka (figure 11.3); these photographs are staged, captured, and shared in a performed way which emulates the Holocaust's visual legacy.[41] These images place the material remnants of the Holocaust at center stage of the visitor experience, and serve as an accessible entryway to the empathetic framework that many visitors use to compose their images. What is more, the materiality of the Holocaust—communicated through artifacts and presented within the museum

Fig. 11.2. "#thenexttimeyouseeinjustice #thinkaboutwhatyousaw #ushmm." The Tower of Faces at the United States Holocaust Memorial Museum. 2017. Printed with permission from Daniela Dumulescu.

environment—forms a behavioral dichotomy: visitors are intended to engage and interact with their surroundings, but they must not touch the artifacts or experience the physicality of the Holocaust's material history through touch. Thus, to photograph is to physically interact with these remnants of atrocity—a physical act which replicates the evidentiary nature of the museum itself, helping visitors through their journey of witnessing.[42]

By photographing the shoes from above and extending her smartphone over the glass barriers which form a pathway through the piles of shoes, the visitor intends to overwhelm the viewer with an image macro that is entirely consumed by the shoes of Holocaust victims, which extends beyond the frame of the image—and (as we know) spills beyond the scenes of capturable imagery.[43] This composition demonstrates the visitor's understanding of the immensity and immeasurability of the Holocaust—an attempt to understand the implications of millions;

this serves as a visual effort to communicate shock, horror, sadness, or any kind of emotion—or even a last attempt to photograph anything in which the visitor finds meaning, before visitors pass through to the end of the exhibition. The shoes of Majdanek are one example of the ways in which visitors emulate a learned Holocaust aesthetic—which can be seen through the ways in which the photography of particular objects or scenes is typified; images showing the shoes are featured heavily in the USHMM's branding and interpretive pamphlets. It is hard to disagree with Jonathan Frater's assertion that "anyone can understand a room full of discarded shoes."[44] This learned aesthetic and its origins are difficult to discern, emerging from a large Holocaust consciousness governed by the prominence of the Holocaust in the media since the liberation of the camps, and its reinterpretation through popular films and media up to this point.[45]

Cornelia Brink demonstrates that images become typified as soon as they are shown or viewed in a cycle of repetition.[46] Attempts to capture the quintessential "Holocaust museum photograph" at the USHMM have manifested in a variety of ways, and all of the examples discussed in this chapter are indicative of that impulse which lies at the intersection of the photographic impulse and the museum's call to action—to think about what you've seen. All of the examples discussed in this chapter contribute to a larger memory pastiche through a learned reproduction of iconic images. There are additional factors at work here, however. I agree with Kansteiner's argument that visitors have little control over the aesthetic arrangement of the pasts they are warned against forgetting, but I argue that they are still able to "craft the images and stories with which they identify, enjoying a considerable sense of cultural power linked to the circumstance that the figures and words on the screen follow commands within split-seconds."[47] The use of framing, filters, and arrangement within their own Instagram feeds—as well as in the larger feed archived under a single hashtag—allows them to connect a sense of individual aesthetic self-fashioning to a wider visual and digital Holocaust narrative. Just as visitors embed their perceptions and experiences in a self-fashioned narrative in connection with wider social structures, the individual tourism photo centers on the perceptions of the tourist body, focusing on the power of the individual visitor in relation to the structure of the hegemonic museum.

PEOPLE: THE TOWER OF FACES AND THE TOURIST BODY

> "When I looked at you as you stood in line, I searched its length amongst the many faces like mine."
>
> —*Visitor comment from the U.S. Holocaust Memorial Museum, Institutional Fonds, October 2, 2002*

Photographs taken in the Tower of Faces—a three-floor installation devoted to the victims of the Jewish community of Eisiskes, Lithuania—feature prominently in Instagram's visual landscape of the USHMM. It is also one of the first places within the permanent exhibition where visitors confront the scale of the Holocaust as a genocidal state plan—something that they do not experience again until they reach the shoe installation toward the end of the third floor. The Tower of Faces extends through three floors of the museum, and visitors pass through the last third of the installation after exiting the pathway through the shoes of victims. A visitor comments: "A short walk away from the collection of shoes is the photo gallery. Above walk living, breathing people, whose shadows and shoes pass soundlessly and unknowingly . . ."[48] Here, the visitors' focus remains on the body of the tourist, rather than the body of the victim; the shadowy presence of the museum visitors and their journey from fantasies of witnessing to witnesses govern their museum interactions.

The interpretive strands of the faces of Eisiskes, the material holdings of the permanent exhibition, and the space and architecture of the museum are tightly wound: the Tower of Faces demonstrates a combination of themes already explored in this chapter—the ways in which visitors seek to combine an emotional human connection with the material history of the Holocaust and the spatial universe of the museum itself—which is already a physical attempt at Holocaust simulacrity. Here, it is important to think through Marianne Hirsch's work on the impact of the image: "[Photographs] produce affect in the viewer, speaking from the body's sensations, rather than speaking of, or representing the past."[49] Tourist photographs taken of or in the Tower of Faces echo this sentiment, and attempt to re-create the bodily sensations experienced when confronted by such an immense number of physical photographs. The hundreds of images rise to dizzying heights, surrounding the visitor on a narrow walkway; the tight quarters, the number of other visitors, and the vertical lines of this installation require that users photograph in one of three ways: with a close focus on the faces of the victims; a wide focus on the immensity of the number of victims; or a close focus on the visitor engaging with the Tower, surrounded by the images of the victims of Eisiskes (figure 11.2).[50]

In these images, the body is the focal point—the tourist body, specifically. [51] Each visitor is centered within the frame, with each image capturing the active engagement with the Tower of Faces or the glass hallways which cross above the Hall of Witness. In images featuring the tourist body, the faces are either hidden or turned away from the camera in a performance of solemnity—gazing beyond the frame, onward to something in the distance. While these photos can range from posed to candid, even the most casual photos are inherently staged—for the photographer is always searching for a particular moment which best expresses his or her experiences within the space of the museum. The memorial image is not about the victim, and is no longer *entirely* about the space; rather, the presence of the tourist body within the frame presents an opportunity to gaze upon the visitor's journey from visitor to witness. Though frozen within the frame, gazing upward or onward, these images inspire movement. They serve as a snapshot of the embodiment of the visitor's journey through the exhibit. These images can also serve an integrative function. In featuring the tourist body or face against a surrounding tower of nameless faces, the tourist body is flattened against and into the memory pastiche that surrounds the visitor. Certainly, this does not place the tourist body within the realm of victimhood—this much is clear, for the tourist body remains as the focal point for the viewer, the person upon whom the viewer can cast their consciousness. A visitor notes, "I saw my loved ones in all the faces."[52] The presence of an identifiable person among the hundreds of unnamed victims of Eisiskes reminds the visitor, the photographer, and the viewer of what was lost: millions of identifiable people, millions of names, millions of lives lost. In speaking of the objects and materiality of genocide, Ulrike Kistner argues that "in the absence of human actors, things lose historical significance and human interest."[53] Here Kistner is speaking specifically of the objects and belongings left behind by victims in the act of genocide committed against them. However, because these reproduced images function as objects of memory in their own right, it is important to remember that the function of the museum cannot be carried out without the visitor or tourist body. The "thingness" and spatial qualities of the museum are wholly dependent on the physical presence of the body of the tourist—and the presence of the tourist within the photograph carries out this same function.

EMBODIED AND PERFORMATIVE: GAPS IN A VISUAL NARRATIVE

> "The train car gave me shivers."
>
> —*Visitor comment from the U.S. Holocaust Memorial Museum, Institutional Fonds, May 23, 2011*

The emergence of the digitally circulated image has called into question the life cycle of the image as both material and physical object. Figure 11.3 can no longer be found on Instagram, though I managed to find it before the user decided to remove it from their profile. The image is composed of a sharp slice of light cutting into an otherwise unviewable scene. It is difficult to even discern what this is a photo of, until exploring the hashtags used at the tail end of the caption: "They lingered everywhere but here. i [*sic*] stayed and tried to settle into the uncomfortableness. This unsettling and undeniable space. #thismuseumisaquestion #holocaustmuseum #boxcarlight #lightbeam."[54] The photographer has attempted to capture the visceral feeling they experienced within a space that is not often photographed at the USHMM—inside the Karlsruhe train car. Pictures of the train car surface very rarely on Instagram. There are many practical reasons as to why the train car is not frequently photographed: it is difficult to capture its image, due to poor lighting or lack of physical space, and many visitors may not feel comfortable lingering or attempting to photograph the space—a space meant to overwhelm the senses. @jolynjanis, however, chose to override their discomfort, recognizing the importance of sharing their images with the wider community. This image serves as an example of the difference between an attempt to photograph an impactful—or even iconic—installation with the purpose of sharing easily recognizable imagery with those online, and the attempt to capture a personal, visceral feeling or reaction to the space or the history itself—despite Barthesian or Benjaminian concerns over the indifference of the camera.[55]

Though the camera itself may be indifferent, the photographer and all possible viewers—present, future, and past—are not. The feminist film theorist Laura Mulvey's recent work on the relationship

Fig 11.3. An image from the inside of the Karlsruhe train car at the United States Holocaust Memorial Museum. 2016. Printed with permission from Instagram user @jolynjanis.

between stillness and the moving image highlights the inescapable presence of the Freudian death drive within the stillness of the photographic image. Mulvey explains: "the photograph's suspension of time, its conflation of life and death, the animate and the inanimate, raises not superstition so much as a sense of disquiet that is aggravated rather than calmed by the photograph's mechanical, chemical and indifferent nature."[56] Indeed, @jolynjanis sought to suspend time in an effort to communicate the physical sensation created by occupying a space characterized by historicized movement and death, but perhaps the act of photographing such a space only added to their sense of disquiet, rendered so by the mechanical indifference of modernity that is partially responsible for bringing about the Holocaust in the first place. When considering only the image itself—separate from the caption and hashtags—the image collapses time and space; this could be any train car, the only difference being that Nazi cars were not photographed from the inside.

@jolynjanis's efforts to "think about what they saw" (and what they felt) embrace the material physicality of the space to connect past to present; the train car—once a space of mobility and movement, and symbol of death, now rests immobile in the USHMM, and frozen within the Instagram image. This image, alongside the other images in this chapter, demonstrates that visitors who photograph the USHMM are driven to share their experiences as witnesses, exerting their own powers over the physical and visual symbols of the Holocaust and shaping their identities as witnesses—if only within a small, square frame and a handful of hashtags. In drawing attention to the "unsettling and undeniable space," @jolynjanis's photograph condenses the materiality and spatial confines of the train car (and by extension, the museum) into a single frame. With a focus on the physical responses felt in the tourist body, this single performance of memory serves as an attempt to pass on the responsibility of witnessing to the viewer. This extends the intent and purpose of the image—and the museum—beyond the walls of the USHMM, and beyond the frame of the image itself.

These images, though housed in small frames, function as fragments of a larger Holocaust aesthetic canon—one that has been heavily engaged with in the public sphere, and which has found its way into the minds of everyday people, and which is reflected in their photographs. What is more, in this age of social media, I agree with Penelope Papailias's assertion that "performative memorializing takes its particular contemporary form as an extension of the experience of mediated witnessing in the era of networked digital media."[57] No two images taken at the USHMM are identical; visual micro-interventions shift the intent of the communicative digital object. While these images and their visual patterns contribute to a wider digital visuality of the USHMM, visitor photography and social media usage at Holocaust memorial sites serve as the front line of visitor engagement with Holocaust memory in the twenty-first century.

The motivation behind these behaviors is not new. Rather, the inspiration to share an image of the USHMM—or Auschwitz, for that matter—on Instagram has much in common with the drive to sign a guestbook, or to write about one's experiences in a travel journal. These images are part of a long trajectory of tourist behaviors, and the presence of thousands of photos on Instagram is not the only aspect of this mobile memory technology which warrants investigation. With the ability to capture individual experiences and engage with sites such as the USHMM, visitors fashion their own experiences as witnesses. While the *subject* of the photograph remains central to discussions of how visual culture remains central to Holocaust memory studies, the *how* and the *why* of the remediated Holocaust memory image are also essential to understanding tourist behaviors at Holocaust memorial sites in the twenty-first century. Visitors can exercise creative input—applying filters to historicize images, or hashtags to archive them. These images may feature different filters, or borders, and some visitors take numerous photos, choosing to create a collage or capture aspects from as many different angles as they can. These micro-interventions are efforts to curate singular encounters with the museum, often within the confined space of the frame itself. What is more, the mode through which we view these images changes their meaning, and their intent. While not all images taken at the USHMM or other Holocaust memorial spaces share in the reverent behavior espoused by these images, many photographic acts at the USHMM demonstrate a consideration for the space as a container for the history and memory of the Holocaust. Through this tension, we can note the ways in which visitors to the museum and audience do not disregard its authority, but rather recognize the museum's importance and seek to collaborate with the institution itself—by sharing in the publicly networked act of digitized witnessing.

NOTES

1. From a very large field, see Marianne Hirsch, *Family Frames: Photography, Narrative, and Postmemory* (Cambridge, Mass.: Harvard University Press, 1997); Marianne Hirsch. *The Generation of Postmemory: Writing and Visual Culture after the Holocaust* (New York: Columbia University Press, 2013); James E. Young, *The Texture of Memory: Holocaust Memorials and Meaning* (New Haven, Conn.: Yale University Press, 1994); Barbie Zelizer, *Remembering to Forget: Holocaust Memory through the Camera's Eye* (Chicago: University of Chicago Press, 2000); Stephanie Shosh Rotem, *Constructing Memory: Architectural Narratives of Holocaust Museums* (New York: Peter Lang, 2013); Janina Struk, *Photographing the Holocaust: Interpretations of the Evidence* (London: I.B. Tauris, 2003); and John Urry, *The Tourist Gaze* (London: SAGE, 2002).

2. Some of these images are also found under the hashtag #holocaustmuseum; differences will be discussed where necessary, though there are far more images shared under that hashtag than under #USHMM, which supports Tim Cole's argument that the USHMM has become *the* Holocaust museum, looming large in American public intellectual life and imagination. Tim Cole, *Selling the Holocaust: From Auschwitz to Schindler, How History Is Bought, Packaged, and Sold* (New York: Routledge, 2000), 146.

3. Lev Manovich, *Instagram and Contemporary Image* (2016), 11, http://manovich.net/content/04-projects/145-instagram-and-contemporary

-image/instagram_book_manovich.pdf. Manovich's work on Instagram corpuses allows us to develop an understanding of visual tropes and typologies which emerge as particular Instagram aestheticisms and styles. Pooled from the collection of thousands of images in major cities all around the world, Manovich's work has demonstrated the replication of particular image types as they relate to food, style, bodies, gender, and space.

4. Menachem Wecker, "U.S. Holocaust Memorial Museum Adopts New Rules to Attract Digital Generation," *Washington Post,* October 3, 2014.

5. United States Holocaust Memorial Museum, http://www.ushmm.org/information/connect-with-the-museum.

6. United States Holocaust Memorial Museum, "Holocaust Education in the Digital Age," https://www.ushmm.org/information/about-the-museum/museum-publications/memory-and-action/holocaust-education-in-the-digital-age.

7. See Elizabeth Edwards, "Thoughts on Photography and the Practice of History," in *The Ethics of Seeing: Photography and Twentieth-Century German History*, ed. Jennifer Evans, Paul Betts, and Stefan-Ludwig Hoffman (New York: Berghahn, 2018), 23–36.

8. See W. J. T. Mitchell, *Picture Theory* (Chicago: University of Chicago Press, 1994). See Elizabeth Edwards, *The Camera as Historian: Amateur Photographers and Historical Imagination, 1885–1918* (Durham, N.C.: Duke University Press, 2012), for an excellent discussion of embodied knowledge and amateur photography.

9. See John Lennon and Malcolm Foley, *Dark Tourism: The Attraction of Death and Disaster* (London: Continuum, 2000); and Michael Haldrup and Jonas Larsen, "The Family Gaze," *Tourist Studies* 3, no. 1 (2003): 23–46.

10. Cole, *Selling the Holocaust*, 159.

11. Wulf Kansteiner, "Genocide Memory, Digital Cultures, and the Aestheticization of Violence," *Memory Studies* 7, no. 4 (2014): 405.

12. Marianne Hirsch's theory of postmemory is explored the most thoroughly in *The Generation of Postmemory*. Hirsch's exploration of this concept is defined by the relationship the second generation shares with the personal and cultural traumas of a generation before. This relationship is comprised mainly of the stories, images, and behaviors of those they grew up around, as well as a propensity for the memory of a cultural trauma they did not directly experience.

13. Figure 11.1. Image copyright Instagram user @keriflaccomio, May 17, 2017.

14. Visitor comments from the United States Holocaust Memorial Museum, Institutional Fonds, June 13, 2003.

15. Cole, *Selling the Holocaust*, 161.

16. There has been some work done on the impact of the digital turn on Holocaust memory—specifically relating to social media use at the Auschwitz-Birkenau State Museum. See Til Hilmar, "Storyboards of Remembrance: Representations of the Past in Visitors' Photography at Auschwitz," *Memory Studies* 9, no. 4 (2016): 455–70; and Imogen Dalziel, "Romantic Auschwitz: Examples and Perceptions of Contemporary Visitor Photography at the Auschwitz-Birkenau State Museum," *Holocaust Studies* 22, no. 2–3 (2016): 185–207. For more on the impact of the digital age on Holocaust studies (and its accompanying anxieties), see Wulf Kansteiner, "The Holocaust in the 21st Century: Digital Anxiety, Transnational Cosmopolitanism, and Never Again Genocide without Memory," in *Digital Memory Studies: Media Pasts in Transition*, ed. Andrew Hoskins (London: Routledge, 2017), 110–40; and Claudio Fogu, Wulf Kansteiner, and Todd Presner, eds., *Probing the Ethics of Holocaust Culture* (Cambridge, Mass.: Harvard University Press, 2016).

17. Weissman notes, "Nonwitnesses are haunted not by the traumatic impact of the Holocaust, but by its absence—by a sense that the Holocaust is not enough with us . . . when nonwitnesses take an interest in the Holocaust, they are not overcoming a fearful aversion to its horror but endeavoring to actually feel the horror of what otherwise eludes them." Gary Weissman, *Fantasies of Witnessing: Postwar Efforts to Experience the Holocaust* (Ithaca, N.Y.: Cornell University Press, 2004), 22–23.

18. This hesitancy is best demonstrated through debates over the appropriateness of particular forms of photography, such as the selfie. See, for example, Breanna Mitchell's infamous selfie at Auschwitz in 2014.

19. Visitor comments from the United States Holocaust Memorial Museum, Institutional Fonds, April 24, 2003.

20. Susan Sontag, *On Photography* (New York: Picador, 1977), 19–20.

21. Figure 11.2. Caption by @wileycoyote8, June 22, 2017.

22. Deborah Lipstadt identified a real fear about the preservation of the memory of the Holocaust in *Denying the Holocaust* (London: Penguin, 1993). Weissman connects this to the need for a Holocaust museum to serve as a physical space in American society, which resulted in the construction of the U.S. Holocaust Memorial Museum; Weissman, *Fantasies of Witnessing,* 6. The literature on the U.S. Holocaust Memorial Museum as a vehicle for memory is substantive. See Edward T. Linenthal, *Preserving Memory: The Struggle to Create America's Holocaust Museum* (New York: Columbia University Press, 1995); Cole, *Selling the Holocaust*; Stephanie Shosh Rotem, *Constructing Memory: Architectural Narratives of Holocaust Museums* (New York: Peter Lang, 2013); Michael F. Bernard-Donals, *Figures of Memory: The Rhetoric of Displacement at the United States Holocaust Memorial Mu-*

seum (New York: State University of New York Press, 2016); and Michael Berenbaum, *The World Must Know: The History of the Holocaust as Told in the United States Holocaust Memorial Museum* (Boston: Little Brown, 1993).

23. Rotem, *Constructing Memory*, 15.

24. See James Clifford, *Routes: Travel and Translation in the Late Twentieth Century*, particularly "Museums as Contact Zones" (Cambridge, Mass.: Harvard University Press, 1997), 188–219.

25. See Tony Bennett, *The Birth of the Museum: History, Theory, Politics* (London: Routledge, 1994).

26. Kansteiner, "Genocide Memory," 405.

27. "Visuality" is used here in the spirit of Nicholas Mirzoeff's analysis of the term: as a collective understanding of multiple visual media and the individual and personalized relationship to those media. In a museum setting, this entails the way the visual—from architecture, the exhibit installation, lighting, historical photographs, artifacts—and the individual conflict and collaborate in any space. This works effectively as a framework of analysis for sources like Instagram, which rely on the communication of multiple aspects of the visual between one individual and many others. Mirzoeff notes: ""The constituent parts of visual culture are, then, not defined by medium so much as by the interaction between viewer and viewed, which may be termed the visual event . . . By visual event, I mean an interaction of the visual sign, the technology that enables and sustains that sign, and the viewer." For more, see Nicholas Mirzoeff, *An Introduction to Visual Culture* (London: Routledge, 1999), 15–16.

28. Rotem, *Constructing Memory*, 186.

29. "DC influencers visit U.S. Holocaust Museum for Days of Remembrance," United States Memorial Holocaust Museum (@HolocaustMuseum) on Twitter, https://twitter.com/i/moments/856210851501682691.

30. United States Holocaust Memorial Museum, "Architecture and Art: Hall of Witness," https://www.ushmm.org/information/about-the-museum/architecture-and-art/hall-of-witness.

31. United States Holocaust Memorial Museum, "About the Museum: Architecture and Art," https://www.ushmm.org/information/about-the-museum/architecture-and-art.

32. Visitor comments from the U.S. Holocaust Memorial Museum, Institutional Fonds, November 7, 2008.

33. Rotem, *Constructing Memory*, 91.

34. James Ingo Freed, "The United States Holocaust Memorial Museum," *Assemblage* 9 (1989): 58–79, esp. 64.

35. Kansteiner, "Genocide Memory," 405.

36. Visitor comments from the U.S. Holocaust Memorial Museum, Institutional Fonds, January 25, 2003.

37. Instagram user @halijisand, September 22, 2017.

38. Ulrike Kistner, "What Remains—Genocide and Things," in *Representing Auschwitz: At the Margins of Testimony*, ed. Nicholas Chare and Dominic Williams (Palgrave Macmillan, 2013), 120.

39. This is akin to Roland Barthes' assertion that "photography has something to do with resurrection." Roland Barthes, *Camera Lucida: Reflections on Photography* (New York, 1981), 80–81.

40. Cole, *Selling the Holocaust*, 160.

41. Cole, *Selling the Holocaust*, 160.

42. For more on tourism and materiality, see Michael Haldrup, "Material Cultures of Tourism," *Leisure Studies* 25, no. 3 (2006): 275–89.

43. Instagram user @tayas13 provides a good example of this image composition: https://www.instagram.com/p/Buhw7AOBsQ3/.

44. Jonathan Frater, "The Shoe Room, and What I Learned There: A Visit to the U.S. Holocaust Museum," *The Rogue Scholar*, August 9, 2011, http://roguescholar.blogs.com/my_weblog/2011/08/the-shoe-room-and-what-i-learned-there.html.

45. Zelizer, *Remembering to Forget*.

46. Cornelia Brink, "Secular Icons: Looking at Photographs from Nazi Concentration Camps," *History and Memory* 12, no. 1 (2000): 142. See also Walter Benjamin, *The Work of Art in the Age of Mechanical Reproduction* (New York: Schocken Books, 1969).

47. Kansteiner, "Genocide Memory," 405.

48. Visitor comments from the U.S. Holocaust Memorial Museum, Institutional Fonds, July 29, 2015.

49. Hirsch, *Family Frames*, 15.

50. Instagram photos of the Tower of Faces fittingly demonstrate the life cycle of a photograph. The Tower features around 1,000 reproductions of images of Jewish life in the town, collected from over 100 families by Dr. Yaffa Eliach. Beginning their lives as physical photographs, captured by Yitzhak Uri Katz, along with his wife, Alte Katz, and their assistant Ben-Zion Szrejder and Rephael Lejbowicz, the images experienced a shift in space and engagement with their reproduction for the exhibit itself—transforming them from objects with a material history in their own right to replications intended for a particular, though very different, context. Lastly, these images experience re-replication as either the sole subject or as the background of other peoples' images. This instance is one of many in which the material objects of the museum fade, settling into the background or flattening into two-dimensional images, synecdochal of the journeyed tourist experience. See Elizabeth Edwards and Janice Hart, *Photographs Objects Histories: On the Materiality of Images* (London: Routledge, 2004).

51. For more on photography and the production of bodies in the social

mediasphere, see Kate Douglas, "Youth, Trauma, and Memorialisation: The Selfie as Witnessing," *Memory Studies* (2017): 1–16.

52. Visitor comments from the U.S. Memorial Holocaust Museum, Institutional Fonds, September 11, 2003.

53. Kistner, "What Remains," 120.

54. Figure 11.7, copyright Instagram user @jolynjanis, October 2016.

55. See Barthes, *Camera Lucida;* and Benjamin, *The Work of Art.*

56. Laura Mulvey, *Death 24x a Second* (London: Reaktion Books, 2006), 60–61.

57. Penelope Papailias, "Witnessing in the Age of the Database: Viral Memorials, Affective Publics, and the Assemblage of Mourning," *Memory Studies* 9, no. 4 (2016): 438.

Notes on Contributors

LORENA AVILA is a doctoral student in the School of Criminal Justice at Rutgers University, Newark. She is a political scientist with a master's degree in public policy from the National University of Colombia. She works on projects related to comparative international criminal justice, human rights, and transitional justice.

TIM COLE is a professor of social history and the director of the Brigstow Institute at the University of Bristol. He is the author of *Images of the Holocaust / Selling the Holocaust, Holocaust City, Traces of the Holocaust*, and *Holocaust Landscapes*, and a coeditor of *Militarized Landscapes, Geographies of the Holocaust*, and *Imagining Regulation Differently*.

ADRIEN DALLAIRE received his doctorate in history from the University of Ottawa and École Normale Supérieure de Paris in October 2019. His thesis is titled "Explaining Survival: The Hierarchy of Persecution and the Jews of the Department of Vaucluse, 1933–1945."

YEHUDIT DORI DESTON is a postdoctoral scholar at the Simon Dubnow Institute for Jewish History and Culture, Leipzig, and at the Hebrew University of Jerusalem. She is the author of *Der Demjanjuk-Prozess: Das Ende der NS-Strafverfolgung in Israel* (forthcoming 2022).

SIMONE GIGLIOTTI is a senior lecturer and reader in Holocaust studies at Royal Holloway, University of London. She is the author of *The Train Journey* and coeditor of *The Holocaust: A Reader*; *Ethics, Art, and Representation of the Holocaust*; *The Young Victims of the Nazi Regime*; *The Memorialization of Genocide*; and *The Wiley Companion to the Holocaust.*

Alberto Giordano is professor of geography at Texas State University and 2018-19 president of the University Consortium for Geographic Information Science. He is a coeditor of *Geographies of the Holocaust* and the author or coauthor of articles and book chapters on the Holocaust, the Armenian genocide, and geographic information science.

Paul B. Jaskot is a professor of art history and director of the Wired! Lab for Digital Art History and Visual Culture at Duke University. He is the author of *The Nazi Perpetrator: Postwar German Art and the Politics of the Right*, as well as the coeditor of *Lessons and Legacies, Vol. XIII: New Approaches to an Integrated History of the Holocaust; Social History, Representation, Theory*.

Anne Kelly Knowles is Colonel James C. McBride Distinguished Professor of History at the University of Maine. She is the author of *Mastering Iron: The Struggle to Modernize an American Industry*, the editor of several books and journal issues on historical geographic information science, and a coeditor of *Geographies of the Holocaust*.

Holli Levitsky is a professor of English and the director of the Jewish Studies Program at Loyola Marymount University. She is the coeditor of *The Literature of Exile and Displacement* and *Summer Haven: The Catskills, the Holocaust and the Literary Imagination*.

Meghan Lundrigan received her doctorate in History at Carleton University in Ottawa, Canada, in 2019, where she focused on Holocaust memory, social media, and visual culture. She is a Historical Research Associate at Know History, Inc. She is writing a book to be titled "Holocaust Memory in the Digital Mediascape" with Jennifer Evans and Erica Fagen.

Nancy Nicholls is a lecturer on memory and contemporary history at the History Institute of the Pontificia Universidad Católica de Chile. She is the coauthor of *Para una historia de los derechos humanos en Chile: Historia institucional de la Fundación de Ayuda Social de las Iglesias Cristianas FASIC, 1975–1991*.

DALIA OFER is the Max and Rita Haber Chair of Holocaust Studies at Hebrew University. She is the author of *Escaping the Holocaust* and *The Dead-End Journey*, the editor of *Israel in the Eyes of the Survivors* and *The Clandestine History of the Kovno Jewish Ghetto Police*, and a coeditor of *Women in the Holocaust*, *Jewish Women*, *The Holocaust: History and Memory*, and *The Holocaust: The Particular and Universal.*

SHARON OSTER is a professor of English at the University of Redlands in California. She is the author of *No Place in Time: The Hebraic Myth in Late-Nineteenth-Century American Literature*. Her essays on American, Jewish, and Holocaust literature have appeared in *English Literary History* and *Prooftexts*.

HANNAH POLLIN-GALAY is a senior lecturer in the Department of Literature at Tel Aviv University. She is the author of *Ecologies of Witnessing*.

ANDREA RUDORFF is a historian and the author of *Frauen in den Außenlagern des Konzentrationslagers Groß-Rosen*. She edited *Das KZ Auschwitz 1942–1945 und die Zeit der Todesmärsche 1944/45*, volume 16 of the documentary collection *The Persecution and Extermination of the European Jews by Nazi Germany 1933–1945*, edited by the Institute for Contemporary History Munich–Berlin.

SUSANNA SCHRAFSTETTER is a professor of history at the University of Vermont. She is the author of *Flucht und Versteck: Untergetauchte Juden in München; Verfolgungserfahrung und Nachkriegsalltag* (*Flight and Concealment: Fugitive Jews in Munich; Wartime Persecution and Postwar Experience*) and the coeditor of *The Germans and the Holocaust: Popular Responses to the Persecution and Murder of the Jews*.

YAEL SIMAN is an associate professor of social and political sciences at Universidad Iberoamericana Ciudad de México, and the author of chapters and articles on victims of violence and the Holocaust in Mexico and Latin America.